D0815553

A PRESIDENTIAL
NATION

Also by the Author

The Student Revolution: A Global Confrontation

A PRESIDENTIAL NATION

Joseph A. Califano, Jr.

W·W·NORTON & COMPANY·INC·

NEW YORK

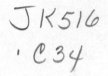

Library of Congress Cataloging in Publication Data

Califano, Joseph A., Jr. 1931–
    A presidential nation.

    Includes index.
    1. Presidents—United States. 2. United States—
Politics and government—1945–   I. Title.
JK516.C34   353.03'13   75-9507
ISBN 0-393-05528-0

For *Mother* and *Dad*

CONTENTS

AUTHOR'S NOTE

For four years I served in various posts in the Pentagon during the Kennedy administration and the early months of the Johnson administration. A significant portion of my responsibilities involved acting as liaison with the White House. From mid-1965 until he left office, I served as President Johnson's Special Assistant for Domestic Affairs.

Since then, like most Americans, I have watched the presidencies of Richard Nixon and Gerald Ford and read about their predecessors. As counsel for the Democratic party in the early 1970s, I had an opportunity to observe the presidential nominating process of a major political party at intimate range.

This book expresses my reflections, informed by those experiences, on the American presidency in the last quarter of the twentieth century—where it is today, how it got there, and some of the things that should be done to make it more accountable and responsive, and to invest it with credible integrity. The central thesis is that the presidency cannot be considered in isolation from the other institutions in American society, national, state and local, public and private, including the media. Ours was intended to be a system of fragmented power, with some checks and balances designed by the original framers of the Constitution and others established by tradition, politics, and collective common sense. For a variety of reasons, concentrated central power has been eroding fragmented power since the presidency of Franklin Roosevelt.

Radical surgery is needed to put the presidency and the power it can exercise in healthy perspective for the continued development of our nation and to preserve the individual freedom of our people. That surgery must be performed not so much on the office itself as on the forces in society that have lost the will and institutional capability to provide checks and balances to the exercise of presidential power. Despite the war in Vietnam, the Watergate scandals, and the turbulence in the minds and hearts of our people that flared repeatedly on the streets of our cities during the late 1960s, the presidency has continued to maintain and enhance its power. It is the other institutions in society—the Congress, the courts, the states and cities, the political parties, the private sector—that have failed to sustain their ability to counterpoint presidential power.

There are several examples in this book that derive from my experience during the Johnson presidency, particularly in the three chapters dealing with presidential personality. Those incidents are recounted as anecdotal evidence to illustrate general propositions, just as a novelist uses characters in an attempt to dramatize basic truths about human nature. To the extent this book provides insights into the Johnson presidency, it offers them as representative of the exercise of presidential power by most recent presidents.

Adoption of the proposals and recommendations in the final chapter of this book would require a major reordering of institutions of American society. There are obviously a number of lesser changes that can be made and have been discussed in the burgeoning literature on the presidency and the balance of American public and private power. My own suggestions are focused on central, basic institutional changes of the kind I believe our nation must urgently consider if it is to face the reality of what has happened over the last forty years and what is likely to occur during the remaining decades of this century. To so much of the legislative and administrative tinkering that has dominated the busy literature of papers, books, committee reports, and political speeches about the presidency, I would address Thoreau's comment: "It is not enough to be busy . . . the question is: what are we busy about?"

Over the past five years, many of the ideas in this book

have been tested privately with men and women, young and old, students and professors, those experienced in the operation of government and the exercise of power and those who have analyzed its exercise. A few thoughts, particularly some of those expressed in Chapters III and IV, have, in other contexts and less-detailed development, been the subject of speeches, congressional testimony, seminars, and articles in the Washington *Post.*

It would be impossible for me to acknowledge all those individuals with whom I have discussed some of the ideas in this book. A few deserve special mention. Elizabeth Drew, one of the most informed observers of the institutional behavior in Washington, was kind enough to review an early draft of the first few chapters. In recent years, Philip Geyelin, the extraordinarily perceptive editor of the Washington *Post's* editorial page, has been a personal sounding board, and he graciously reviewed portions of this manuscript. Gregory Craig, a bright young lawyer and friend, was of immense assistance in his research and comments on Chapter VIII. These individuals, of course, bear no responsibility for the thoughts and ideas in this book. That responsibility is solely mine.

It is customary for an author to express gratitude to his editor, but the time, energy, and thoughtfulness that Evan Thomas has invested during the writing of this book have been so special that it is difficult to express my appreciation adequately. An enduring bonus of our work together has been that both Evan and his wife Anne have become dear friends. My secretaries Evelyn Furgerson and Sonia Ryerson not only lived through the several drafts, but helped check out those gritty but relevant facts that are so difficult to nail down, and did it all with great good humor. The considerate patience of my law partners, particularly Edward Bennett Williams and Paul R. Connolly, has been much appreciated.

Finally, I would like to express my deepest appreciation to my wife Trudy and my three children, Mark, Joe, and Claudia. All of them bore up well under the strain of my requests for silence and solitude during the months of intensive reading, writing, and thinking that have gone into this book. My wife, both severest critic and greatest comfort, has more often than she realizes forced me to think through several of the issues discussed on the following pages.

Washington, D.C.
April 1975

A PRESIDENTIAL
NATION

I

———⚬⚬⚬———

THE PRESIDENCY
IN PERSPECTIVE

The final decades of the twentieth century may be the best of times for the enhancement of presidential power—and the worst of times for regeneration of the constitutionally inspired checks on the exercise of that power.

The modern presidency stands in a contemporary jungle of degenerating social and economic compacts, floundering governments and religions, splintering elemental units of society (like the American family), and agnostic, if not despairing, civilizations. Strong leadership is sought—and needed—not only to redress the maldistribution of fewer resources among more expecting people at home and abroad, but also to lift the spirit of our nation and draw the best from its citizens. Economic problems effectively resist the politics of self-interest. The technology of war persistently maintains its pace at least a few steps beyond the ability of man to find enduring peace. Communications, particularly television, rivet our attention on the president and the most desperate problems he seems unable to solve. It is in an environment of unprecedented social and institutional Darwinism that we bear witness to the manifestations of presidential power. No perspective on the exercise of that power can be informed in an ahistorical time capsule that is insulated from the searing realities of our time, the recent past, and the near future.

Nor can the potential of presidential power be reckoned in a political vacuum. It must be assessed in terms of the executive branch over which the president presides, the Congress and the federal judiciary which are theoretically separate and equal, the states and cities which are supposed to provide decentralized sources of power, the press, the special-interest institutions of our society, the political parties, and the people. The relationship of the man to the office, his personality, ideology, and experience are of special importance; but the measure of their importance must be taken in the algebra of institutional forces at work on the presidency. Despite the Watergate scandals and the Vietnam War, virtually without exception those forces are presently poised to accept the maintenance and growth of presidential power. The target of our national energies should be the restructuring of those institutional forces more than the reshaping of the presidency, if we truly seek to put presidential power in a healthy democratic perspective.

The personal characteristics of George Washington and Richard Nixon present a contrast as sharp as the Federalist papers and the White House tapes. The lofty goals and high hopes that blew so freshly through the first presidency of the newborn republic stand in stark relief against the musky air of amorality and criminality that polluted the presidency in the early 1970s. The significance of personal immorality has been frequently underestimated in contemporary analyses of the Nixon presidency.

Nevertheless, a man does not lie when he thinks others will tell the truth and catch him in his falsehood. Professional politicians do not seek candidates for office who have no chance of winning elections. Men do not ordinarily wage war unless they believe they have the weapons with which to win. The opportunity for success and the means to take advantage of that opportunity must be available to the potential actor, whether man, politician, warrior—or president.

The presidential office today is not the office to which George Washington was first elected in 1789. Its powers are vastly more extensive; its dominance of American political life daily apparent to most citizens and all politicians; its reach into our economy, our social and political institutions, and our personal lives far deeper than Washington could have conceived.

It is not simply that the power of the presidency has multiplied beyond calculation since the early days of our nation. The originally conceived counterpoints to presidential power have also changed. The relative decline has been sharp for some. None has grown in power and influence as the presidency has. Watergate's service to our nation may, in the final analysis, rest in its tragic dramatization of the tilt of the balance of power to the presidency. In the early 1970s, the institutional forces of our society were postured to permit a Watergate to happen. The executive branch itself was in such organizational disarray that the president felt the pressure—and sensed the freedom—to bring more power personally to himself and to enlarge his staff to control its exercise. The Congress had for years permitted its capability to hold the president accountable to atrophy. The states and the cities were weak financially and impotent politically as counterpoints of decentralized power. Despite the brilliant investigative work of a few news organizations, television demonstrated how the media could be turned more into an instrument of presidential power than a persistent skeptic of its exercise. The special-interest forces of society, such as business, labor, and the educational institutions, had become increasingly regulated by or dependent on the president and his branch. As a result, we approach the final decades of the twentieth century more as a presidential nation than as a republic of deliberately fragmented power.

But this was not the design of the original framers of the Constitution.

The robust debate among the founding fathers about the presidency ended in a clear, but by no means unanimous, victory for those who favored a strong, independent, one-man chief executive. They rejected the committee chairman concept that characterized the president of Congress system under the Articles of Confederation. They fashioned what James MacGregor Burns would aptly call, in his 1965 book *Presidential Government,* "one of the most powerful political institutions in the free world." But not without concern.

There was concern about the powers inherent in the commander-in-chief role even though the standing army of the proposed United States numbered less than one thousand at the time. The "unrestrained power of granting pardons for treason, which may be used to screen from punishment those whom he had secretly instigated to commit the crime, and thereby prevent a discovery of his own guilt" was, as *The American Heritage History of the Presidency* points out, a matter of grave apprehension to anti-Federalist New York Governor George Clinton. Delegates feared that the president would be controlled by "minions and favorites." There was particular anxiety that he would enter into sinister foreign alliances in secret, perhaps in part inspired by the fact that the fifty-five delegates themselves held their sessions behind the closed doors of Independence Hall (it was not until 1840, more than fifty years later, that James Madison's notes of the proceedings were first published).

Jefferson worried that the ability of the president to run for re-election might turn the chief executive into a lifetime officeholder. The four-year term itself was thought by others to be an overreaction to the no more than one-in-three year term of the president of Congress under the Articles of Confederation. Most concerns were capsulized in fears of creating another "despotic monarchy" of the kind that Thomas Paine had so thoroughly discredited and devastatingly ridiculed in his best-selling pamphlet, *Common Sense.* All the delegates shared one concern: They wanted to make certain that the president would be accountable and responsive to the people.

The ratification votes in the states reflected the many disagreements during the secret debates in Philadelphia. Rhode Island rejected the Constitution. Despite George Washington's uniquely persuasive support, the Virginia state legislature approved it by only 10 votes, 89 to 79. The arguments that a strong Congress, a life-tenure judiciary, independent states, and a president both impeachable and indictable for improper conduct could hold the presidency in check were of special significance in persuading the necessary nine of thirteen states to ratify a document with a one-man chief executive officer and commander in chief vested for a four-year term with "the executive Power." Ratification took two years and occurred in June 1788.

From its beginning in 1789, with George Washington, to the present, the presidential shield has been held by a host of diverse men: some idealistic, others imperialistic; some woefully inept, others astonishingly able; some ideological, others pragmatic; most honest, a few corrupt. The men who have stood behind this shield have, more often than not, risen to the occasions history has thrust upon their presidencies. As an institution, the office of the presidency has, until recently, survived the judgment of historians with more distinction than most of the men who have occupied it.

Historically, the powers of the presidency have expanded in times of war and domestic crisis. For the most part the American people have enthusiastically bestowed additional powers on the president during such periods; often they have not bothered to rescind them. Men like Abraham Lincoln, Woodrow Wilson, and the two Roosevelts have been among our strongest presidents and have exercised enormous power at the peaks of their careers in office. The great power inherent in the office has made superb moments of leadership possible. But even those men, to say nothing of the founding fathers, could hardly have conceived the total power that would be vested in the modern presidency at the time of our nation's bicentennial.

During the term of Chester Arthur (1881–1885), just before the turn of this century, Woodrow Wilson wrote of a weak and innocuous presidency in his book, *Congressional Government*. The chief executive and the branch he headed were, Wilson noted, "taken into partnership with the legislature upon a salary which may be withheld, and . . . allowed no voice in the management of the business." The presidency, as Wilson saw it then, was "simply charged with the superintendence of the employees." Wilson's view changed

over time, of course; he died defeated in what then seemed
to many an overreaching attempt by the president to put the
United States in the League of Nations.

Yet Wilson, at his most ambitious moments, would have
been hard pressed to consider actions on the scale of American involvement in Korea or Vietnam without a formal declaration of war. It is doubtful that even Henry Lockwood in
his book favoring *The Abolition of the Presidency* thought
such actions remotely possible when he wrote in 1884, "Let
a person be chosen to an office, with power . . . equal to that
of the Presidency . . . and it will make but little difference
whether the law actually gives him the right to act in a
particular direction or not. . . . He acts. No argument that the
law has been violated will avail."

The foundations of the presidency for the final decades of
the twentieth century were set more in the terms of Franklin
D. Roosevelt than in the terms of George Washington or any
of his intervening successors. To be sure, Jackson, Lincoln,
Theodore Roosevelt, and other strong presidents provided
some precedents for Franklin Roosevelt. But the combination of domestic crisis (depression) and global war focused
ever-increasing power in the White House during his unprecedented four-term presidency. The presidency would
never be the same again. Emergency war and economic
powers, many in effect to this day, set precedents for Korea,
Vietnam, and the first peacetime wage and price controls of
the early 1970s. The New Deal's involvement in business,
labor, social welfare, and housing set the stage for Lyndon
Johnson's Great Society to embark upon the most pervasive
and profound intervention of the central government in an
attempt to equalize opportunity and redistribute wealth and
power in America.

Judged by his deeds, Franklin Roosevelt saw the presidential office as the power center of American government. But
even he could not have foreseen the array of political, social,
and technological forces that would further concentrate
power in the presidency. The cold-war pressure persisted
with the same intensity during most of the term of John
Kennedy that it unyieldingly exhibited during the time of

Harry Truman. Modern industrialization, communications, science, technology, and concentrations of economic power —to say nothing of racial and social tension—worked not simply to maintain but to enhance the power of the central executive as the people turned to strong presidents like Roosevelt, Truman, Kennedy, and Johnson to solve their problems.

The relatively somnambulent years of Dwight Eisenhower might have brought a sigh of relief to those concerned about the depth and breadth of presidential intrusion into American society. But the many presently intransigent problems that festered during his tenure set the stage for an unprecedented surge in presidential power. The Johnson presidency saw more power over domestic matters flow to the White House than during any other comparable time span in this century. If Roosevelt strengthened the president vis-à-vis the potential counterforces in our republic, Johnson tilted the balance of power in our federal system to the point where the presidency was the source to which everyone looked who wanted the central government to intervene in domestic society. And most everyone seemed to want intervention for one purpose or another.

Since the time of Franklin Roosevelt, the presidency has grown in power much more rapidly and extensively than any other part of the system, dwarfing the Congress, the states, the cities, the special interests; and far more than holding its own with the judicial branch and the media. Whether that growth has deformed or enhanced our political system is the key political question our nation faces. The presidency is meant to be part of an intricate system of checks and balances. It cannot be considered in a political isolation, a thing apart from the Congress, the courts, the states and cities, political parties, the press, and most importantly, the people. Only when the presidency is considered as part of an institutional, political, and social system can we have a sense of whether and to what extent it is out of balance, and whether it is time for the American people to cry "halt" before their institutions become too weak to turn back the tide of executive power. Whether Lord Acton's overused aphorism about absolute power corrupting absolutely exaggerated the point, it is clear beyond reasonable doubt that power creates a desire and perceived need for more power and strong men with such desires and perceived needs will act to fulfill them. Along with the overdue concern and attention to the development of presidential power in modern times, the actions of three presidents—Kennedy, Johnson, and Nixon in connection with the war in Southeast Asia, and the uses of power by Nixon in the sordid political nightmare referred to as Watergate—have spawned a great deal of analytical nonsense about presidential power. The persistently debilitating implications of the war in Southeast Asia and the amoral and criminal elements of Watergate and its related abuses of power cannot be denied. Those who assess these two events as major tragedies for the American democracy also have an obligation to consider carefully what went awry in the office of the presidency and our political and social systems that should be changed. They must recognize the difference between a corrupt man in control of a sound institution and a good man corrupted by a bad institution.

A failure to recognize the distinction between the presidential office and the man who holds it or the blurring of that distinction can be very much in the interest of the occupant of the office or his opponents at any particular moment in time. Confusion of the person and the office can lead partisans to emphasize the need to strengthen the office held by a Kennedy or Johnson during the 1960s and then to demand that the wings of the imperial presidency of Richard Nixon be trimmed in the early 1970s. But such confusion has no place in an analysis of presidential power. Recognition of the distinction between the office and the man is essential to any pragmatic attempt to put presidential power in perspective.

Any analysis of the presidency must recognize the limits of civil and criminal law and the inherent fallibility of human nature, however well- or ill-intentioned. Careful attention must also be paid to people, politics, and institutional relationships. These are the relevant points of departure. The creature comforts and occasionally regal ambiance that attend the presidential office are of symbolic, not systematic, importance to the kind of analysis the potency of presidential power deserves in these times.

A strong presidency is essential to the future of this nation and the freedom of our people. American citizens should appreciate the need for a strong presidency and understand its benefits as well as its dangers. Accepting the obligations of citizenship in a presidential nation is essential to deriving those benefits. There have certainly been corrupt and inept men in the Oval Office and on White House staffs; but most who have served there have done so with integrity and good intentions. Those with talent and social conscience who serve there must have the power to achieve, through legitimate means, the ends they believe desirable for this nation—ends which in most cases are well within the mandate they were elected to fulfill. Indeed, as often as not, the reason such men fail to fulfill their mandate is lack of power. The federal government and the United States changed irrevocably in some respects during the 1960s and the efficient operation of government, as well as the achievement of our democratic ideals, requires that the office of the president remain strong enough to lead the nation with accountability and credibility and to execute the laws passed by the Congress with responsive compassion.

The Constitution is flexible enough to accommodate these changes and the conflict that inevitably accompanies and sometimes survives them. The central context of constitutional accommodation without excessive concentrations of power is the system of checks and balances. The balance conceived by the founding fathers was among different branches and levels of the government and between the public and private sectors. The framers heeded Montesquieu's warning in his book, *The Spirit of the Laws*, that, "when the legislative and executive powers are united in the same person, or in the same body of magistrates, there can be no liberty." The Congress was given the power to legislate and was bicamerally divided. The Senate was to provide whatever special wisdom and insulation from immediate pressures attend a six-year term. The House of Representatives, with a brief two-year term, was devised as a more direct respondent to the wishes of the American electorate. The members of the federal judiciary were given lifetime tenure, the better to judge specific cases of individual rights and duties and individual guilt or innocence, free of contemporary political and social pressure.

The original hope was that the three branches would have sufficient powers to check abuses by one another and that appropriate increases in the power of one might be countered by an increase in the power of another to check and balance. The flexible language of the Constitution provided growing room for the separate but less than equal branches to increase their own power at any given point in time. The Congress has always had the power to organize itself in whatever way it desires and to appropriate funds for its own use. The failure to exercise that power effectively should not be confused with its absence.

There is a fourth place at the table of American democratic power which the framers tried to set independent of the three branches of government. The First Amendment provides, quite simply and straightforwardly, that the "Congress shall make no law . . . abridging the freedom of speech, or of the press." The press—in modern terms, television, radio, newspapers, magazines, and books—was conceived of as the people's eyes and ears and often their voice. Its license to criticize those in power was given unique constitutional preference.

The men who drafted the Constitution and its early amendments were also conscious of the need for decentralization. They gave the states (and through them, the cities, counties, and boroughs) special constitutional protection. Article V permits amendments to the Constitution only "when ratified by the legislature of three-fourths of the several states, or by Conventions in three-fourths thereof." In the Eleventh Amendment, they reserved to the states or the people "The powers not delegated to the United States by the Constitution, nor prohibited by it to the states."

This was all done in the context of economic, technological, and social development at the end of the eighteenth century. If, in their extraordinary foresight and wisdom, the young men in Philadelphia foresaw many of the nineteenth-century developments, certainly most of what has happened in the twentieth century was beyond the political and intellectual ken of even the most prescient of them. What they fortunately did recognize were the intricacies of human nature. In addition to the need for compromise, this insight into man's nature is doubtless why so many provisions in our Constitution are so ambiguously drafted, to give human beings in changing circumstances the ability to adjust their condition within certain fundamental commandments of freedom. But it is also why the president was given real rather than ceremonial power.

To put the presidency in contemporary perspective, it is important to understand what happened to the American people and the American nation during the turbulent decade of the 1960s. When John Kennedy and Lyndon Johnson took charge of the executive branch, the federal government was not involved in manpower training programs; social security did not include medicare; less than $2 billion was being spent on health and education programs; defense expenditures represented some 60 percent of the budget; there was no antipoverty program; the environment was a matter of concern to a few professors and perhaps those students entranced by Thoreau.

Regardless of what anyone thought of the Great Society, when Lyndon Johnson left government, it was a political, social, institutional, financial, and bureaucratic reality. The central government was training more than 1.5 million men and women each year for jobs. Medicare for the aged was in place and medical care for everyone was almost within reach. The central government had become involved in American education at every level with billions of dollars and countless forms and regulations. Johnson inherited an executive branch that operated less than fifty domestic programs; his legacy was a central executive operating some five hundred such programs. The Brookings Institution analysis of the fiscal 1975 federal budget tells the story dramatically. From 1960 to 1975, the national government's budget had increased, in cash income maintenance, from $20.6 billion to

$98.2 billion; in helping people buy essentials, from $1.1 billion to $33.2 billion; in aid for social programs (including revenue sharing), from $1.4 billion to some $20 billion; and in investments in the environment, from $5.4 billion to $17.3 billion. Once appropriated, control over these funds settled in the president's branch of government.

By the early 1970s technology and population had brought us to the point where state lines often were at best irrelevant and at worst counterproductive in the solution of such problems as air and water pollution, transportation, congestion, economic development. As a result, the federal government moved into each of these areas, not as an apprentice laborer, but as the foreman on the job directing the social and economic work of our nation.

Something else happened on the way to the end of the twentieth century. We discovered that natural resources were not inexhaustible and that the price of self-sufficiency in energy, for example, required expensive and risky investments in nuclear and solar power that made no sense for near-bankrupt states and cities. Such colossal investments could only be financed by a self-insurance program distributed across the entire nation and regulated, if not operated, by the federal government.

Economic power in the late 1960s and early 1970s had no more respect for state and city boundaries than environmental problems. Our giant corporations, such as those in communications, transportation, electronics, and pharmaceuticals, were far beyond the ability of the states to regulate effectively. The individual gross product of General Motors and some other multinational corporations had surpassed the gross product of several of our states. No longer were Sears and Roebuck and the Atlantic and Pacific Tea Company the only distributors of goods and foods at the retail level across our nation. Scores of powerful corporate colleagues had joined that once-exclusive club. Larger unions were formed to assemble workers in stronger bargaining units. The banks that financed these enterprises came to control more money than most of our cities. As the people became concerned about these large concentrations of economic power, they looked to the federal government for protection, in the form of consumer laws and wage and price controls. The Congress responded by giving the president wide discretionary power over the economy and by enacting consumer protection legislation that covered everything from auto safety and truth-in-lending to children's toys and flammable fabrics. Big business provided less resistance than was expected because there were advantages in dealing with one set of regulatory standards at the national government level rather than with fifty sets established by the fifty states. Individual and institution, large and small, turned to the president's executive branch for help and protection. Fine-tuning the economy— the dream of a few brilliant economists like Walter Heller, Gardner Ackley, and Arthur Okun only a decade before— became the consuming political responsibility of the president.

The American nation also established some major national objectives far beyond the capabilities of private enterprise and private resources, notably the National Aeronautics and Space Administration program to put a man on the moon and the eventually aborted supersonic transport project. Kennedy and Johnson ignited public support for these efforts. Business and labor (which had to some degree spurred Kennedy and Johnson to action) enthusiastically joined the federal government in these programs. Another industry, space, was created, totally dependent on the central government. At the same time, the miserable failure of the Interstate Commerce Commission in its regulation of the railroads and the similar default of state and local public transportation authorities resulted in the creation of Amtrack, a government railroad system for much of the nation, and opened the door for the central government to become the controlling investor in local mass transit systems. By the early 1970s, aping the railroads, the airlines turned to the Civil Aeronautics Board in an attempt to ease their economic woes.

The response of the central executive—the president's branch—was to increase its size, power, resources, and talented personnel to deal with these problems. The response of the states and cities was to turn to the central government and to grow even faster in size and dependence on that government. Little wonder, then, that over the course of the 1960s government became the fastest growing business in the United States. Although most of the employees went to work for state and local government, many of them became *de facto* agents of the Federal government because most of the money and power was placed at the disposal of the federal executive. Ultimately, that meant the White House. Harry Truman's desk plaque, "The buck stops here," took on cogent new meaning. The presidency needed more authority than ever to stay abreast of the political and social responsibility that the electorate placed on the office and the man who held it.

Much of that responsibility was also self-imposed by presidential promises that far exceeded performance capabilities under existing legislative and administrative authority. Here modern communications played a critical role. The president was visible to the people almost every night on national television and he naturally wanted to proclaim some good news or promise better news. The desperate fight for a minute or two of national television time by those who aspired to succeed incumbent presidents led them to promise even more if elected. For every ill, from ending the war in Vietnam to providing day-care centers for working mothers, there was a presidential solution. The more savage the storm, the more the people looked to their president for relief—and the more inclined the president seemed to imply that, once the storm was weathered, the gold at the end of the rainbow would be within reach.

The explosion of the White House staff was inevitable. Woodrow Wilson had his Colonel Edward House, but Franklin Roosevelt is generally regarded as the president who had the first substantive White House staff. When Roosevelt died, Truman divided the tasks among several permanent aides, including Clark Clifford, Charles Murphy, and George Elsey. Eisenhower adapted the military staff system to the presidency. Sherman Adams became the chief of an extensive executive staff system that Eisenhower considered essential for the efficient conduct of a relatively passive presidency.

With the activism of John F. Kennedy came the contours of the present White House staff structure. The National Security Council staff under McGeorge Bundy became a little State Department. Larry O'Brien built a sophisticated legislative staff to work with the Congress. Under Theodore Sorenson the counsel to the president assumed new powers, and Ralph Dungan opened a White House personnel office to scout the talent needed to fill increasing numbers of presidential nominations and appointments in the cabinet departments and agencies.

Lyndon B. Johnson increased the size and potency of this staff system as he reorganized it. The press secretary to the president was assigned aides whose primary interest was television, or special advance work, as well as newspapers and magazines. In addition to being special counsel to the President, Harry McPherson directed a stable of speech writers. The National Security Council staff remained much the same under Walt Rostow as it had been under Bundy. I was directed to assemble a comparable staff for domestic affairs to develop legislative programs for submission to the Congress and to coordinate and help develop domestic and economic policy and the federal executive response to domestic crises.

The Johnson domestic affairs staff never exceeded five or six people. It remained for Richard Nixon to enlarge it into a domestic council of some seventy professionals. Under Henry Kissinger, the National Security Council publicly became the *de facto* State Department and moved as deeply into defense as foreign policy. By November 1972, the Nixon White House staff soared to an astonishing 607 people; it leveled off thereafter at between 500 and 550. Gerald Ford replaced Nixon staffers almost (if not quite) as fast as they departed.

The explosion of the presidential staff, in part, reflects the increased difficulty of directing the executive branch with its myriad responsibilities so often irrationally scattered among many departments and agencies. It also dramatically evidences the unprecedented powers that have been assumed by the presidency and vested in the central executive. The preservation of freedom in America in the last quarter of the twentieth century requires a strong presidency, but one checked and balanced by energized institutions, public and private. The viability of these institutions is as essential to our freedom as adherence to the Constitution that set them in motion. Whether this nation has the same appointment in Samarra that history has made for other civilizations that concentrated power in the hands of one man may well depend on its ability to revitalize and reshape the counterpoints of presidential power.

I I

---·◦◦◦·---

THE PRESIDENT'S
BRANCH

"I can assure you of one thing: You will never work for or with a more complicated man than Lyndon Johnson so long as you live. I guarantee it."

With those words, then Secretary of Defense Robert S. McNamara shook my hand and wished me well as I left his office to become special assistant to the president of the United States in July of 1965. If McNamara's words aptly captured the personality of Lyndon Johnson, they provided no hint of the stunning complexity of the domestic side of the federal government. What neither he nor I appreciated was how rapidly and geometrically that complexity would grow as Great Society programs proposed by the president sailed like legislative boomerangs through the Congress and back to the White House for signing ceremonies and execution. What happened to the executive branch during those Great Society years increased the potential of presidential power more significantly than during any other five-year period in our history. With the Johnson programs, the president's branch reached into all the nooks and crannies of American life and acquired leverage over institutions, public and private, that had not previously felt the benevolence—or the pinch—of presidential power.

The tilt of power to the president had begun long before Johnson took the oath of office for his first elected term in January 1965. From 1930 to 1965, the American population rose from 123 million to almost 200 million; and the gross national product rose from $90 billion to $900 billion. But during that same thirty-five-year-period, the executive branch changed even more dramatically:

> —Expenditures on the domestic side of the government rose from $2.7 billion to approximately $100 billion, more than 59 times faster than the rate of increase in population.
> —Federal grant-in-aid programs rose from 24 to almost 200, almost 14 times faster than the rate of increase in population.
> —The number of government civilian employees rose from 600,000 to almost 3 million, more than 7 times faster than the rate of increase in population.
> —The military evolved from a relatively small number of adventurous soldiers, sailors, and marines to a standing Army, Navy, Air Force, and Marine Corps that approached 3 million men and women.

From 1965 to 1968, the domestic side of the executive branch changed even more dramatically. In the First Session of the 89th Congress, of 87 major measures proposed by the president, 84 were passed. In the Second Session, of 113 presidential proposals, 97 became law. To those 181 new legislative programs passed in 1965 and 1966, the 90th Congress would, at the president's recommendation, add more than 100. When the Johnson administration ended on January 20, 1969, there were some 500 social programs operated by the federal government to quench the American thirst for new solutions to persistent public problems.

The funding was often inadequate and some programs did not achieve their objectives. But when Johnson left the White House, grant-in-aid programs were available for everything from flood control to birth control to rat control. For poor children there were school breakfast, Head Start, day care, and foster grandparent programs. For the elderly, there were nursing homes, medicare, and special housing. For the minorities, there were civil rights, voting rights, and fair housing laws. For the consumers, there were truth-in-packaging and truth-in-lending acts and all sorts of safety legislation ranging from automobiles and highways to children's toys and housewives' draperies. For the environmentalists, there were scenic rivers and trails, clean air and water legislation, and any number of conservation and wilderness area preservation bills. The people in the country got rural development grants; the urban dweller a safe streets act; and the American Indians, their own Indian Bill of Rights. The federal government began training more workers than did the Fortune 500 largest corporations. Its position as the single most important factor in financing and building the homes in which most Americans live was cemented and enhanced. Legislation was passed to help drug addicts, retarded children, students, teachers, and scientists. We often said the president could not be the mayor of every city and the governor of every state, but to future historians it may well appear that was exactly what Americans were trying to make him.

After the Great Society programs became part of the executive bureaucracy, the constitutional mandate that the president "take care that the Laws be faithfully executed" took on dramatically new proportions of social justice. The president who seeks to fulfill the letter and spirit of that mandate discovers that effective control of the executive branch is aggravated by the organizationally incoherent way in which many of these five hundred domestic programs are scattered throughout a crazy quilt of bureaus and divisions in the more than one hundred executive departments and agencies. The decisive factor in situating a new program in a particular department or agency often has little to do with rational concepts of management. One congressional committee may be considered more receptive to a proposed idea than another, or simply be less busy than another. One cabinet or agency head may have more influence with the president, the White House staff, or the Congress; another may be more able as an administrator than those of his peers vying for the same program.

With hundreds of new programs passed in five years, a certain degree of confusion and error is inevitable. As a result, executing presidential programs is not without occasionally telling, if preposterous, incidents. Shortly after the Congress enacted legislation which authorized the president, subject to congressional veto, to designate "wilderness areas" that would be held sacred from any development, President Johnson wanted to announce the first areas he selected with some fanfare and publicity. He particularly wished to emphasize how close these areas would be to population centers and how many million people would be able to visit them and return home in the same day. Since he wanted this done within hours of his decision, an otherwise routine letter to the Congress was redrafted in frenetic haste.

When the president had edited and approved the letter, he told me, "Get Udall over here right away and the two of you brief the press. This is an important event, not only for the conservationists, but for the several million Americans who can visit these areas." I immediately called Secretary of the Interior Stewart Udall and he rushed to the White House within a few minutes. He reviewed the material quickly and we went to the Fish Room to brief the press. By the time I returned to my office, my secretaries, Peggy Hoxie and Evelyn Irons, excitedly chorused, "Secretary [of Agriculture] Freeman wants to talk to you right now. Boy is he boiling!"

I went into my office, picked up the phone and asked the White House operator to connect me with Orville Freeman. As soon as Freeman got on the phone, he said, "What in hell is going on over there? I just saw the wire service tickers saying that you and Udall briefed the press on the new wilderness areas. Wilderness areas fall within the jurisdiction of the Agriculture Department." I apologized to Freeman and checked back with Udall to discover that not one of us—the president who had signed the bill, the interior secretary who was the administration spokesman on conservation, the senior White House aide who had worked on the legislation— had realized that the wilderness areas program was being administered by the Department of Agriculture and not by the Department of Interior.

Smaller federal agencies and numerous bureaus within large departments respond to presidential leadership only in the minds of the most naïve students of government administration. Under the myth of reporting directly to the president, more often than not these agencies operate as independent fiefdoms, responsive to their own constituencies, pet theories, and the congressional subcommittees to which they look for oversight and appropriations, rather than to presidential leadership and the broad national interest. While serving as presidential assistant for domestic affairs, I doubt that I ever met, much less consulted or helped guide, more than one-third of these noncabinet agency and commission heads. Hyperactive as he was, President Johnson met even fewer of them. And, as House Appropriations Committee Chairman George Mahon has said, "LBJ knew more about the federal government and the line items in the budget and had his finger in more agencies than any other president in this century."

For the chief executive, the problem of loyalties to constituencies and members of Congress, as distinguished from responsiveness to presidential policy direction, is not limited to smaller agencies that receive little or no personal attention from the president and his staff. The middle-level bureau chiefs and the regional administrators in large government departments are often predominantly concerned about the attitudes of the substantive or geographical constituencies they serve and the senators and congressmen with whom they must work, particularly those in positions of power on the oversight and appropriations subcommittees and those who reside in their region. In short, these smaller Federal agencies and bureaus within larger executive departments are presidentially unaccountable. Since the president is the elected chief of the executive branch, the condition precedent to rendering such agencies accountable to the people is, in the first instance, to render them accountable to him.

Marshaling all the programmatic tools available to attack a broad national problem can be a bureaucratic nightmare. If, for example, a president were to decide, as a matter of national policy, that every man and woman in this nation

capable and desirous of working should be given the necessary training and employment, the intelligent implementation of that decision would involve a number of federal departments and agencies. There are manpower training
programs of one kind or another in the Department of Labor, the Office of Economic Opportunity, the Department of
Health, Education and Welfare, the Veterans Administration, the Department of Defense, the Department of Commerce, and, to lesser degrees, in other departments, like
Agriculture (for certain rural Americans), Interior (for
American Indians), and the Economic Development Administration in distressed areas. The Justice Department's
Civil Rights Division and the Equal Employment Opportunity Commission would be involved because of their roles
in eliminating job discrimination. A president should thus
consult all those departments, devise a coordinated program,
and then order its implementation. It is not surprising that
there have been more interdepartmental committees attempting to coordinate domestic programs than anyone has
been able to count or hope to be aware of. In 1966, a Department of Agriculture study revealed the astonishing fact that
its secretary was chairman or a member of at least 306 inter-
agency committees.

It is not surprising, then, that shortly after assuming office,
presidents so often conclude that their most difficult task in
carrying out their mandate from the American people is to
inspire, persuade, cajole, urge, and, too rarely, order the
federal bureaucracy to follow their policies. Harry Truman
expressed his frustration when he commented that he spent
most of his time trying to convince people to do what they
should be doing anyway. The enormous potential power inherent in the Great Society programs is bound to make the
difficulty in exercising it even more frustrating for an incumbent president in the late 1970s and 1980s.

What Americans must recognize is that the same bureaucratic nightmares in the executive branch that make it impossible for the president to assess responsibility among fragmented authorities, make it difficult for the Congress, as
legislative representative of the people, to hold the president

accountable for the actions of the branch he heads. The president who wishes to be responsive to the needs of his people is often frustrated by the tenacious strength with which organizational disarray informs bureaucratic attempts to protect parochial interests at the expense of national needs. Irrational fragmentation should not be confused with intelligent decentralization. The former tends to centralize and concentrate more power in the presidency and the White House staff; the latter provides an environment for the healthy dispersion of executive power.

Seated atop this bureaucratic Tower of Babel, a president who seeks to fulfill his enlarged mandate for the faithful execution of the laws and to be responsive to the needs of the people will strive for control and policy direction of the executive branch. If he can reshape the government departments and agencies into sensible functional organizations, then he will have gone a long way toward consolidating his power over the executive branch and providing himself with department heads who can truly and fairly be held responsible for program areas, like manpower training or the development of natural resources. But he cannot get this job done alone. Most major reorganizations require legislation or formal congressional acquiescence.

And the president needs some help from his own cabinet and agency heads, which is rarely forthcoming. With one exception (John Gardner), in the scores of reorganization proposals I considered while on the White House staff, the cabinet officer or agency head destined to lose a program in a reorganization opposed the plan. With one other exception (J. Edgar Hoover), the cabinet officer or agency head who was gaining jurisdiction through a reorganization favored it. Gardner believed the water pollution control program belonged in the Interior Department rather than in the Department of Health, Education and Welfare. Hoover did not want the Bureau of Narcotics moved into the FBI because he felt too many Treasury narcotics agents were corrupt or inadequately trained.

President Johnson became painfully aware of the need to

reorganize the government to better control it, and of the difficulty in eliciting the necessary congressional agreement. He was successful in some areas: in the creation of a Department of Housing and Urban Development, bringing together several formerly independent agencies, and a Department of Transportation, consolidating more than thirty independent agencies and programs throughout the federal government; in establishing the Bureau of Narcotics and Dangerous Drugs, assembling the enforcement elements in the Departments of Treasury, Health, Education and Welfare, and Justice in the Justice Department; and in effecting several other consolidating reorganizations, including those related to better operation of pollution and civil rights programs. Johnson's recommendation that the Post Office Department be dropped from the cabinet and recast as a hybrid government-private operation was adopted by Richard Nixon and approved by the Congress during Nixon's first term. These achievements, remarkable as they were, would be regarded by most experienced government observers as only the beginning of a serious effort to make the executive branch more efficient and to provide the institutional structure essential to render the exercise of presidential power more responsive and accountable.

The need for vast executive reorganization has long been recognized. The task force established by President Johnson in 1964 recommended that the government establish a Department of Natural Resources and a Department of Housing and Community Development. A subsequent presidential task force, chaired by Northwest Industries Board Chairman Ben Heineman, recommended the establishment of a Department of Natural Resources and Development, a Department of Economic Affairs, and a Department of Social Services. The recommendations of President Nixon's reorganization commission, headed by Roy Ash, were similar. As a cornerstone of his new American Revolution, Nixon asked the Congress to enact the commission's proposals to consolidate several of the twelve cabinet departments and various agencies into four domestic departments: Community Development, Natural Resources and Development,

Human Resources, and Economic Affairs. Joined by State, Treasury, Defense, Justice, Agriculture (which survived even at the proposal stage for political not organizational reasons), and Transportation, the cabinet departments would have been reduced only from eleven to ten and several other agencies and bureaus would have been abolished. More importantly, they would have been reorganized along functional lines and lesser independent agencies would have been consolidated under their control. The strong bipartisan support these proposals received from many members of prior Democratic and Republican administrations was not surprising. Where one stands on the issue of executive reorganization is determined by whether and where one has sat in the executive branch. Anyone who looks at the problem of running the federal government, particularly from the viewpoint of its chief executive, is likely to come to many of the same conclusions. Anyone seeking an accountable and responsive presidency should agree.

Whether because of political naïveté or rhetoric unsubstantiated by effective lobbying, Nixon made such sweeping proposals to the Congress at one time that they were destined for early congressional demise. Reorganizations are enormously difficult to achieve politically. In the Congress, committee members covet their jurisdiction as bees protect their hives; taking away any honey without being stung is no task for political amateurs. They have potent allies among their parochial cohorts in the legislative branch, the executive bureaucracy, and the special interests that are aroused by any attempt to disturb existing cozy relationships.

The investment of political capital is so great and the risk of loss so substantial that a president can at best achieve one or two major reorganizations during his years in office—if he selects his targets shrewdly. The two major Johnson achievements, the Department of Housing and Urban Development and the Department of Transportation, were reorganizations of separate agencies, virtually all of which fell within the jurisdiction of the same House or Senate oversight committees before and after congressional approval of the reorganization. The constituent agencies folded into the De-

partment of Housing and Urban Development were all sub-
ject to the jurisdiction of the House Banking and Currency
Committee and the Senate Banking, Housing and Urban
Affairs Committee.*

All but two of the major constituent elements Johnson
proposed for inclusion within the Department of Transportation were within the jurisdiction of the Senate Commerce
Committee and the House Committee on Interstate and Foreign Commerce. Those two elements were the Coast Guard
in the Treasury Department (the House and Senate Banking
Committees had jurisdiction) and the Maritime Administration in the Commerce Department (on the House side, the
Committee on Merchant Marine and Fisheries had jurisdiction).

Johnson was able to convince the Congress to include the
Coast Guard in the new Department of Transportation not
entirely because of the careful staff work that preceded the
submission of the proposal to the Congress and his political
shrewdness and persuasive power. The Coast Guard itself
wanted to move into the Department of Transportation and
the secretary of Treasury at the time, Henry (Joe) Fowler,
was a team player. Once the decision was made, he did everything in his power to help pass the legislation.

The Maritime Administration, however, was never folded
into the Department of Transportation, despite a strenuous
legislative battle by Johnson himself. The unyielding opposition of the American labor movement (backed by maritime
industry management) found fast friends on the House Maritime Committee and among the career civil servants in the
Maritime Administration angered by then-Administrator
Nicholas Johnson's enthusiastic support of the president's
proposal and maverick attitude toward maritime industry
sacred cows. That committee was already distressed by the
failure of the Johnson administration to provide additional
funds for the maritime program. Its chairman was infuriated
by the thought of losing jurisdiction over the bulk of the
committee's work. Key committee members were depend-

*At that time, it was called the Senate Banking Committee.

ent on the maritime-industry-labor combine for political financial support.

The House Government Operations Committee did report out a bill which would have included the Maritime Administration within the Transportation Department. But House Maritime Committee members won their cause on the House floor by a resounding 260 to 117 vote with a potent argument: "If LBJ's transportation reorganization puts us out of business this year, then he may send up another proposal which will put your favorite committee out of business next year." The tenacious floor manager of the Johnson bill, California Democrat Chet Holifield, called the struggle over the Transportation Department the toughest, roughest fight during his many years in the Congress. He was right. But most reorganization attempts signal such fights.

Johnson's third major reorganization attempt never got off the ground. His 1967 State of the Union Message proposed the creation of a combined Department of Labor and Commerce. The proposed consolidation was not founded in the painstaking staff work that had preceded the earlier reorganization proposals. But it was discussed in advance with some businessmen and AFL-CIO President George Meany. Among others, I talked to Edgar Kaiser and Henry Ford, while the president himself talked to labor leader Meany. The businessmen cautiously gave their tentative approval and the president told me that Meany agreed to support it. The proposal was sent to the Congress where it was killed without hearings, largely because of labor opposition. The long-term relationship with Meany was of such importance to Johnson that he never revealed Meany's prior clearance of the proposal. Instead, he accepted the criticism for making a rare legislative blunder.

The unsuccessful attempt to combine the Commerce and Labor Departments teaches an important lesson for purposes of this analysis. When the elimination of a decidedly constituent-oriented department is contemplated, a Herculean presidential effort will be required; and even such an effort may fail. The sense of constituent concern on the part of labor, eventually shared by powerful business elements, in connection with the proposed Commerce and Labor reorganization, served to confirm the president's skepticism of recommendations coming out of those departments (and others, like Agriculture). An incidental result was further to strengthen the role of the domestic staff at the White House and the Bureau of the Budget in reviewing their recommendations and guiding their work.

The Johnson administration experience demonstrated that congressional passage of reorganization measures through the Congress requires a significant investment of political capital by the president himself, and even then significant structural reform is likely to elude his grasp. That experience was confirmed under Nixon. Nixon's 1971 call to eliminate the constituency-oriented Departments of Commerce, Labor, and Interior and to sharply trim the jurisdiction of the Agriculture Department, fell on deaf congressional ears. Lacking Johnson's legislative genius and determination, Nixon made proposals so sweeping that the entrenched triangles of congressional committees, permanent executive bureaucracy, and special private interests were able to perform effectively under their sweetheart contract to maintain the institutional status quo. With so much less political capital to spend, Nixon soon withdrew from the battle.

The Congress can thwart executive reorganization. But it cannot offer alternatives to satisfy a president's natural appetite for one man with enough authority to be held responsible for a specific functional area. Richard Nixon announced the establishment of a super cabinet. Certain cabinet officers were given broad functional authority over their colleagues and responsibility to report directly to the president in those areas. Treasury Secretary George Shultz, for example, was designated to supervise the formulation and conduct of economic policy. But Nixon discovered that cabinet officers regard themselves as equals in their access and responsibility to the president and take seriously those laws that vest jurisdiction over certain matters to their departments. Perhaps lulled by their supine acceptance of directives from White House aides Bob Haldeman and John Ehrlichman, Nixon did not realize that cabinet officers will not take orders from one of their peers. The Nixon plan had about as little success as Johnson's abortive attempt to put Housing and Urban Development Secretary Robert Weaver in charge of his administration's attack on urban problems. When coordinating urban programs became a significant drain on White House staff time, Johnson issued an executive order explicitly vesting the secretary of Housing and Urban Development with the power to convene the resources of other cabinet departments and agencies for a coherent response to urban problems. The order was shortly ignored and the responsibility for coordinating the administration's urban programs fell back on the White House staff.

Where bureaucratic infighting is a serious threat to the carrying out of non-self-executing presidential directives, White House aides offer to a president two distinct advantages over *ad hoc* super-cabinet-officers. They speak as agents and in the name of the president of the United States, who is the legally constituted superior to all cabinet officers, and they do not have jurisdictional operations turf to protect and expand or bureaucracies and constituencies to appease. In 1966 and 1967, for example, when Johnson was concerned about the pressure that increased capital investment was exerting on interest rates, he decided to restrict the access of federal agency borrowers to the money market. Federal paper is issued by a number of federal departments and agencies to raise funds for capital projects in the private market. Not simply Treasury, but others like Housing and Urban Development, Agriculture, and the Federal Home Loan Bank Board issue such paper. Sister departments and agencies balked at having the Treasury Department control the extent to which they entered the money markets. As a result, Johnson established a system whereby, for almost two years, the immediate White House staff cleared the amount and timing of every offering by a government agency to raise funds in the private markets.

Beginning at the end of 1966, through the time Lyndon Johnson left office on January 20, 1969, the White House Domestic Affairs staff devoted less time to devising new programs and helping gain their enactment than to the problem of implementing and coordinating the cornucopia of Great Society legislation that had been and was still being enacted. With some three hundred items of new domestic legislation, we began the process of determining who would operate, supervise, or coordinate those programs, many of which put different departments and agencies in the same functional areas, for instance, education, pollution control, manpower training, and urban rehabilitation.

Seemingly interminable meetings were held in my White House office with four major figures: Labor Secretary Willard Wirtz; Health, Education and Welfare Secretary John Gardner; Housing and Urban Development Secretary Robert Weaver, and Office of Economic Opportunity Director Sargent Shriver. Most of that time was spent (often to the great frustration of Gardner and Shriver) on such bureaucratically thorny issues as who would do what and who would have how much authority over which programs. Arguments at the highest levels of government can also often be reduced to absurd bickering.

At one point, President Johnson announced that he would establish "one-stop service centers" in every ghetto in the nation, to provide neighborhood access to all the federally available social services at single locations. Partially as a result of the Watts riots, but also as a result of the angry discontent fermenting in other cities, Johnson gave high priority to bringing together the Labor Department job-training program which was at one end of the city, the Office of Economic Opportunity Job Corps application center which was at the other end, and the Health, Education and Welfare vocational education program which was in a third section of the city. Sometimes the locations of the three offices formed a perfect triangle of maximum distance.

The attempt to achieve his objective precipitated a bureaucratic Donnybrook. OEO wanted the service centers to bear its name. Secretary Wirtz wanted the Labor Department posted across the entrance (and, indeed, at one point threatened to withhold funds unless there was some indication on the door that the Labor Department was providing

the funds). Weaver thought Housing and Urban Development should operate the centers under its banner. The least
bureaucratic individual was Gardner who, having concluded
that the centers should go forward, wanted to make certain
that whoever controlled them would do so in fact as well as
in bureaucratic decor. On those occasions when the Washington bureaucrats finally reached agreement, moving
offices from one part of the city to another met with the same
kind of parochial resistance locally, with the vigorous support
of individual congressmen where shifts among different congressional districts were involved. Bureaucratic bickering
delayed the opening of these centers so long that few were
ever put in operation. What progress was achieved in Watts
may be attributable not only to the almost dictatorial authority the Justice Department was given by the president over
other departments in the wake of the 1965 rioting, but also
to the fact that Justice had no operational programs and
hence no bureaucratic turf to protect. Its only function was
to effect some convenient and effective collocation of Federal services and then move out.

Virtually all bureaucratic disputes of this sort are resolved
by the Office of Management and Budget or the White House
staff with minimal, if any, presidential involvement. For the
most part, the participant cabinet officers and agency heads
do not want the president to know how deeply and emotionally they have become involved in petty bureaucratic issues.
White House aides do not like to report to their boss that the
reason they cannot get the program off the ground sooner is
because top presidential appointees are trying to plant new
sod on their own turf or keep others from walking on their
bureaucratic lawns.

But presidents understand. They share a distaste for such
arguments in their presence among their cabinet officers.
Indeed, the more spirited the debate within the government
becomes on any matter, the more likely a president is to want
the issues narrowed and much of the spirit taken out of the
arguments before he has to face the two, three, or four opposing cabinet officers in the Oval Office. There are any number
of obvious techniques for this, but the one most often used

is to have the arguments thrashed out through White House aides. John Kennedy and Lyndon Johnson frequently employed this technique, although on major substantive issues they would also speak individually to the cabinet officers involved to make certain they understood departmental views. With rare exception, however, they would not meet with a discordant group until the issues had been narrowed. In part, this is a means to force busy cabinet officers to think through their own positions on the merits; and, in turn, to preserve as much of the president's time as possible for the irreconcilable issues.

Tasks such as these require personnel on the White House staff who are able and sensitive and who can master the substantive as well as the bureaucratic issues. A cacaphony of fragmented programs and the bureaucratic voices they amplify must be coordinated, and all else failing, the president needs a staff to do the job. As Clinton Rossiter has noted in his book, *The American Presidency,* in such an environment, the White House staff becomes an essential tool "to rescue not merely the administration, but the presidency itself from the babel and bedlam of the modern state."

As a president's frustration with operational fragmentation increases, he discovers with each missed objective that there is no one person in his government he can hold bureaucratically and politically responsible. That frustration peaks in times of immediate or persistent crisis when the presidential perch on top of the fragmented executive branch feels particularly insecure. Whether Republican or Democrat, liberal or conservative, the presidential reaction will be instinctively identical: Get someone in the White House to handle it. So common is this reaction in national security matters that we hardly notice it. But the same orders are increasingly issued in domestic affairs.

The president seeks to create a post, institution, or person that can reasonably be held accountable to achieve some specific, urgent objective. As environmental matters became public issues of pressing concern, President Nixon created an Environmental Protection Agency and a Council on Environmental Policy, both reporting directly to him. As inflation became a persistent and prickly crisis, Nixon found responsibility for economic policy formulation and implementation scattered about the Office of Management and Budget, the Council of Economic Advisers, and the Departments of Treasury, Commerce, and Labor. He initially established the Cost of Living Council, then the Price Commission and the Pay Board, all reporting directly to the president. These new agencies were nominally situated in the White House because it was the only place that could effectively commandeer the resources and obedience of the other government departments and agencies with bureaucratic fingers in the economic policy pie—and even then, they had difficulty obtaining cooperation from constituency-oriented departments like Agriculture. Similar action was taken when the Federal Energy Office/Administration was established to handle the energy crisis. As the economic crunch persisted and tightened, both Presidents Nixon and Ford appointed White House assistants (Kenneth Rush and William Seidman) to coordinate and monitor the development and implementation of economic policy.

When faced with serious and immediate economic problems, Lyndon Johnson chose not to impose across-the-board wage and price controls. He decided to use every other tool available to bolster the wage-price guideposts and to hold prices in the basic industries, to break material bottlenecks and to increase the supply of available personnel in the labor force. His administration's jawboning was enmeshed in repeated price rollback crises, involving aluminum, copper, steel, and other major industries. The president's personal prestige was often at stake. The program frequently required departments to act against their constituents' narrow interests (Agriculture Secretary Freeman, for example, was asked to condemn a rise in food prices). It became clear that the program involved several major executive departments and agencies and would have to be conducted from the White House indefinitely. When I could no longer do this job effectively on a part-time basis, John Robson and Stanford Ross (who succeeded Robson) were added to the White House staff to devote virtually full time to the jawboning program of the president to hold down wages, prices, and interest rates.

The late 1960s were liberally sprinkled with crises that required the attention of the federal executive and often involved the president's political and personal prestige. There were water shortages and power failures, civil disturbances, ghetto rebellions, and major strikes. The crisis-inspired federal involvement often engaged several departments and agencies. White House staff direction was considered essential to effective response and so these crises made their special contribution toward further concentration of power there. While the domestic crises dwindled in the early 1970s, the need to be prepared lingered on. The intractable lethargy of acquired bureaucratic power and the fragmentation of departmental and agency authority made it inevitable that succeeding administrations and the executive bureaucracy would agree that the White House staff would and should continue to handle such "sensitive" problems.

Presidents also make room for pet programs in the White House, to take on politically inspired crises or to focus attention on presidentially perceived urgent national problems. Nixon's White House Office on Drug Abuse and the strengthening of the office of the White House assistant for communications are reflections of that. Johnson located a special assistant for consumer affairs in his executive office. He wanted the Office of Economic Opportunity there when it was launched, in part to dramatize his personal commitment to the war against poverty and to rivet the nation's attention on the problem. Such an organizational structure achieves four important goals for a president: It sends a message to the American people that their chief executive is personally interested in the field; it tells the federal bureaucracy (and state and city bureaucracies) that the man who runs these programs can give orders with a White House command urgency; it helps insulate the new operation from early erosion in bureaucratic wars by placing it above the other warriors; and it gives the president direct control over the favored project.

Thwarted by the Congress in attempts at executive reorganization, frustrated by the fragmentation of authority and responsibility among the inefficiently organized departments and agencies, harassed by crises they are expected to resolve, tempted by the potential of effectively exercising the increasing powers laid at the White House door and by their personal ability to focus attention on pet programs, it was inevitable that presidents would take that action solely within their control: They would enlarge their own staffs to make their power felt. This was the alternative chosen by Presidents Kennedy, Johnson, and Nixon, and accepted by Gerald Ford. The president can control the number of people on the White House staff and organize them as he pleases. They may not all nominally be charged in budgetary and bookkeeping terms to the White House; many of them may be technically on the payrolls of the various departments and agencies of the government. But they are, in Patrick Anderson's precise term, *his* men.

Since the time of Franklin Roosevelt, the concept of the White House staff has been that a president is entitled to have a group of people whose loyalty runs only to him, whose power derives solely from him (not the Congress or constituent pressure groups which often vie for the attention of cabinet and agency heads), and who can be trusted to share the president's perception of his interests and carry out his orders to protect them.

Whether the White House staff is small, as in the days of Roosevelt, or numbers in the hundreds, as in the days of Nixon and Ford, there will be a few staff members in daily contact with the president and totally dedicated to him. Their power comes from the ability to say with authority, "The president wants . . ." These intimate few do not maintain the ability to use those three words with authority unless they are doing what the president wants and tells them to do. Without that authority, the personal and press secretaries, the top national security and domestic affairs advisers, and the other senior staff are useless to the president. With more than two thousand presidential appointees scattered in more than one hundred departments and agencies, the president could not run the government without a few such aides.

Every president seeks tight control over his immediate staff in recognition of the power those men have to help or hurt him. James Rowe, a White House aide in FDR's administration and an intimate of Lyndon Johnson, told me of a conversation with Kennedy aide Kenneth O'Donnell shortly after the 1963 assassination. O'Donnell was trying to decide whether to stay on with the new president. Rowe remarked, "One thing for sure is that Johnson will run a tight ship; he'll keep everyone on a short string just the way Roosevelt did. It won't be the freewheeling staff you boys had with Jack Kennedy."

"Are you kidding?" O'Donnell whipped back. "Kennedy kept all of us on a string about five feet long. Everytime we stepped out beyond it, he jerked us back!"

The framework of the large White House staff of the mid-1970s began to take shape under Kennedy and Johnson. By mid-1965, two fine staff operations were in place. Kennedy, with the aid of McGeorge Bundy, the able and articulate former Harvard dean who was to become president of the Ford Foundation, had rebuilt and expanded the National Security Council staff. Bundy had assembled bright and imaginative young aides and established the precedent for the Henry Kissinger operation in the Nixon administration.

The other superb organization was Larry O'Brien's. Early in his administration, Kennedy recognized the need for a strong congressional relations office if he were to maintain a liberal and aggressive posture toward the Congress. O'Brien headed that operation over the thousand days of the Kennedy presidency. After the arrival of Lyndon Johnson, he and O'Brien molded what was unquestionably the finest legislative staff in the history of the executive branch. But in the mid-1960s the rest of the White House was not functionally organized.

There were a number of talented people: Bill Moyers, Jack Valenti, Harry McPherson, and Doug Cater, to name a few. The press office had just gone through an emotionally wrenching reorganization in which George Reedy, the president's long-time friend and press secretary, had resigned and Bill Moyers had replaced him. Moyers had never been a press

secretary before, but with his talent and his father-son relationship with Johnson, Moyers was able to organize a sophisticated press office in short order.

With the impending departure of Richard Goodwin and
Moyers's preoccupation with the press office, Special Counsel
Harry McPherson emerged as Johnson's chief speech writer.
Valenti was Johnson's appointments secretary and utility in-
fielder. Doug Cater worked thoughtfully to help develop and
monitor Johnson's health and education programs. For economic policy, the president relied heavily on the Council of
Economic Advisers, and was well served by three chairmen:
Walter Heller for a brief period after the Kennedy assassination; then Gardner Ackley from the University of Michigan;
and, finally, Arthur Okun, who came from Yale.

But in July 1965, nowhere in the White House were the
legislative program and the coordination of domestic departments brought together and related to economic policy. The
new domestic programs created the need for such an office
and that was my assignment. The president gave me three
tasks: to prepare legislative programs, to assist him in developing and coordinating domestic programs and related economic policy, and to guide the response of the federal executive to domestic crises. The relationship between these three
jobs was something that he called "not a job description, but
an opportunity to help get the White House domestic operations shaped up." Johnson and Defense Secretary Robert
McNamara recognized how important it was to build a
domestic staff and encouraged me to do so. That recognition
was expressed in a discussion McNamara and I had about my
successor as his assistant at the Pentagon. There were two
likely and eminently qualified candidates, Lawrence Levinson and John Steadman. Levinson had been my deputy on
and off while I worked as McNamara's special assistant and
had the edge over Steadman by reason of that experience.
But McNamara closed that discussion by saying, "You take
Levinson to the White House. You'll need him more than I
will. That job over there is going to be infinitely more difficult
for you than this one has been."

Few people appreciated the enormous problems that

would result in attempting to coordinate the Great Society programs and operate them cost-effectively once they were enacted by the Congress and funds appropriated for their execution. Even fewer had a sense of how critical it would be to relate domestic programs to economic policy. Among the few who saw the need to "put it all together" were Charles Schultze and his deputies, Elmer Staats, and Phillip (Sam) Hughes.

At about the same time I joined the White House staff, Kermit Gordon left the Bureau of the Budget to become president of the Brookings Institution. Gordon's act was hard to follow, but Shultz did it brilliantly. An economist by profession, he was a staff manager of the first rank. He needed all his acquired skills and native talent to deal with the mountain of legislation that was enacted by the 89th and 90th Congresses. Fortunately for the president (and for ourselves), Schultze and I worked as well together as any two men ever have. We were both systems-oriented and shared a sense of the importance of a strong presidency.

We both recognized that a domestic affairs staff in the White House had become an organizational imperative for the president. In relatively short order in 1966, Levinson and I were joined by James Gaither, Matthew Nimetz, and Fred Bohen. Gaither, a Supreme Court clerk from the Justice Department, staffed health, education, poverty, and job-training problems; Nimetz, another Supreme Court clerk out of Harvard Law School, worked on urban and environmental programs and criminal justice; and Fred Bohen, from the Woodrow Wilson School at Princeton, worked on urban programs, government reorganization, and government employee problems.

By the mid-1970s, the Nixon White House staff had ballooned beyond a size that could assure the kind of accountability to the president (and through him, to the people) essential to a responsive central executive. When the intimate few who have White House telephones at their fingertips becomes six hundred, most of whom never see the president and many of whom do not see the senior four or five White House aides often enough to assure even minimal supervision, there is a serious problem not simply for the president, but for the people he was elected to serve.

Watergate involved a corrupt abuse of presidential and White House staff power that can occur with a staff of fifty as well as with one of six hundred. Nevertheless, the sheer size of a White House staff can provide a virtually impenetrable measure of deniability for a president or top domestic or national security aides who wish to put in motion questionable activities. Swollen staffs offer frightening opportunities where intentional deception to cover illegal activities is involved or where the president's concept of the function of government is essentially antidemocratic. This is particularly true where a president is surrounded with a large number of aides who lack the instinct, experience, maturity, or judgment to temper presidential orders.

But there are serious problems even with an oversized White House staff that is honestly attempting to achieve legitimate national and presidential objectives. Size itself can create a measure of confusion in the interpretation of lawful presidential orders. Where the presidential staff is relatively small and when its two largest segments (national security and domestic affairs) are tightly controlled, the members in daily contact with the president, necessarily a few, have the ability to assure that those who work for them understand the president's objectives. As the size of the White House staff expands, the ability of the president to maintain taut control is weakened. Senior presidential aides, who themselves supervise large staffs, find it difficult to control the use of the president's name by their own staff members. Large numbers provide fertile soil for mistakes and excesses that crop up out of perceived views of what the president wants or what would be good for the president.

Individual responsibility and public accountability tend to become lost in large staffs. When presidential orders are passed to senior assistants, then to middle-level aides, and then to their juniors, it can become difficult to determine who ordered what action. The confusion about what the president desired, what spin a senior aide added or subtracted, and what those aides carrying out the order perceived was desired, can make it impossible to pick up the pieces of responsibility when something goes wrong. When all goes well, everyone takes a share of the credit; but as John Kennedy noted, while success may have a thousand parents, failure is a bureaucratic orphan.

Reading presidential words for their true meaning is a major function of White House aides, as is making certain that the president understands the ramifications of each exercise of power. Access to a president is essential to inform presidential directives with precision, to argue for or against particular courses of action, and to acquire the personal intimacy that assures an understanding of the true meaning of presidential directives. Presidents do not always verbalize that meaning; they do not always mean what they say.

Any president who sits in the White House is first and foremost a human being. Like any of us, he has good days and bad; highs and lows. He can be hurt and he gets angry. His problems seem unyielding. In a relatively short time after he assumes office, his critics question his ability to solve monumentally complex problems quickly enough. Each day he reads or listens to some commentator who questions his judgment or his motives. It is difficult for any of us to imagine what it is like to live and work in that kind of an environment. Most of us assume that any man who rises to be president should recognize that he will have to live with this problem. But anyone who has been in the high reaches of government, has known politicians intimately, or has ever read a story written about himself, recognizes how easy it is to become annoyed about perceived inaccuracies, slights, distortions, or unfair criticisms. Within weeks after assuming office such stories are a president's daily diet. On the day he is inaugurated, he knows that a fast clock is already running against his honeymoon with the press. He finds little solace in his basic recognition that the same First Amendment that nourishes the press is certain to give him political indigestion.

Presidents often express their anger, usually to the aides closest to them. Few, if any, are consumed with the vicious and concealed rage that marked the vindictive presidency of

Richard Nixon. But most lose their tempers in pursuit of legitimate, if controversial, national objectives. Anyone who has served on a presidential staff has been subject to commands inspired during instants of anger. Most who have served there recognized that, when such orders were issued, it was best to ignore or at least to sleep on them, and wait until the president raised the matter again in a cooler moment. Doubtless Pierre Salinger wishes he had slept on John Kennedy's order to ban the New York *Herald Tribune* from the White House in response to the newspaper's persistent needling of the president's personal and political style. In early months of service, most presidential aides relay any number of presidential orders they later wished they had not.

Some situations are obvious. At a time when the nation was steeped in controversy over Vietnam, President Johnson read on the AP wire that Senator Clifford Case had declared publicly against the war. He told me to call Case and tell him the president would take his dovish advice from Senators Ernest Gruening and Wayne Morse who had opposed the war from the beginning. "Tell him the president doesn't need advice from someone who waits until the New York *Times* editorial board decides to change its mind." Of course, I didn't make the call and Johnson never expected me to. Indeed, he would have reproached me royally if I had. But there are many more ambiguous situations with serious implications for the abuse of presidential power. Junior White House aides, who rarely see a president, are likely to lack the personal relationship and repeated direct exposure to avoid such abuses.

Subsequent to March 31, 1968, when Johnson removed himself from the presidential campaign, he decided that the executive branch should remain neutral during the fight for the Democratic nomination, so that it could function during the ensuing months. Johnson made the neutrality decision in the context of a memorandum he received one morning from Agriculture Secretary Orville Freeman. Freeman's memo reported his intention to announce that afternoon his support of fellow Minnesotan Hubert Humphrey for the 1968

Democratic presidential nomination. Upon receiving the memo, Johnson called me and said that he wanted the executive branch to remain neutral. He asked me to contact every cabinet officer immediately and tell them not to support any of the Democratic candidates.

"If they want to support a candidate, then they can leave the government," Johnson said. "I can't have the government torn apart by cabinet officers and presidential appointees fighting among themselves about Kennedy, McCarthy, and Humphrey."

Eventually, Freeman got the word, but not before his speech had been released to the press. On the afternoon of that same day, Agriculture Undersecretary John Schnittker was speaking in Indiana, about to announce his support of Robert Kennedy. Shortly before the speech, I called Schnittker and told him the president's wishes. But Undersecretary Schnittker, like Secretary Freeman, had already informed the press of the Democratic candidate he intended to support.

During the rest of the day I was able to contact most cabinet officers, but Wilbur Cohen was making a luncheon speech at the National Press Club. In the course of the question and answer session that followed, Cohen declared for Hubert Humphrey. All of this aggravated Johnson who regarded these public statements as violations of a directive he had given earlier in the day. He evidenced no appreciation of the time it takes to transmit such an order.

That evening, when the president and I were in the Oval Office, he was still fuming over the dangers of disrupting the executive branch, because cabinet officers and other high administration officials announced support for a variety of presidential candidates and thus "put narrow partisan interest above the public interest." He bent over to read the AP and UPI tickers clattering in his office. One of the wire services ran a light item which reported that Secretary of Agriculture Freeman had declared for Humphrey; Undersecretary John Schnittker had declared for Robert Kennedy; and an obscure assistant secretary had come out for Hubert Humphrey. The article speculated breezily about who would win a poll among the Agriculture Department top hierarchy.

Johnson was furious. He immediately reached for the telephone and told the White House operator to get the assistant secretary on the phone. To my knowledge, Johnson had never spoken to him before. Johnson excoriated him for violating a direct presidential order by declaring for Humphrey, and asked him to come to the White House that evening and submit his resignation to me.

As soon as I left Johnson's office, I called the assistant secretary, a mild-mannered and dedicated man, and told him to hold his resignation and forget about what happened unless he heard from me in the morning. He said, "No, no, the president directly ordered me to bring this resignation to you." I told him that the president was concerned about various individuals in the executive branch of the government coming out for various presidential candidates and thus making it difficult, if not impossible, to govern during the last several months of the administration. "Because of a variety of circumstances over which you had no control, you became the focal point of the president's annoyance that so many major officials declared for candidates today," I added.

He repeated, "I have a direct presidential order."

"Forget it for now," I urged.

"I can't."

"Look," I said, "I was with the president when he called you." I told him I would take full responsibility for not accepting the resignation. "Just go back to your job in the Agriculture Department." With trembling reluctance in his voice, he agreed.

That, of course, ended the matter. Johnson never expected to receive the resignation and, I am sure, he would have felt ill-served by me had I accepted the resignation on his behalf. After three years of serving on his White House staff, he would have expected me to have some sense of how to measure his true meaning when he spoke in anger. At the same time, the Agriculture Department assistant secretary had every reason to take the president of the United States at his word. The same kinds of commands can be taken just as literally by a lower-level White House staff aide who is young, relatively inexperienced and sees the president rarely during a year. The larger the presidential staff, the larger the number of aides with limited access there will be, and the greater the danger such commands will be followed.

The size of the White House staff can affect the nature, depth and number of problems to which a president is exposed. This, in turn, can have a serious impact upon the policies he eventually pursues or rejects. There are times when presidents will accept or reject policies out of hand. Only a very limited number of aides—four or five at most—have an opportunity to talk through the president's initial reaction with him. Aides working below the top five or ten on any presidential staff have little, if any, opportunity to discuss directly with the president their views on policies within their responsibility. They must make their case to the senior White House staff.

The selection of these senior aides is more important to the exercise of presidential power and the conduct of presidential policy than the selection of most cabinet officers and agency heads. During the early Johnson years, Jack Valenti was the man through whom virtually all papers went to the president. He understood that the timing of the president's receipt of certain papers could affect his psychological ability to review them objectively. On one occasion in 1966, I forwarded a proposed new higher education program to the president. Valenti called and said, "Joe, I think you'd better hold that education program for a few days. The president is not exactly overjoyed [a typical Valenti euphemism] about the statement put out today by those college professors on the Vietnam War. If you want him to consider it dispassionately, you ought to wait a few days." Knowing that Jack was as sensitive a barometer of Lyndon Johnson as ever served him, I held the program back. A few days later the president reviewed the memorandum and approved it enthusiastically.

Those few aides at the top of a White House staff are singularly important in terms of the issues that go to the president for full discussion. In the preparation of the legislative program, for example, even a president as immersed in detail as Lyndon Johnson must be general in his guidance and largely dependent on his staff to bring major issues to his attention on a timely basis. In the early summer of 1965, when I first joined the Johnson staff, his guidance was quite limited. While we were swimming in the pool at his ranch, Johnson said, "There are three areas of urgent concern for the 1966 legislative program. The transportation system of this country is a mess. I want to do something about it."

Holding two fingers up out of the water, he continued, "Second, we must show the people of this nation that the cities can be rebuilt. I want a program to totally rebuild the ghettos of the nation."

With three fingers jutting out of the water about an inch away from my chin, he continued, "We need an open housing bill. School desegregation and equal employment are not enough. We'll pass voting rights this year. But people have to live together, smell each other, to understand they have the same ambitions and insecurities and plans and hopes, whether they are black or white or red or green or purple!" He concluded by stating, "You get me good, workable programs in those areas and I'll pass them and the rest of the stuff you liberals want. Get all the other programs you can convince me are right and I'll pass them. But give me something big in each of those three areas."

That was the extent of the guidance on the selection of programs until we met again, day after day, and night after night, in December 1965 and early January 1966. There were, of course, numerous discussions during the intervening months and a healthy unfinished agenda of campaign promises yet to be fulfilled. We kept Johnson informed of our progress with scores of memos, and presented a number of critical issues for his decision. But, the whittling down of hundreds of legislative suggestions to the final hundred or so that were presented to the president in December was left to me, my staff, the other senior presidential aides like Harry McPherson and Doug Cater, and Budget Director Charles Schultze.

Access to the president can be decisive on any number of

issues. Whatever the problems of the Johnson staff, lack of
access was not one of them. The president read every memorandum he received from a cabinet officer. Every senior
White House aide and some junior ones had access on paper,
and often in person, to the president on every subject, sometimes to the irritation of those who believed an issue had
been resolved, only to have the president reopen it on the
basis of a memorandum from another staff assistant or cabinet or agency head. Nixon may have done some of the greatest damage to his presidency by so limiting the access of his
cabinet officers and most White House aides that he received
only the narrowest of input from a few men: H. R. (Bob)
Haldeman, John Ehrlichman, Charles Colson, and Henry
Kissinger in the early years of his presidency; Alexander
Haig, Ronald Zeigler, and Henry Kissinger in the later years.

Senior presidential aides must select carefully those issues
on which they "go to the mat" in attempts to persuade the
president. A president can engage the Congress in tough
legislative battles only a few times in any legislative session.
These fights are costly to the delicate relationship between
the man in the Oval Office and the congressional leadership.
The same sort of problem faces a senior White House assistant in his relationship with a president. There are only so
many arguments that a White House aide can have with the
president before he begins to be regarded either as a pest,
a man unable to make the judgments essential to the performance of his duties, or someone who argues indiscriminately
for every program he favors.

The selection of which matters to take to the mat with the
president plagues every conscientious senior aide. Most try
to make the decision on the merits of the issues involved. But
as a White House senior aide becomes more engaged, his
decision to press the president on a particular matter is more
likely to be influenced by other issues he has pending before
the president, his relations with particular cabinet officers,
his problems with key congressmen important to some unrelated legislative program, some immediate crisis, the time
of night, or personal considerations such as the chronic strain
most such aides feel in holding their families together when
they are consumed with work.

As larger numbers of energetic junior White House assistants probe more deeply into the departments and agencies
of government, they are inclined to take more issues to their
superiors for consideration. This, of course, further erodes
the time and ability of senior White House aides to thoughtfully sift issues down to those matters that raise public policy
issues truly appropriate for presidential resolution. In the
absence of a strong cabinet officer, like Secretary Robert
McNamara in the Kennedy and Johnson administrations, the
temptation of junior White House aides to increase the scope
and depth of White House involvement in departmental activities can be irresistable, particularly in face of the functional disarray of the departments and agencies.

White House aides tend to be bright, mostly young, energetic, and aggressive. Whether they serve in a conservative,
socially *laissez-faire* administration or a liberal, interventionist one, their instinctive tendency will be to involve themselves in as much detail in as many matters as time permits.
When they discover that most department and agency officials will follow their decisions on minor matters, they tend
to become seduced by the allure of power and they revel in
its exercise. To the extent the president and his aides become
involved in the minutia of government, they have less time
to focus on problems of true presidential import. As George
Reedy notes in his book, *The Twilight of the Presidency*,
presidents themselves are repeatedly tempted to reach out
for control over the details of government. Such involvement can divert a president from attention to the central
objectives of his administration.

One of the most difficult problems for any president is to
hold his administration steady on course toward the achievement of central objectives established during his political
campaign and usually announced in his State of the Union
and other major messages. There are any number of distrac-
tions for the White House incumbent: international crises,
monetary crises, economic problems at home, strikes, natural
disasters, scandals, personal tragedies. Too large a White
House staff multiplies the opportunity for inviting diversions
from his central objectives and major problems. In this sense,
the difference between a White House staff of six hundred

and one of fifty can be qualitative for a presidency.

Other factors also contribute significantly to the depth of White House intervention into operational activities. Often, the goals of the president exceed the objectives of the authorizing legislation and he decides to hold the cabinet officer accountable in a demanding way. Johnson, for example, frequently set specific goals, particularly in the wake of new legislation, or to deal with some crisis. In 1967 and 1968, he established a weekly reporting system on the number of federally assisted new housing starts. Where the weekly reports of the Department of Housing and Urban Development indicated a failure to meet presidentially established goals (which significantly exceeded congressional ones), the White House staff dug deeply into the operation of the housing programs to find out why. With a large White House staff, there are plenty of young assistants to do the digging.

Limited tenure for senior White House aides is also important to the priorities selected for the deployment of presidential power. In late 1965 and early 1966, President Johnson, Lee White, and I were enthusiastic about the proposal for a Department of Transportation as the initial step in a major reorientation of the nation's transportation policy. Bill Moyers expressed doubts about whether we could persuade the Congress to enact such legislation and whether it was worth all the effort to try. In January 1965, Johnson had promised a new maritime subsidy program to modernize our obsolescing fleet of merchant ships. Moyers's attempts to put such a program together had been an especially frustrating experience for him and ended in utter failure (as did attempts by others in later years). At the time, I felt Moyers had no appreciation of the importance of our Transportation Department proposal and was rolling over too quickly in the face of his recent unpleasant experiences in attempting to formulate a new maritime program.

In late 1966, after the Department of Transportation legislation passed the Congress, one of the nation's top transportation economists visited me at the White House. Now that the new executive department had been formed, he suggested that the president propose a total reorganization of the inde-

pendent transportation regulatory agencies as the next logical step. I told him that his suggestion was out of the question.
The Transportation Department bill had been the toughest
legislative fight of the 89th Congress, it had taken perhaps 15
percent of my time in 1966 and required almost daily presidential attention. We could not afford an effort like that
again. Shortly after the economist left, I thought back to the
Moyers incident in 1965. If Moyers had still been working on
the legislative program in 1965, I mused, we probably would
not have a Department of Transportation. If I had not been
working on the legislative program in late 1966, perhaps my
successor would have done bloody battle with the transportation industry in the 90th Congress and produced a sorely
needed reorganization of the transportation regulatory
agencies.

What, then, is the presidential perspective of the executive
branch?
From his window in the Oval Office, the president looks
out on a jumble of irrationally organized departments and
agencies. History has demonstrated the inordinate difficulty
of obtaining congressional approval for the major reorganizations essential to the functional rationalization of the executive branch he has been elected to lead. Politics teaches him
about the inherently divided loyalties of cabinet and agency
heads who must testify before congressional oversight and
appropriations committees and live with cross-pressures
from their peers, their constituencies, and the bureaucracies
they administer. The Great Society programs provide him
with the potential to intervene at the national, state, city,
neighborhood, and family level to achieve his objectives. He
sees technology and the aspirations of the people changing
so much faster than the institutions over which he presides
that he fears major crises unless some institutional adapta-
tions can be made promptly. His own personal experience
confirms his political instinct to place power in the hands of
men whose loyalty runs decisively to him, and what better
way to assure that than by making certain their power derives solely from him. Inevitably, Republican or Democrat,

conservative or liberal, he will perceive a substantial and powerful White House staff as the best means of exercising presidential power to achieve his public policy objectives and render responsive the erratically organized executive branch over which he presides.

III

THE SEPARATE BUT UNEQUAL BRANCH

Pitched in constitutional conflict with the presidency, the Congress comes off as the separate but unequal branch of the federal government. Discussion in the press and on Capitol Hill about this sorry condition has centered on a variety of controversial issues: the passive role of Congress during the Vietnam War, the inability of the Congress to act forcefully on inflation, the difficulty in formulating campaign reform legislation in the face of the most pervasive political corruption in our history, the constitutionally demeaning dependency of the legislative branch on the executive branch for the information on which major legislative judgments are made.

Congressmen and senators rise on the floor of the House and the Senate almost daily to blame the executive branch for withholding information from the Congress, for intentionally misleading its members, for having too much power in relation to the Congress, and for waging or inviting war without consulting with the Congress. The Watergate scandals added a sharper and more acrimonious tone to such congressional statements. The freshman Democratic class of 1975 deposed three committee chairman and moved to "democratize" the House of Representatives, but it remains to be seen whether a "democratic" House can deal more effectively with the president than a "seniority" House. Rhetorical and symbolic attacks by congressional leaders, embattled committee chairmen, and liberals and conservatives have echoed on Capitol Hill for the better part of the twentieth century. Increasingly discordant notes of frustration have been blown on congressional trumpets since the time of Franklin Roosevelt.

The more tempestuous congressional reactions to the executive branch are directed at presidential actions perceived as usurpations of the constitutional prerogatives of the legislative branch. For Roosevelt, it was the tilt to England and France before World War II and how we became involved in the war; for Truman, Korea and the firing of General Douglas MacArthur; for Kennedy, the Bay of Pigs and muzzling the military's right to speak out; for Johnson, too much Vietnam with too little information and too many poverty program workers stretching congressional authorizations with too little regard for establishment political power; for Nixon, (even before impeachment proceedings for criminal actions) too much more Vietnam and too many arrogant assertions of executive privilege and presidential power to withhold expenditure of congressional appropriations. The basis of all these attacks has been a deeply felt and vividly expressed congressional conviction that the president was simply too powerful, not providing the Congress with enough information, and trampling over congressional prerogatives.

The Congress postures itself as the rhetorical bulwark against presidential overreaching, while it continues to vest the president with real power. In the face of a strong presidency, members of Congress often look, as Washington commentator Elizabeth Drew bluntly wrote in the New York *Times Magazine,* like "walking cartoons." It is not the executive branch that is responsible for the congressional bended knee, hat-in-hand position toward the president. Nor does the basic reason for the decline in congressional effectiveness and status lie with federal bureaucrats whose concern is often for the approbation of constituencies independent of the president and the Congress, nor with the coverage of the press and pollsters who simply recorded the fact that in the early 1970s the American people thought less of the Congress than of the most corrupt presidential administration in our history. Responsibility for the separate but unequal status of the Congress of the United States rests with the Congress of the United States.

The reasons for the congressional acquiescence in second-class constitutional citizenship—some would say lack of will and spine—are complex and both institutional and informational. Its status vis-à-vis the executive was not always unequal. Speaking of the capitol city fifty years ago, Washington reporter Raymond Brandt is quoted by Fletcher Knebel as saying, "We never covered Washington in the twenties. We covered the Senate. You wasted your time downtown." With Franklin Roosevelt, the downtown Oval Office became the chief source of information about the national government. The entire story may not be contained in Walter Lippmann's statement that "nothing affects more the balance of power between Congress and the President than whether the one or the other is the principal source of news and explanation of opinion." Nevertheless, the consuming focus of the media on the president has contributed mightily to the futility some congressmen sense in attempts to restore the legislative branch to its equal status.

But there are deeper reasons for the lack of congressional will. The collegiate nature of the House and Senate is constitutionally indigenous. Any representative legislature is likely to house ideological differences that can hamper its ability to act with single-minded authority and debilitate its collective will. In times of confusion about national goals and persistent difficulties in solving national problems, a sense of growing despair accompanies and often sharpens ideological discord. The Congress is the branch most vulnerable to fragmentation in periods of doubt about national purpose, particularly in the absence of strong leadership. Consider, for example, how much more effective the overwhelmingly Democratic 94th Congress would be if there were an aggressive Democratic president in the White House.

To this muddled ideological situation must be added the

lack of party discipline in the House and Senate. Conservative and liberal views are strongly held within both parties. Conservative John Jarman, elected as a Democrat from Oklahoma, moved comfortably to the Republican party in the wake of the liberal House revolution in 1975; liberal Lowell Weicker, elected as a Republican from Connecticut, mused aloud about a possible switch to the Democratic party early this same year. Economic and racial stress frequently add severe regional and human pressures to the forces arrayed against collective solidarity, even on institutional issues. Increasingly sophisticated and powerful private interests, such as segments of business and labor, contribute their share to the fragmented pursuit of legislative branch self-interests. As a result, it is rarely the presidency with or against the Congress as an institutionally coherent force. It is the presidency and some of the Congress, often a majority, against the rest of the Congress. The tools available to the president in such circumstances are enormous—information, discretionary grants, an almost unlimited grab bag of personal favors, and a relatively solid executive front. The problems of the president with the executive bureaucracy fade when compared with the difficulties of the Democratic and Republican leadership on the Hill with many members of their own party.

This is not to say that the Congress is sentenced to supine impotency against the executive juggernaut. Powerful committee chairmen do have the power to say "no." Wilbur Mills held up the Johnson tax surcharge for almost two years in the 1960s in an attempt to slow down the Great Society programs, reduce government spending, and get better congressional control over the federal budget. In his 1966 State of the Union message, Johnson proposed a four-year term for members of the House of Representatives. The proposal was greeted with louder cheers and more extended applause than any other item mentioned that evening. In our delight at this enthusiastic reception, we failed to notice House Judiciary Committee Chairman Emmanuel Celler sitting on his hands and remarking to one of his colleagues, "It will never come out of my committee." It never did.

But negative power alone is not sufficient for the Congress

to regain its constitutional composure in the presence of the executive branch. The Congress has oversight responsibilities and appropriations powers as well as the constitutional right to advise and consent on treaties and major appointments. It has virtually unlimited subpoena authority. The impact of televising the work of the House Judiciary Committee (and its superb legal staff) during the 1974 impeachment hearings demonstrated the potency of what Douglass Cater described in his book, *The Fourth Branch of Government*, as "publicity power." Its legislative muscles were gently flexed in 1974 in placing restrictions on executive branch arms sales, food grants, and foreign trade credits. But with rare exception, the Congress has chosen not to inform and organize the exercise of those powers. There are a number of actions the Congress could take to assume a much higher ground from which to perform its constitutional function to help check and balance the executive.

The informational and institutional problems should be clear to any careful observer of the Washington scene. The judgments of the 535 members of the Congress, like anyone else's, can hardly be better than the information on which those judgments are based. The Congress is dependent upon the executive branch for most of its information, with occasional and, too often, superficial assistance from outside experts and special interests. Of the three branches of government, the Congress is the most inadequately staffed and the least efficiently organized. To some extent, ineffective organization is endemic to any representative legislature, but there is no excuse for inadequate staffing.

The Congress has a Congressional Research Service, but the function of that service is to provide documentary research and put into statutory language any idea, inane or ingenious, any congressman wants drafted into a bill he can introduce. The Congressional Research Service is substantively neutral.

The General Accounting Office serves as the investigatory arm of the Congress. It is excellent in exposing waste, cost overruns on government contracts, and office furnishings excessively luxurious for federal employees. The General Accounting Office has repeatedly attempted to acquire a substantial analytical capability. From 1972 to 1974 it assumed major new responsibilities in assuring compliance with campaign reform legislation. But its main work remains exposure of waste in the federal government.

In 1972, at the urging of Senator Edward Kennedy, the Congress established its own Office of Technology Assessment to assist in anticipating the consequences of technological advancements on public policy. This can be an important step toward arming the legislature with the analytical tools necessary to deal with the executive. Whether the Congress staffs and funds this office properly will reflect the extent to which its members understand its potential in assessing public policy alternatives and assuming the legislative initiative.

The staffs of the committees of the Congress have improved significantly in recent years. This is particularly true in the Senate, where most committees and important subcommittees can and frequently do compete successfully with the best law firms for first-rate young lawyers and with universities and foundations for economists and analysts. While not up to the Senate, the House committee staffs are, on the whole, appreciably better than they were in the early 1960s. But these more substantial and better trained committee staffs with their limited analytical tools are no match for the presidential and executive staffs who have at their disposal the most sophisticated analytical techniques and the resources to assemble the array of computer data required for intelligent public policy formulation. They can help congressional committees expose waste, corruption, and bungling, but they are at a distinct disadvantage in producing carefully considered and well-informed legislative programs.

The Congress has virtually ignored the revolution in analytical technology and, as a result, wrestles with the president on the mat of public policy with one arm tied behind its back. As Iowa Senator John Culver has pointed out, in the early 1970s the Congress had only a few computers and they operated in large measure on congressional payrolls and housekeeping matters. The vote-taking in the House of Representatives was computerized in the early 1970s to save an hour or two out of most legislative days. But even at that late date, the Congress had no central systems-analysis office and only a scattering of such analysts among its committee staffs. Many of these analysts left the executive branch when administrations changed in 1969 and have every intention of returning should the Democrats assume control of the White House. Entering the last quarter of the twentieth century, the Congress had not made its intention to assume a stronger role in national policy formulation serious enough to attract a permanent staff of top-flight analysts.

By contrast, in the early 1970s the president had at his disposal in the executive branch more than four thousand computers working almost entirely on substantive policy issues. Sophisticated analysts and programmers held key staff positions, not only in the Office of Management and Budget and the Department of Defense, but increasingly in the domestic departments of the government. The Pentagon, both within its own walls and in its think tanks (like Rand and the Institute for Defense Analysis), could "war game" any number of strategic budgetary alternatives, while the Armed Services and Foreign Affairs Committees of the House and Senate still based most of their decisions on the work of small staffs and the gut reactions and idiosyncrasies of key committee members. Essential as that experience is and empirically informed as many of these gut reactions may be, they are inefficient bases for the performance of oversight functions, particularly when complicated scientific and financial data are involved.

The unique analytical capability of the president and the branch over which he presides has made the federal executive by far potentially the most significant force in our society for the conception, development, and enactment into legislation of new substantive programs. Without almost total reliance on the informational and analytical resources of the executive branch talent at the president's disposal, neither the Congress nor any of its committees has the consistent capability of developing coherent, large-scale federal programs.

As George Reedy has pointed out, the 1958 Space Act,

which was almost totally the work of Lyndon Johnson and his
Senate Preparedness Subcommittee staff, is one of the few
examples in the last fifty years of a statute establishing a
major program that originated on Capitol Hill rather than in
the White House. In time of economic crisis, the Congress
can replace presidential programs with its own, but it seems
incapable of acting on a timely basis and cannot force the
executive to administer the spirit as well as the letter of price
and wage control programs or rationing legislation. Today,
the kind of legislation that originates in the Congress is essentially consumer legislation (with a big assist from disaffected
young executive branch staffers and public interest attorneys
like Ralph Nader), restrictive riders emotionally attached to
foreign aid and trade legislation, and relatively minor statutes of particular interest to a region or limited constituency
of importance to powerful congressmen.

Shrewd legislators like former Ways and Means Committee Chairman Wilbur Mills at his peak had to turn to the
Department of Health, Education and Welfare and its computers (or a systems-oriented research center like the Urban
Institute which, in turn, is largely dependent on executive
branch contracts) when they wanted detailed information on
the financial impact of various welfare reform alternatives.
The Joint Economic Committee has done a remarkable job,
particularly when it is realized that virtually all its basic data
comes from the statistical offices of the Commerce and Labor
Departments, the Council of Economic Advisers, and the
Federal Reserve Board. Yet, think for a moment what the
situation might be if that committee had the statistical and
analytical capability to do their own computer runs, their
own independent analyses and projections. It is not necessary to duplicate the capability that exists in the Bureau of
Labor Statistics or the Commerce Department's Office of
Business Economics, but simply to have the kind of capability
that exists in most large banks and is available to the staffs of
most major corporations.

The more sophisticated members of the Joint Economic
Committee in the 1960s and early 1970s, like Senator William
Proxmire and Congressman Henry Reuss, were convinced

that inflation was getting out of hand in the Johnson administration and that the Nixon economic game plan of the late 1960s would go awry. They sensed simultaneous recession and inflation as early as 1970. But their conviction was essentially instinctive, based on their own economic sense and shrewd perception informed by whatever their wide range of contacts in the private sectors of banking, business, and labor wished to contribute. Their ability to develop their own projections and economic scenarios, supported by detailed analyses and statistics, was sharply limited because they lacked the staff and the computer technology.

This problem affects the Senate Finance and House Ways and Means Committees as well. It is true that a high degree of professionalism has historically marked those committee staffs as well as the staff of the Joint Committee on Taxation. But they have been forced to rely on analytical components of the Internal Revenue Service and the Assistant Treasury Secretary's Office for Tax Policy. The use of the Internal Revenue Service for political purposes during the Nixon administration dramatizes how legislatively irresponsible it can be for the Congress to rely on executive branch staff work. Even without such corrupt practices, no congressional committee should have to rely so heavily on the analytical capability of the executive branch staffs. In the final analysis, those staffs must maintain their loyalty to the president whom they serve. It is that president's program they support and work to enact into law.

The executive branch is, of course, not the only source of information available to congressional committees. Today the right of petition is exercised by well-informed, powerful, and persuasive interests. But particular interest groups who are helped or hurt by a government program invariably offer self-interested presentations. During the national dialogue over health care in the 1960s and early 1970s, the Congress heard many different voices: hospitals, doctors, pharmaceutical and insurance companies, pharmacists, labor unions. Their inputs of information and judgment were essential to the Congress as it sought to improve the delivery of health care and to exercise its oversight responsibilities with respect to executive branch implementation of existing health-care programs. However, such parochial interests are likely to be too self-centered to effectively counterbalance the executive on many broad policy issues. Take drug prices as an example: Drug companies want to maintain their prices to protect research capabilities and profits; pharmacists want to protect their own profit margins; hospitals want to protect the profit centers that their own pharmacies have become; doctors want to protect what they consider their right to practice medicine and the sanctity of the doctor-patient relationship; and the elderly want special concessions for senior citizens, the blacks for the poor urbanites, the unions for low-income workers. The Congress should have a public policy analytical capability to assess these varying claims, to measure them against each other and against the claims of the executive branch for the programs already enacted as well as those proposed by the president.

Most politicans, like most lawyers, doctors, and businessmen, realize not only that knowledge is power, but that, today, acting in the absence of knowledge almost guarantees disaster. Where public policy is concerned, to act on major issues without independent knowledge is to play Russian roulette with our democratic system. The president's power vis-à-vis the Congress takes on a frightening perspective in a continuing environment where the president has most of the knowledge and the Congress must go to him or his executive branch to get most of the facts.

Any congressman who has been in Washington for any number of years can recount incidents where a recalcitrant executive branch has successfully refused to furnish information to congressional committees and, as a result, the committee has either been unable to act or has acted in uninformed support of an executive action that it later regretted. Delay in providing information is itself a potent weapon, for the attention span of most senators and congressmen and their committees tends to be far shorter than the persistent interest of entrenched executive branch bureaucracies. It is only natural that the president use that knowledge to achieve his objectives. One of the most effective presidential techniques can be to withhold information when its release could have an adverse impact on his legislative objectives, prematurely show his programmatic hand, or limit his policy options.

Lyndon Johnson faced this problem in the 1960s. The Bureau of the Budget had established a system under which domestic departments projected new and existing legislative programs for a five-year period, much along the lines of the five-year planning-programming-budgeting system introduced by Defense Secretary McNamara in the Pentagon. When new legislative proposals were made, whether for Model Cities or clean air or water programs, their costs were projected not only for the first year, but for the four succeeding years. By the end of 1966, similar projections were made for most existing government programs.

Proud of our newly developed capability, when the Model Cities program was sent to the Congress in early 1966, we revealed its five-year cost projections. First year costs to provide funds for selected cities to analyze their proposed Model Cities areas totaled only $10 million. The projections revealed that in three years, the federal costs of the program would exceed $.5 billion and, in the fifth year, would reach at least $1 billion. Whether that $1 billion would be a plateau depended on the number of cities that entered the Model Cities program. Under any circumstances, the program would have been controversial. But the opposition attack on the "astronomical" costs of the Model Cities program revealed by the five-year projections almost blocked its enactment. As a result, Johnson decided not to release similar figures for future programs he recommended to the Congress. "A congressman is like a whiskey drinker," he said. "You can put an awful lot of whiskey into a man if you just let him sip it. But if you try to force the whole bottle down his throat at one time, he will throw it up."

Several senators appreciated the importance of these five-year projections. Led by Senator Abraham Ribicoff, particularly with respect to urban programs, they repeatedly attempted to obtain them. Ribicoff was convinced that the people had to understand how expensive it would be to re-

build the cities. He argued that the Johnson administration
was probably not spending enough to do this and that release
of the numbers, even in the billions, would help get the
programs passed and funded. Johnson sharply disagreed with
Ribicoff's political judgment. He believed revelation of these
projections would make it more difficult to enact Great Society programs and fund them at satisfactory levels, particularly when the Congress was becoming increasingly concerned with the mounting costs of the war in Southeast Asia.

Johnson successfully kept the five-year projections from
the Congress. He regarded them as internal planning documents. He argued that they contained the tentative numbers
of "analysts and intellectuals" in the government. Since he
could not give his approval or disapproval to every five-year
spending plan in the federal government, he felt he should
not have to take personal responsibility for such projections.
Mere release, he complained, would constitute an assumption of political responsibility no matter what the caveat.
Since the legislative branch had the power to appropriate
funds year by year, he concluded, no one knew how much
money would be spent in future years until the Congress
acted.

Is it proper for the chief executive to withhold such estimates from the legislature? It would be outrageous for the
president of an American corporation, who was urging that
a new project be mounted, to refuse to tell the board of
directors how much money he estimated would be needed
five years in the future. But politics and government are not
businesses. In business, the objectives are narrow and common: to maximize return on an investment. Business success
is measured against that easily quantifiable standard. In politics and government, particularly where new legislative
proposals are involved, the objectives are neither narrow nor
common, and the results are not readily quantifiable. Estimates are rarely solid, particularly five years forward on a
new program. A president inevitably will be able honestly (if
self-servingly) to rationalize that the new legislative program
he proposes is in the public interest; that if it works well, he
wants certain high levels of expenditure for it; but that if it

does not work well, he will have enough sense to request lower levels of expenditure or terminate the program. Therefore, he can point out, there is no reason why the Congress should have this information at the start, especially where the Congress has the power to grant or withhold funds each year. The Congress, a president will say somewhat ingenuously, can make its own projections.

The congressional lack of analytical prowess has the effect of debasing its political dialogue with the executive branch. In 1967, President Johnson decided to develop a program to close the housing gap in the United States as rapidly as possible, without distorting the capital markets of the nation and putting too much pressure on the construction labor force. Months of analytical work by the Council of Economic Advisers and the Department of Housing and Urban Development were necessary, first to determine the size of the housing gap, and then to establish the scope and length of the program for closing it. When the Housing Act of 1968, with its goal of closing the housing gap in ten years, was sent to the Congress, there was little discussion of the validity of the time and cost projections. The Congress and its committee staffs were simply not equipped to analyze the program intelligently in these terms and to conduct a dialogue on the merits with the White House and the Department of Housing and Urban Development. Most discussions in the Congress involved the parochial rivalries of interest groups that had been jousting for decades in the housing arena. Congressional debate essentially constituted a search for some means to balance the relatively narrow interests of banks, home builders, real estate brokers, and trade unions. Congress, of course, is the proper forum for such interests to make their views known on a legislative program proposed by the president. But the Congress should also be sufficiently informed independently to evaluate presidential analyses and programs on their merits.

Moreover, the president and his executive branch are in better condition to outmaneuver the Congress in the street fighting among the special-interest groups. The executive has some measure of discretionary power over many grant-in-aid programs and other federal benefits that can be bestowed upon or withheld from such groups, or the congressional districts of key members, during a legislative battle over a presidential program. In virtually all legislative poker games with the Congress, not only can the president closely hold the informational cards. He also has a stacked deck he can cut in favor of special-interest groups that support him.

The most awesome tilt of power in favor of the president's branch involves the military budget. Under Kennedy and McNamara, the Pentagon began to make decisions on the basis of program packages related to the capabilities of combinations of forces from all three military departments to meet different potential threats to the national security. This is the context in which McNamara presented his annual defense posture statements. Yet, for appropriations purposes, these program packages were retranslated into budgetary line items. The president of the United States and his chief advisers in the Defense Department analyzed defense problems as they should, on a systems, threat-oriented basis. But, because of obsolete appropriations procedures and analytical techniques, the traditional line item budgets to which the Congress was accustomed had to be ressurected.

As a result, a kind of meat ax approach has often characterized congressional efforts to cut the defense budget. "The budget must be cut by $5 or $10 billion," is the cry of too many congressmen and senators—not out of demagoguery which might be politically understandable, if intellectually unsavory, but out of self-imposed ignorance which is politically and intellectually inexcusable. There are, of course, a few exceptions. In 1969 and 1970, for example, some senators focused with sophisticated specificity on selected programs (like Senator Walter F. Mondale's attack on the nuclear carrier program of the Navy). But such small successes were in good measure due to the expertise of former Pentagon and Budget Bureau analysts, who were willing to assist senators on the Hill and provide the data and analysis essential to the use of the scalpel in place of the ax. Those analysts had access to old friends and contacts with executive branch information that the president probably preferred not have been made available to them. The coherent dialogue that should mark congressional consideration of the defense budget cannot depend on such chance encounters. It requires that detailed military budget information be available on a regular basis to a much larger number of congressmen than those on the Armed Services Committee.

Perhaps the best sense of perspective of presidential power over the Congress can be gained by reflection on the complexity of relating issues such as military spending, domestic programs, and economic policy to each other. The president's branch has by no means solved that problem. But throughout the 1960s and early 1970s the White House (with its Office of Management and Budget) climbed closer to the top of the mountain, while the Congress (with its fragmented committees) remained below sea level. In the context of a gross national product approaching $1.5 trillion and a federal budget far in excess of $300 billion, the expenditure by the Congress of even $100 million to develop, over a period of time, its own analytical capability would seem to be the minimum response necessary to fulfill its obligation intelligently to legislate and to respond with an informed degree of skepticism to programs proposed by the president.

Belatedly, the Congress has begun to take some action. Of enormous potential significance is the Congressional Budget Act of 1974. In the 1960s and early 1970s, in January of each year the president sent to the Congress the budget for a fiscal year beginning on July 1. The Congress divided the budget among a variety of appropriations subcommittees, which lacked the central staff necessary to analyze hundreds of pages of complex data. The 1974 act creates a Congressional Office of the Budget, comparable in analytical potential to the president's Office of Management and Budget. The Congressional Office of the Budget can provide the House and Senate Budget Committees established by the act, as well as others, with staff resources sufficient for a sophisticated analysis of the president's budget. The budget committees and staff review the budget as a whole, relate it to priorities and goals, and issue a concurrent resolution by April 15 of each year to set spending ceilings in major program categories (such as health and defense), and to establish aggregate spending and revenue totals. Then the various appropriations subcommittees go to work. By early September, the budget committees must review that work to reconcile it with the spending ceilings in each of the major program categories. If appropriate, the Congress could enact a reconciliation bill cutting expenditures, raising taxes, or some variation of both. The process ends by September 25 in time for the start of the new fiscal year on October 1.

Some have criticized the bill as inadequate. Even if it is not the panacea senators as diverse as Edmund Muskie, Charles Percy, Harry Byrd, and William Brock believed when they urged its enactment, it is clearly a major step in the right direction. But whether its potential can be realized will depend in large measure on the willingness of House and Senate committee chairmen to cooperate. The early skirmishes between Senators Edmund Muskie and John McClellan provide some indication of how difficult it may be to secure that cooperation.

Congressional oversight of the executive branch and the president has been performed through a series of fragmented and overlapping standing and select committees and subcommittees. They have often been organized in response to the jurisdictional protocols of executive departments and agencies, with plenty of leg room for powerful committee and subcommittee chairmen to expand the scope of their responsibilities. The White House staff and Office of Management and Budget are well aware of their ability to draft proposed legislation in a manner likely to steer it to a friendly committee. In this sense, the Congress has provided the president with some Trojan horses on Capitol Hill.

Most members of the House and Senate are totally dependent on committee reports to obtain a sense of the legislation on which they must vote, but which they have no time to read, much less study. For the evaluations of existing executive programs, these committees depend largely on studies made by the General Accounting Office, special- and public-interest groups, and often the executive branch itself. It is next to impossible for an executive department head responsible for a program to provide an independent, objective review of the manner in which he is operating it. (A fortiori, he can provide no such analysis of whether he should be operating that program.)

During the 1960s the committee structure of the United States Congress lost its relationship to the realities of American life. Committee jurisdictional lines became a major inhibition to the functional, problem-oriented analysis of our national problems. Today, the antediluvian congressional committee structure bears major responsibility for the second-class citizenship of the Congress vis-à-vis the executive branch. Senator Hubert Humphrey made a proposal in 1971 for a National Security Committee in recognition of the fact that diplomatic and military affairs, foreign aid, international economic policy, and U.S. intelligence activities are all threads of the same foreign policy fabric and cannot be evaluated intelligently unless they are considered together. Under the chairmanship of Representative Richard Bolling and against the determined opposition of most existing committee chairman, the Select Committee on Committees of the House of Representatives has recommended a restructuring of the fifteen major standing committees essentially along functional lines: for example, education, public works and transportation, energy and environment, science and technology. The proposals are not likely to satisfy the functionally oriented purists because they take account of some of the political realities. Nevertheless, their adoption would be another indication that the Congress intends to get up off its knees and try to stand face to face with the president and his branch. But that adoption is not likely to come easily or soon, for in late 1974, the House resoundingly rejected the first attempt to effect the Bolling proposals, in favor of a hollow compromise.

The political problems in altering congressional committee jurisdiction are severe. As the powers of one congressional committee are altered, each unaffected committee fears it as an opening to trim its own jurisdictional sails. Constituents are interested in knowing that their congressman is chairman of some particularly powerful House committee or subcommittee, like Ways and Means or Defense Appropriations. The broader the jurisdiction, the more opportunities the chairman has to help his own congressional district. As Washington *Post* congressional correspondent Mary Russell noted after the House rejected the Bolling reorganization proposals, "When the House finished six torturous days of debate on reforming its committee system . . . one thing was clear—why it's been 28 years since the last time the House tried to reform itself." Votes on these issues do not split along ideological or party lines; members vote their jurisdictional interests. Thus, for example, the two House committee chairman who voted to support the Bolling reforms in 1974, George Mahon of Appropriations and Thomas Morgan of Foreign Affairs, either lost no jurisdiction or gained some. As indicated in Chapter II, this importance that committee chairmen and senior committee members on both sides of the aisle attach to maintaining the integrity of their jurisdictional turf in turn generates tenacious opposition to proposals for executive departmental reorganization.

The congressional seniority system, although under increasingly effective challenge in the House of Representatives, continues to make its contribution to resisting change. Congressmen, who have been elected for eight or ten terms and who are at last secured in safe districts, usually have remained on the same committees, working their way to the chair or ranking minority status. They are not readily persuaded to vote for any reorganization that might increase pressure on the Congress to alter the jurisdictional scope of committees on which they have acquired an influential voice by reason of sixteen or twenty years of service.

Where a member stands on the issue of seniority is likely to depend on how long that member has been sitting in the Congress. Senator Walter F. Mondale, at a dinner in New York, was delightfully candid when asked by a liberal supporter what he thought should be done about the seniority system in the Congress. "The longer I am in the Congress," Senator Mondale quipped, "the less I am concerned about the seniority system." Whether one is for or against the se-

niority system can also change in response to views on substantive policies. With the congressional committees in the
hands of conservative chairmen like James Eastland, John
Stennis, and John McClellan, liberals press to have committee chairmanships determined on the basis of majority vote
rather than seniority. But as the liberals in the Senate, like
William Proxmire and Edmund Muskie, assume committee
chairmanships (and others like Stuart Symington, Edward
Kennedy, Walter Mondale, and Birch Bayh approach them),
it is likely that the conservatives will complain about the
seniority system and the liberals will be satisfied to maintain
"a system that has served the Congress so well for so long."

The January 1975 unseating of three House committee
chairmen should be seen in perspective. Two autocratic, personally unpopular, and conservative chairmen—F. Edward
Hébert of Louisiana and Armed Services and H. R. Poage of
Texas and Agriculture—were unseated in favor of popular
and more liberal and democratic House members, Melvin
Price of Illinois and Thomas Foley of Washington, respec-
tively. The old populist Wright Patman, was deposed by
Henry Reuss, largely because of age, but also because so
many of the liberal new Democrats believed Reuss would be
far more effective in achieving their goals and more responsive to their new liberalism.

These actions, and other changes in House rules relating to
the selection and power of subcommittee chairmen and the
role of the Democratic Caucus, are certainly calculated to
render senior House leaders and committee chairmen notably more responsive to the needs and desires of younger and
more recently elected members. In these terms, the constitutional role of the House as an instant barometer of the
public may be more fully realized. But it is unlikely that
democratically elected committee and subcommittee chairman will be less jurisdictionally jealous than their seniority-
selected predecessors. In this perspective seniority seems
more a superficial and tactical issue than one of fundamental
substance. Debates over the seniority issue are lively and
charged, but they tend to confuse the central need for an
institutionally systematic reorganization of the House and

Senate committee jurisdictional structure. Such a reorganization is essential to congressional assumption of equal
ground with the executive.

The numerous duties of congressmen and senators—their
various committee assignments, their responsibilities to constituents, and the chronic campaigning that often attends the
brief two-year term of House members—contribute to the
separate but unequal status of the Congress in relation to the
presidency. By the early 1970s, there were some 148 House
subcommittees under 36 standing, select and joint committees. Over the course of a three-month period studied in
1973, there were 1,189 committee meetings. Most such meetings take place on Tuesday, Wednesday, and Thursday (938
of the 1,189 during the April–June 1973 period) because most
House members and a large number of senators return to
their districts and states to politic with their constituencies
from Friday through Monday.

The Congressmen's harassed life-work style makes them
easy prey for a president intent on imposing his will on the
Congress. With the exception of Dwight Eisenhower, all recent presidents have fully appreciated their advantage here.
In the Second Session of the prolific 89th Congress, some
White House aides and a few congressional leaders expressed
concern about sending to the Congress an even more extensive legislative program than had been submitted to the First
Session. Johnson's response was blunt and to the point: First,
we may never have another Congress with a liberal (as distinguished from a merely Democratic) majority in the House
during my presidency; second, if we don't keep them frenetically busy with our legislative business, they will spend their
time investigating us. As a result, the Second Session of the
89th Congress passed even more legislation than the first.
From the perspective of presidential power, the White
House effectively characterized the issues for the Congress.

Congressmen are so busy and understaffed that a strong
president can virtually set their complete agenda. Not only
does the executive branch provide the initial drafts of legislation (except for the tax-writing House Ways and Means Com-

mittee which has customarily declined to accept draft legislative language from the executive). In addition, the White House staff and executive departments under its direction write speeches for congressmen and senators introducing and supporting legislation and frequently sit in the cloakrooms during critical debates to provide facts, figures, and rhetoric to floor managers and supporters of administration bills. This is usually done at the urgent request of congressmen and senators who simply lack the staff resources and data to do it for themselves.

The absence of independent and adequate staffs is particularly debilitating to a Congress controlled by the party out of power in the White House. The edited Nixon tapes provide candid testimony of the awareness of the president and his staff of the sharp advantages this situation gives the office of the president—and the fact that presidents are not about to help the Congress change the situation. An interesting exchange between Nixon and John Dean on February 28, 1973, is directly to the point:

P. Congress is, of course, on its (inaudible). And yet they are so enormously frustrated that they are exhausted. Isn't that the point?

D. I think there is a lot of that.

P. It is too bad. We can take very little comfort from it because we have to work with them. But they become irrelevant because they are so damned irresponsible, as much as we would like to say otherwise.

D. Yes, sir. I spent some years on the Hill myself and one of the things I always noticed was the inability of the Congress to deal effectively with the Executive Branch because they have never provided themselves with adequate staffs, had adequate information available—

P. Well now they have huge staffs compared to what we had.

D. Well they have huge staffs, true, as opposed to what they had years ago. But they are still inadequate to deal effectively—

P. (Expletive deleted) Don't try to help them out!

D. I am not suggesting any reserve money for them. I ought to keep my observations to myself.

When subjected to the grossest presidential affronts the Congress has acted. When President Nixon submitted an insultingly unqualified man like Harrold Carswell to sit on the Supreme Court, the Senate denied him confirmation. When Nixon refused to spend large sums of money appropriated by the Congress, he acted in illegally and politically blatant defiance of its legislative mandates. Congressmen went to court to obtain orders that appropriated money be spent. But most cases are not so dramatic and in the impoundment controversy the Congress sought out another branch for decisive help in its battle with the president.

Where there has been an egregious breach of constitutional comity by a weak and mistrusted president, the Congress has been able to pass legislation purporting to limit his power. The 1973 War Powers Resolution is a recent example. It is doubtful that the resolution would have been passed over a presidential veto in November 1973 if Nixon had not been so deeply entangled in the Watergate scandals. Yet, as Senator Thomas Eagleton has written in his book, *War and Presidential Power: A Chronicle of Congressional Surrender,* that resolution may prove to be more rhetorical gesture than a *de facto* curb of presidential power. Despite the congressional hurrahs, the resolution may have little impact on presidential ability to commit U.S. forces to combat without a declaration of war. Within forty-eight hours of any such commitment, the resolution requires the president to notify the Congress of the need for the commitment, the authority on which it is based, and its estimated scope and duration. Subsequent periodic reports must be made to the Congress. The president must terminate the commitment within sixty days unless the Congress specifically authorizes its continuance for a longer period or is "physically unable to meet" because of hostilities on U.S. soil.

The rhetoric of the War Powers Resolution is dovishly resolute. Its practical impact is another matter. It is a near-certainty that no president would commit troops without prior consultation with the congressional leadership and their assurance of support. Absent a level of distrust as deep-seated as the congressional attitude toward the Nixon administration at the peak of the Watergate scandals, the president is likely to be taken at his word. Senator Wayne Morse often stated that Lyndon Johnson gave the Congress ample advance notice in 1964 and 1965 about the extent of potential U.S. involvement in Vietnam. What Congress needed then was a prescience no War Powers Resolution can provide.

The Congress has taken other actions utterly inconsistent with the thrust of the resolution in terms of presidential power. The rhetoric of the War Powers Resolution should be contrasted with the major impact on presidential war-making power implied by congressional termination of the draft and establishment of the volunteer army.

The greatest inhibition on the decision of a democratically elected leader to wage war is the need to have the people's support. It took Roosevelt years of persuasion and the Japanese sneak attack at Pearl Harbor to bring the nation to a point where they were willing to wage war in the South Pacific, North Africa, and Europe. Truman's decision to fight in Korea was one he had to make with the concern that, as the war progressed, it would likely be unpopular and costly to the political fortunes of a party that depended upon the support of the American people in order to retain control of the White House. In both cases, the need to draft middle- and upper-class young men into the military required that the president maintain the support of their families.

The concept of a volunteer army—paid at a rate just high enough to attract those at the lower economic levels of our society and ending a draft which exposes every economic and social level to possible military service—lifts from the president the most potent inhibition on a decision to wage war. It is appalling that so many antiwar congressmen climbed on the volunteer army bandwagon. Many did so because of their revulsion at the Vietnam War and because they can rationalize the concept as providing that only those who "volunteer" will have to go to war.

This is a gross misreading of one of the central historical lessons of the war in Southeast Asia. What turned this nation around on Vietnam was neither demonstrations in the street nor the rhetoric of David Dellinger, Tom Hayden, and Benjamin Spock. It was, in quite readable political terms to the presidents who agonized over Vietnam, the realization that the vast middle class of America would not permit its sons to be drafted to die in a war that it considered meaningless. It was middle- and upper-class Americans, who knew how to contact congressmen and to influence their local communities, most all of whom vote and many of whom help finance campaigns, that posed the sharp dilemma to the president: Get out of Vietnam or get out of office. An all-volunteer force that permits the middle- and upper-class Americans to avoid military service will effectively reduce the need for future leaders to be concerned about the more affluent majority of America and its judgments about foreign adventures, at least until those adventures are so far along that they will be virtually impossible to stop.

Moreover, the Congress has stood by for decades as presidents have replaced treaties with executive agreements that do not require ratification by two-thirds of the Senate. Indicative of so many other issues that concern the executive and legislative branches, the Congress has largely permitted the president and his Department of State to decide the category into which arrangements with foreign nations fit. Thus, the White House has decided whether Senate ratification was necessary in each case. A few congressional actions in 1974, such as the requirement that the executive submit certain foreign arms sales to the Congress for possible veto, the redirection of much of the food aid program, and the restrictions on Soviet trade agreements, provide some hint of change in this aspect of the relationship of the Congress to the president, as does the flare-up over the exodus from Vietnam. But the Congress is divided on the wisdom of such restrictions and congressional action in the economic arena in the early 1970s provides some strong evidence to the contrary.

The price and wage control and federal energy office legislation of the early 1970s sharply dramatizes the contrast between legislative reality and congressional rhetoric. In the context of speeches about imperial presidencies, overweaning White House power, and presidential dictatorship, the

Congress literally imposed on Richard Nixon vast discretionary authority over wages and prices. When the energy crisis of 1973 arrived, the Congress was only too willing to turn over to the president wide powers to allocate fuel among industry and home use, transportation modes, and states and cities. Aside from congressional restrictions on the president designed to hold down energy prices, the continuing debate on energy and economic issues is characterized not in terms of whether to give the president more power, but rather in terms of what power to vest in him.

There are indications that this trend will continue and move into other areas. For instance, despite the Russian trade restrictions, the Congress is giving the president increasingly wide discretion to negotiate foreign-trade agreements, authority which carries with it the power to make and break millionaires and determine the futures of large corporations. Discretionary economic, energy, and foreign-trade powers properly belong in the executive branch since the Congress cannot (and should not) administer wage and price controls, operate fuel allocation programs, or negotiate complex trade agreements. But without usurping executive power, the Congress can certainly provide more clearly defined standards of accountability for the presidential exercise of such power, both in the legislation it enacts and in the performance of the oversight function by its committees. For example, it could provide explicit wholesale and consumer price index targets in connection with price and wage control legislation.

The relationship between the president and the Congress is not necessarily affected by whether the Congress is Democratic and the president Republican. Nor does it depend upon whether the president is conservative, like Nixon, or liberal and aggressive, like Johnson and Kennedy. Indeed, under the most conservative occupant in recent years, the presidency has acquired unprecedented peacetime powers.

Legislative deeds (what the Congress does) not only belie recent congressional rhetoric (what the Congress says). More significantly, they confirm the increasing congressional difficulty in legislating with the kind of precision necessary to set standards sufficiently specific to measure presidential performance. These are contemporary symptoms of a festering, persistent congressional impotence, aggravated by its dependent reliance on the informational and analytical resources of the executive branch. What is so disturbing is that this unfortunate congressional condition is self-imposed.

Toynbee tells us that the civilizations he studied were not destroyed by foreign enemies. They deteriorated and crumbled from within. So it is with institutions. Like people, they tend to bring their problems on themselves. They carry within them the seeds of their own destruction. As the Congress thrashes about in frustration at its separate but unequal status among the branches of government, it must understand that its houses are made of fragile glass. Before its members throw too many stones at the presidency, they must recognize that they hold in their own hands the power to vote themselves the staffs and analytical capability they need, to establish central systems-analysis and program-evaluation offices, to reorganize their committees along functional lines that reflect the needs of modern American society, to assume their constitutional role as the most effective and responsive legislature in the history of mankind, and to assess the impact on presidential power of each major legislative action. Such recognition is essential if the Congress is to perform, consistently and rationally, its critical role of putting presidential power in healthy constitutional perspective.

If the Congress fails to act, increased power will flow to the office of the president, and not simply the kind of warped and criminally exercised power revealed by the Watergate scandals. What should be a greater concern to most Americans is that the Congress continues to grant the president more and more power and render him less and less accountable for its exercise. Effective accountability in the last quarter of the twentieth century will depend in large measure on the ability of a coequal branch of the government to review the work of the chief executive. That kind of capability does not exist in the Congress today and will not come in the future unless the Congress provides for itself.

Future historians may ruefully conclude that there was nothing more effective or responsible the Congress was capable of doing. So blinded had it become by its self-deceptive rhetoric and internal battles that it did not see how weak had it become in relation to the president and his executive branch—until its only recourse was to lodge power in the president and let him answer perhaps to the governors and mayors and, ultimately, to the people.

I V

---·◦◁∞▷◦·---

THE PRESIDENT
AND THE GOVERNORS
AND MAYORS:
Caesar among Centurions

In the early years of our republic, the states provided effective counterforces for the president and the central government. It was from the states that political strength was gathered, from the state houses that so many early political leaders came. The central government provided some important threads to help weave the states together. But the states were the fiber of American life. They functioned in consonance with the original design of the founding fathers, as deliberately decentralized checks and balances to the power of the presidency and the national government. Subdued during the Reconstruction era that followed the Civil War, they retained sufficient political vitality to resume this role and perform it well in the early years of the twentieth century.

Then Theodore Roosevelt put the Sherman Anti-Trust Act to work and he gave the American people an early glimpse of the use of federal power on economic and conservation issues. In 1916, the federal government was vested with the power to raise money through the income tax. In the 1930s and 1940s Franklin Roosevelt used the tax power to raise and spend money, initially for the problems of human misery born of economic depression and then to wage war. During the 1950s the Supreme Court put the racial discrimination issue in the hands of the federal executive, and Dwight Eisenhower made it clear to Orval Faubus and the state of Arkansas that the federal government was supreme over the states in this area. With the Great Society programs of Lyndon Johnson, the heavy machinery of the federal executive dug deeply into the soil of state and local issues.

During the early years of our nation, states and cities were regarded somewhat like shells to embryonic chicks: They provided essential protection for economic, social, and human development. Today, the economic, technological, and social forces at loose in our troubled society have left those shells shattered on the ground. As states, cities, and counties have increasingly failed as viable instruments of local government—either in political leadership, financial resources, or ability to cope with the problems of their people—they have become the political chicks of a mother-hen central government, dependent on her for financial and other succor. The federal government alone collects and spends about two-thirds of the funds devoted to the public sector of our economy and is now a major source of financial support to local communities across this country, for programs ranging from family services for the poor to local public transportation for the entire community.

Technological advances and human congestion have enormously complicated our problems with nature. They can no longer be effectively confronted within the confines of political boundaries drawn more than a century ago and gerrymandered in the long-forgotten local political battles of succeeding generations. The forces of the twentieth century—technological and human, institutional and political—have combined to render the states political eunuchs in the performance of any role as serious counterpoints to the power of the central executive and the president who presides over it or to the national Congress which controls the purse strings for so many programs that intimately affect state and local communities. As presently structured, the combination of the fifty states with their arbitrary boundaries and the jigsaw puzzle of twenty-five thousand cities and counties, many of which are more populated than some states, is no match for the relatively affluent and powerful presidential and legislative branches of the federal government.

This is true despite the fact that, in economic terms, state and local government is monumentally big business and getting bigger. By the early 1970s, state and local government employed well over ten million Americans. Roughly half of those Americans worked in general government jobs at the state and local level; the remaining half were affiliated with public education. The payrolls for state and local government in those years exceeded $7 billion per month, some $250 million per day. Total expenditures at the state and local level in the early 1970s approached $200 billion per year. During the 1960s, state and local government was the fastest growing sector of the American economy. Over that decade, all jobs in the American economy increased 19 percent. State and local government employment skyrocketed by 64 percent. Growth projections for the decade of the 1970s are even more dramatic.

The explosion in the numbers of state and local bureaucrats has been necessary to staff the array of new departments and agencies established by their governments. But there is not strength in those numbers in dealing with the central government. In public policy decisions allocating domestic program resources, these numbers work to help divide them. With the federal executive increasingly entrenched as the cornucopia of domestic program funds for distribution to states and localities, the fifty states and twenty-five thousand cities and counties become aggressive supplicants as their fragmented departments scramble for federal funds. In turn, the president's executive branch has been placed in a position to divide and conquer the lower levels of government with each grant of federal funds it dispenses.

The dry numbers of the president's budget tell the story of state and local dependence on the national government. In the fiscal year ending June 30, 1950, federal grants to the states for social programs (there was no revenue sharing) totaled $300,000. In the fiscal year ending June 30, 1960, such grants and revenue sharing totaled $1.4 billion. For the fiscal year ending June 30, 1974, the total reached $20.6 billion: $14 billion for grants-in-aid for social programs and $6.6 billion for revenue sharing. The branch over which the president presides has some two million people administering these programs and monitoring the performance of the states and cities.

But even those figures do not provide sufficient appreciation of the dependent status of state and local government on federal financial resources. If all federal funds to assist state and local government are totaled, the climb is from $7 billion in 1960 to an estimated $51.7 billion for the fiscal year ending June 30, 1975, an increase of more than 700 percent. It is true that state and local government expenditures have been rising even more sharply than federal expenditures over this same period. Nevertheless, from 1960 to 1975, federal aid as a percentage of state and local government expenditures has grown from 13.5 percent to 22.4 percent, a 66 percent increase.

Nor do financial statistics alone adequately express the impact of federal aid on state and local governments. In many cases, funds are available only where states or cities agree to take specific actions dictated by the executive branch. As the fiscal 1975 Special Analysis of the president's Office of Management and Budget points out,

> The influence of Federal grants is substantially greater than the figures alone indicate. Many grant programs are intended to encourage innovation by State and local governments by testing and demonstrating a new concept's validity in "demonstration" programs. Other programs unnecessarily restrict States by requiring them to establish and maintain specific agencies, though many of these provisions are being phased out. Most importantly, many programs require the recipient government to match Federal aid funds with its own resources. In the last few years, State and local governments have al-

located about 10% of their own revenue to match Federal grant moneys.

The financial plight of the states and cities is now so serious that it has sharply eroded their constitutional standing as counterpoints to presidential and executive branch power. This condition is likely to persist as far into the future as anyone can see. Increasingly, governors and mayors are reaching the limits of their ability to raise money in the public sector without, as more than one politician has concluded, committing political suicide. Too often tax increases are proposed by governors and mayors not at a time when they recognize their need, but at a time when they have decided to retire from office and ought to do this for their people as a final act of their political career, to make up for their failure to obtain sufficient funds for the public sector in the past.

Revenue sharing is not likely to put the states and cities back on their constitutional feet. Proponents of revenue sharing consider it as an effective means by which the states and cities might reclaim their economic viability. If correct, they would have a potent argument for revenue sharing, because economic viability is an essential ingredient of the political strength the states and cities need to counterpoint presidential power in the last quarter of the twentieth century. But this argument assumes that revenue sharing will come from the federal government without strings and in amounts sufficient to render our states and cities economically (and to that extent, politically) solvent institutions of decentralized power. History teaches that with federal funds come federal guidelines. Initially, there is broad legislative guidance, but detailed executive branch regulations follow fast on the heels of legislation.

The Congress will simply not tax and tax and let the governors and mayors spend and spend. It is the taxing authority that hurts politically and the spending authority that helps politically. No politician is going to reach for the taxing end of the stick without the benefit of some control over the spending end. Indeed, he should not. Such a system further

contributes to the confusion our people already have in trying to identify which political leaders are accountable for
what political actions. A governor, mayor, or county commissioner is not likely to be more responsible in his selection and
operation of social programs if he does not have to raise the
money to mount them. He is forced to make the hard priority
choices much more carefully if he must procure taxpayer
funds to finance them.

So long as the amounts of federal revenue to be shared are
not plentiful, the states and localities will stand divided,
fighting for larger pieces of the pie from the president and
the branch he heads. The political difficulties of the governors and mayors in raising taxes are mirrored at the national
level. The pressures to hold the federal budget down are
likely to last indefinitely, with the result that revenue sharing
funds will not be generously available for state and local
governments. As the courts began in the early 1970s to put
certain state and local property taxes in constitutional jeopardy, the response of the federal executive was a desperate
search for some new tax. In 1972, President Nixon studied
and almost proposed a national system of sales taxation to
finance local public school systems in the face of these court
cases. Interestingly, the most discussed technique was a val-
ue-added tax, to be placed on each element of incremental
value in the production and distribution of goods, a tax which
renders irrelevant the states and localities in which the goods
are produced and distributed. It was the same sort of tax
President Johnson had considered and almost proposed in
1968.

The public dialogue over revenue sharing, like the cold
figures and interventionist policies, demonstrates the special
power of the president and his branch over state and local
government and the dependency, still on the increase, of
state and local government on the central executive. Yet,
there is at least some measure of ambiguity to the impact of
federal funds on state and local government. One can argue
that, as we have acknowledged national responsibility in so
many spheres of local community life during the 1960s, we
have also recognized that the effective application of federal

power often requires the insulating conduit of state and local government. To some extent this breeds a political atmosphere of mutual dependence.

No such hypothesis can be postulated with respect to the other forces in our society that significantly affect the power balance between the president's branch and state and local government. The environmental, population congestion, and technological forces of the 1960s and early 1970s have combined to render state and local governments incapable of fulfilling their constitutional function as forceful counterpoints to the central executive.

A century ago, it made no difference that rivers ran through the politically inspired boundaries of the several states. In the 1970s, modern manufacturing methods, automobile emissions, and the tons of waste that come from population congestion have made water pollution a major and urgent problem. Pollution cannot be eliminated from part of a river anymore than leukemia can be purged from part of a blood stream. No individual state or city, acting alone, can effectively deal with this problem. The states, reluctant to relinquish any of their sovereign power to one of their peers, have turned to the federal government for help.

Air moves in air sheds, a fact not known or considered relevant over much of the past two hundred years of political and bureaucratic maneuvering by governors and mayors to establish their own jurisdictional fiefdoms. Today, we realize that it is no more possible to clean the air in Chicago without cleaning the air sheds and currents in the surrounding suburbs and Gary, Indiana, than it is possible to clear cigarette smoke only from the driver's seat of an automobile. Neighboring states and cities in air-polluted metropolitan areas look increasingly to the federal executive to establish and enforce clean air standards and help establish superjurisdictional authorities.

Human congestion has carried with it transportation problems of unwieldy proportions. They cannot be alleviated by cities, or in some cases even states, acting alone. New York City, for example, can have at best only a marginal impact on its own traffic congestion problem; it must work with suburban cities and counties, as well as Connecticut, New Jersey, and probably Pennsylvania. The congestion problem is not as severe in the District of Columbia, but the political problem of working with Maryland, Virginia, and the surrounding suburban counties and cities is.

Problems of human congestion become even more jurisdictionally complex when they assume regional proportions. The long Northeast corridor, which extends from Washington through Maryland, Delaware, Pennsylvania, and New York to Boston, is the most congested in the nation. With the limited resources available, intelligent formulation of transportation policy requires, on a regional basis, the systematic selection of the best mix of transportation modes to move people and material. How many people and which materials can most conveniently and efficiently be moved by automobile, truck, railroad, ship, or airplane? Over what routes? At which times of day or night? With what frequency? Not one of the states or cities involved can rationally analyze, much less resolve, the problems. Here the federal executive acts in a variety of ways: grants to railroads, control of air routes, subsidies for highway construction and maritime programs, pressure on the states and cities to form regional and metropolitan compacts and authorities. But the president's branch always acts as the most affluent and powerful member of the family of government, the domineering planner and provider for the political household.

As the states and cities are now organized, there is no other way to deal with present-day environmental and transportation problems. To the extent state and local boundaries inspire and perpetuate parochial loyalty, more often than not they complicate and impede effective action on these problems. As a result, the people in those areas increasingly turn to the president and the central government either to solve their problems, or to force the states, cities, and counties to work together toward their solution.

As congestion and pollution spread into suburban areas, metropolitan and regional authorities have begun to form across our nation and to erode, at least for these limited purposes, the relevance of state and local jurisdictional lines. Metropolitan transit authorities help to solve the congestion problems of central cities. Regional clean air and water authorities provide an organizational framework to confront environmental problems. But they offer little in terms of an effective counterbalance against central executive power. To some degree, these authorities become competitors with states and cities for federal funds. In this sense, the central executive faces yet further division among its constituent parts and an increase in its potential to divide and conquer. More significant are the detailed federal standards and guidelines under which these authorities are required to operate because of their predominate dependence on the federal government for financing. From this perspective, they are more an agent of the federal executive administering funds than of the constituent states and cities they were created to serve.

Modern technology's corporate corollary of capital concentration is serving to increase the power of the president and the branch he heads vis-à-vis the states and cities. Communication, production, and computer technologies have precipitated unprecedented concentrations of wealth in a relatively small number of national corporations. Those who are concerned about corporate power and want it restrained, those who manage that corporate power and want to maintain or increase its strength, and those who seek to use that corporate concentration for the economic development of their states and cities are all turning to the president's branch to achieve their objectives.

Not only consumer advocates, but most thoughtful academics and commentators on corporate America recognize that few, if any, states are equipped to protect the public interest in the face of increasingly large concentrations of corporate power. It is no longer only General Motors that has a gross product and income that far exceeds the gross product and tax income of several individual states. Today, virtually all companies on the "Fortune 500" list of the largest corporations have far more resources, power, and single-

mindedness of profit-oriented purpose than the state of Delaware, where most of them are incorporated. Accordingly,
many (but not all) consumer groups have pressed for a federal incorporation law to replace, at least for major corporations, our current system of state incorporation. In terms of
controlling concentrations of corporate wealth, there may be
strong arguments in favor of such a law. (Awed by the resources and power of multinational corporations, some have
even argued that the time has come for international incorporation.) However, in terms of enhancing the value of states
as constitutional counterpoints to central executive power
directed by the president, the impact of effecting such
proposals will be to give the federal executive additional
power and funds, in this case directly at the expense of the
states.

Since 1966, consumer groups have urged that the president be given new and increased power to regulate American corporations. The men and institutions these groups wish
to subject to government regulation would, quite naturally,
prefer less "government interference." But increasingly, if
they must live with more regulation, they would prefer it at
the federal level rather than at state and local levels. Top
corporate managers have long recognized the irrelevance of
state and local boundaries to the manufacture, distribution,
and consumption of most American goods, which are produced and distributed nationally and advertised on network
television, in national magazines, or in national campaigns
through the newspapers of a dozen or so major cities. To
these managers, state and local lines have become unnecessary irritants (except to the extent that they provide the
comforting harbor of tax benefits when new plants are
located within their boundaries). To network television itself,
the most powerful communication force in American society, such boundary lines have never been, and are never
likely to be, of any relevance.

By the late 1960s large corporations became resigned to
increased federal involvement in consumer protection programs. They also began to appreciate that, from the corporate point of view, when the federal government decides to

move into an area of consumer protection or occupational safety, it makes more sense in terms of cost, irritation, and time to try to assure that such legislation will be pre-emptive of similar state or local activity. Pre-emptive legislation eliminates state and local rules in the same areas and gives the large national corporation an opportunity to deal one-on-one with the federal executive. States and cities, except where consumer protection agencies are politically desirable and effective public relations devices, are more than willing to permit the federal government to intervene with the complex and (in their terms) sometimes expensive regulatory apparatus necessary to enforce certain consumer protection laws. They are so pressed for lack of funds and have such difficulty recruiting the necessary talent, that they seem delighted to leave to the federal government any task it is willing to assume.

There was a day in this nation when economic and social planning was done at the neighborhood level; then there came the day when it was done at the city or county level; and then it was done at the state level. Today, however, our economic and social planners are aware of the inhibitions state and local boundaries impose on economic development and social progress. The Tennessee Valley Authority of Franklin Roosevelt's administration was an early reflection of this awareness. In the 1960s, the federal government established programs under the Economic Development Administration and a number of regional bodies, like the Appalachian and New England Commissions, to stimulate economic development. These commissions recognized the technological and population changes of the past fifty years and attempted to accommodate those changes to the economically and socially relevant natural characteristics of different regions, irrespective of state lines. The development program for Appalachia and the commission to oversee it, for instance, involve all of some states and portions of others.

Their lack of financial resources has placed significant pressure on states and cities to regionalize some public services

and programs once considered sacredly local. But virtually
every action toward regionalization is being taken at the
instigation of the federal government and with the central
executive as the decisive voice in each functionally oriented
regional grouping. Prompted by its own limited resources,
the federal government has sought to encourage the states
and cities to organize joint regional and community efforts in
the hope of reducing public expenditures. The Safe Streets
Act of 1968, as originally conceived and proposed, contemplated the establishment of regional training centers for state
and local police forces to ease the financial burden of police
training on individual states and cities. The Fire Safety Act
of 1968 was initially conceived, in part, to make fire-fighting
training and equipment uniform on a regional or metropolitan basis. Both legislative recommendations would have
given the central executive decision power to establish man-
datory guidelines for states and cities that received federal
funds.

There is a healthy measure of participation in the planning
and implementation of regional development programs by
the states in the region covered by a commission umbrella.
But, for purposes of the present analysis, it is essential to
recognize a paramount characteristic common to these types
of regional organizations. The president's executive branch
speaks not simply as a partner, its voice carries the authority
of the senior partner. The central government provides the
matching funds for regional development and, with those
funds, usually selects the regional development projects to
be undertaken. When these regional commissions were amply funded in the mid-1960s, the federal voice was often that
of the president or a White House assistant.

Lyndon Johnson proposed legislation under which the federal government was to help organize community development districts, whereby several counties could band together, rise above their county lines and pool their common
human and material resources to provide services at a level
otherwise not achievable in rural America. As Johnson described the proposal to the Congress, its purpose was to demonstrate how a common effort could provide the needed

district vocational school in one county, the hospital in another, police training in a third, an adequate library in a fourth. "This effort can avoid the waste of duplication—or worse still, the total lack of such facilities or services because of a failure to pool common resources."

The proposal never reached full fruition. But it is probably still the only way to significantly and efficiently upgrade these kinds of social services in rural areas. The troublesome question is whether the president's hand should loom so largely. Yet, without carrot (money) and stick (no money, Mr. County Commissioner, unless you forego some of your petty jurisdictional authority) inducements from the federal government, it is difficult to see how some of these services can be provided at any reasonable public cost.

The economic and political realities of providing adequate public services during recent years were accompanied by the social and moral awakening that exploded on the American conscience. The social forces of the 1960s and the early 1970s, with a big assist from the federal judiciary and the failure and political inability of the states and cities to respond to these forces, left a moral and political vacuum which the presidency filled. The legal, human, and moral issues of racial discrimination in America swept across state and local lines as though they did not exist and exposed states and cities as politically impotent or obstructionist in the face of a major national problem. Then, in the early 1970s, the courts began to ask what the constitutionally and legally mandated rights of equal protection and nondiscrimination meant in the context of municipal and county boundaries. Federal district judges in Richmond and Detroit concluded that those boundaries were irrelevant in terms of achieving school desegregation in Virginia and Michigan. Their judgments were reversed, but they stand as symbolic evidence in the increasingly convincing case presented by the forces and events of the sixties and seventies which established the artificiality of state and local boundaries in America. Moreover, the issue is by no means closed; other federal judges, as well as state and local political officials, will have to face it in varying circumstances in other metropolitan areas. The city of Richmond, in annexing portions of neighboring Chester-field County to dilute the voting power of inner-city Blacks, demonstrated the irrelevance of local boundaries—and sent the issue back to the courts.

The Richmond and Detroit school-district decisions also reflect the constitutional implications for states and cities of racial integration in America. They point up the difficulties of achieving equal opportunity, rights, and protection only within the boundaries of a single state or city. The achievement of true equality of educational opportunity and school desegregation in the metropolitan areas of Washington, D.C., or New York City, may well require that school systems be recast (if not through court decree then through enforcement of fair housing laws) to take in neighboring Virginia and Maryland, or Connecticut and New Jersey.

School desegregation in the 1960s and early 1970s was only the sharpest cutting edge of the fight for social justice that pressed all three branches of the federal government to pierce the state and local government veil. The plight of thousands of Blacks and poor whites in Harlem, Detroit, and Chicago did not begin in these cities, anymore than it is likely to end there. It began in large measure in the rural poverty of Alabama, Mississippi, and Louisiana, and in the hills and mountains of Appalachia. Social justice for these disadvantaged Americans requires commitment and action on a scale that has nothing to do with lines on maps that define the geographical limits of Northern cities and Southern states.

As this nation is now constituted, those who fight for government intervention in the cause of social and racial justice urge the central government to act. Once again, the central executive, here with repeated congressional mandates, has moved in ways that have the effect (perhaps unintended) of weakening existing state and local power centers. Under the 1964 Civil Rights Act, the president was given authority to withhold federal funds from school systems that discriminated. The poverty program gave the president the power to establish community-action agencies outside the existing state and local political establishment. Under federal legislation concerning health care, the president's branch is acquiring increasing increments of authority to impose controls on the medical profession, a once sacred preserve of doctors and state boards.

During the past fifteen years, legislators and political leaders on the whole have been distinctly more cautious than the federal district judges in Richmond and Detroit in suggesting (much less taking) any actions to circumvent state and local boundaries. The proposals to establish regional commissions for economic development, to alleviate air and water pollution, or to set up metropolitan authorities and community development districts have been neatly couched in the comfortable rhetoric of states' rights. That rhetoric has provided the politically acceptable setting in which presidents have been able to disregard bureaucratic boundaries. Whenever such rhetoric and subtle approaches have been lacking, direct attacks on state and local power by the central executive have met with stiff resistence.

One of Lyndon Johnson's major thrusts took on established state and local power directly. The most controversial redistribution of power attempted by his administration involved the community action programs of the war on poverty. These programs by law required the "maximum feasible participation" of the poor in planning and carrying out projects designed to help them help themselves move out of poverty. When the Congress enacted the Office of Economic Opportunity legislation in August 1964, there was nothing subtle about the purpose of the community action programs. They were conspicuously, proudly, and deliberately designed to redistribute power at the state and local level and to operate outside the traditional federal, state, city, and county power structure.

At their 1967 peak, there were more than nine hundred federally financed community action agencies throughout the nation. These agencies were perceived by social planners as an effective means of giving the poor a forceful voice in the planning and administration of local antipoverty efforts. Less than a hundred of these community action agencies were administered by state and local government agencies. Most were dependent upon the federal government directly for assistance; and most put sharp pressure on state, city, and local government to change their way of doing business.

The governors and mayors did not like this kind of political intrusion and they acted to control or eliminate it. So severely had the state and local political tendons been strained, that two years after the law was enacted, the Congress changed the original community action concept, in an attempt to shift much of the control and power from poor and neighborhood groups to the mayors and governors. It amended the antipoverty statutes to provide that governors and mayors could take over community action agencies if they so desired.

When the Nixon administration took office in January 1969, many (but not all) governors and mayors were on the steps of the White House urging the new president to close these community action programs down completely (and, incidentally, give them any of the money that might be saved). Unfortunately, the governors and mayors acted negatively. For eliminating community action programs did nothing to strengthen or improve state, city, or county government. It merely removed one of the irritants that local political leaders perceived as parochially dangerous.

Volunteers in Service to America (VISTA), another program of the Office of Economic Opportunity, provides a similar example. VISTA was originally conceived as a domestic Peace Corps. Young, largely white, middle-class college graduates would live and work for two years in ghettos and pockets of rural poverty to help the disadvantaged there to help themselves. The assistance was to be for social purposes: health, education, child care, family budgeting, and the like. But, with an inexorability that was more surprising to local political officials and their congressmen than it should have been, these young, white, middle-class college graduates began to recognize that what the poor needed as much as anything else at the local level was a vote in elections and a voice in government. Inevitably, many VISTA volunteers became active in local politics. The established system worked against the VISTA program: Congressmen and senators argued on behalf of politically nervous sheriffs and county commissioners that VISTA was spearheading the creation of a "third world" political organization, one independent of the traditional parties which dominated a given state or district. The result was to trim back and reduce the efforts of VISTA. As with respect to the community action agencies, the political establishments of the states, cities, and counties acted negatively.

These poverty program examples illustrate one of the major problems with the reactions of states and cities to the increase of federal power. First, they perceived the problem in the narrowest possible sense as a danger to the personal and political careers of their elected officials. Second, they acted negatively to destroy the introduction of the new force, rather than strengthen themselves to deal with or co-opt it. These are isolated cases where the president acted overtly and aggressively to redistribute power at the local level through federal programs deliberately and publicly designed to do so. They made insignificant contributions to the erosion of state and local power in favor of the central executive. Except for an occasional state or local spasm in response to a direct presidential thrust of this sort, in the near term there is not much likelihood that the states and cities will resist the more subtle carrot-and-stick overtures of the president's branch, much less resume the role they performed in the early days of the republic as one of the key constitutional balances to central executive power.

As a nation, we react forcefully to attacks (such as the community action agencies of the poverty program) that we perceive as dangerous usurpations of sacred state and local prerogatives. But we are persistently reluctant to evaluate, or face coldly, the total impact of these different programs on the ability of states and cities to counterpoint the power of the president and his central executive. In the hindsight of history, the failure to recognize the continued erosion of state and local authority vis-à-vis the president and his branch of the federal government and to examine alternatives such as regional and metropolitan government may turn out to be one of the most serious oversights of the late 1960s and 1970s.

This failure stems from a combination of institutional lethargy, entrenched bureaucracy, and an understandable desire to do something now about urgent problems like racial discrimination or pollution, while putting aside the profound implications of how we go about doing it. These considerations are underlined by unrealistic acceptance of the idea that, whatever the difficulties of the present state, city, and county structure, the nation as a whole is better off to leave them as they are. We tend to fall back on the false security of the exhausted cliché that, inefficient as our system is, there is no better structure available.

But these United States are not the city-states of Thomas More's *Utopia* or the societies of Plato's *Republic*. The common characteristic of the ideal societies of the past—the utopias—was that they were static. Change might initially have been necessary to achieve the ideal; once achieved, however, time itself came to a stop. To the contrary, change —social, economic, and scientific—is the most pervasively significant force operating in our nation today. Change has always been the very heart of the human and political condition. But the pace of change today is startling and the prospect is that its pace will quicken, affecting every facet of life, including those things which seem most remote from technology, such as political values, personal morality, and religion. So swift is the acceleration of change that more than one commentator has speculated that trying to make sense out of change may soon become our basic industry.

Our private-sector institutions, our corporations and labor unions, are, largely because of the capitalist economic structure of our nation, required to accommodate change in order to survive. Unfortunately, our governmental structures are not forced to accommodate social change or face extinction in the same way. States maintain their geopolitical status on maps as states, cities as cities, and counties as counties, even though they increasingly appear, for all practical purposes, like so many hen scratches on the solid ground of political reality.

There are any number of ways by which the state, city, and county structure of our nation could be reshaped. It is essential to examine the way in which they should be changed, promptly and carefully. As constituted, there seems no realistic possibility that states, cities, and counties will become effective counterpoints for presidential power. In immediate terms, therefore, it is not fruitful to look to them as effective balances to the American presidency. This nation can, over the short run, survive this situation, which has developed over a generation or two, a relatively short time in the span of history. But it cannot survive this condition over a more extended period of time without recognizing that the president and the central government will become so singularly powerful that he and his men will no longer work through the states and localities on federal programs that intervene deeply into local communities and personal lives. It will seem best, increasingly, for the central government to deal directly with the people involved, bypassing what it perceives as the politically meddling states, cities, and counties, obsolete relics of another age. The president and his men will, indeed, become the mayors of every city and the governors of every state.

State and local officials are, of course, aware of the problems they confront with inadequate financial resources. They are becoming increasingly aware of the problems created by the arbitrary jurisdictional lines that preserve their political fiefdoms. But they rarely seem to perceive the broad constitutional implications of their condition. They evidence little appreciation of the constitutional function of their states and cities as counterforces to presidential power. Their responses seem predominately motivated by parochial bureaucratic politics that inspire negative reactions to attempts by the federal executive to encroach on their personal political territory.

Some states have rewritten their constitutions. There have been attempts by some cities, particularly larger ones under the unyielding pressures of human congestion and urban decay, to change their charters and reorganize their departments. These steps are important. But they hardly constitute the march toward regionalization that Dwight Macdonald has recommended. They do not even constitute a significant step toward redrawing state and local boundaries so that they make sense, in view of the problems of technology, human congestion, transportation, and the environment that so heavily burden our society.

The question is not whether states and cities are overburdened; it is whether they are politically and jurisdictionally relevant or obsolete. The problem is not how to preserve them as self-sufficient political entities, for the pyramiding problems of crime, health care, education, racial tension, and traffic congestion honor few artificial boundaries in a society as mobile as the money it takes to make a down payment on a motorcycle or an automobile. The issue is not centralization or decentralization, but what to centralize and what to decentralize, how, and at what level. The search should not be for perfect political jurisdictional entities to deal with pollution, transportation, economic development, and public education, but for the most effective mix of different governmental entities to deal with such problems—a mix that provides safeguards for our individual freedom.

This nation must examine new organizations of the fifty states and the twenty-five thousand cities and counties that have been perpetuated within their borders. The sooner that examination begins in earnest, the sooner something effective can be done to provide a decentralized counterbalance to the power of the central executive and the president who presides over it.

V

——————∞——————

THE MEDIA:
Adversary or Instrument
of Presidential Power

We have noted how certain public institutional forces—the executive branch, the Congress, the states and cities—tend not only to squint in the glare of presidential power, but, particularly in the past fifteen years, to turn to the president for sunglass prescriptions. But what of the people the president is elected to serve and the private institutions through which they express their interests to him and through which he communicates his policies to them? What is the form and substance of presidential power in this perspective?

The relationship of a president of the United States with the people he is elected to govern is his most complicated and one central to our democratic system. It involves people at all levels: the 220 million American citizens as individuals, with one person casting one vote; as men and women with stations in life that affect their political views; as homeowners, apartment dwellers, fathers and mothers, students and workers. In an ideal concept of majoritarian democracy, citizens as individuals are the ultimate balance of power.

As individuals their capability to assess presidential power is exercised with decisive finality only once every four years.

Presidential power is exercised (and influenced) everyday in more intimate relationship with groups of people who wield power through the private institutions that they manage or control: with the press, with people of influence in communications and in setting fashionable intellectual and life styles in our nation, with corporate managers and labor union officers, with special-interest groups. Those who control aggregates of wealth or influence large blocks of voters can be important to the attainment of presidential power and can help shape its exercise.

A president's relation with the people also involves his connection to his political party: to the elected governors and mayors; to the state, city, and county chairman who dominate his regular party structure at the local level; to the national committee of the party he leads; and to the rank-and-file Democrats or Republicans who ring doorbells, distribute campaign literature, or perhaps just vote the straight party ticket, or even a split ticket.

A president's opponents can also influence his relationship with the people and his exercise of power. These are the adherents of the major opposition party, splinter parties, and politically sophisticated interest groups. In pursuit of the public policies he seeks to implement and the personal aims in which he believes, the president must, as he exercises the power of his office, alienate in greater or in lesser degree the opposition party and the interests who seek protection under its banner.

These, then, are the people and their private institutions, to whom the president must relate. Any president will attempt to craft the dimensions of that relationship with meticulous calculation. The first step is communication, and that, of course, depends upon the media—television, radio, newspapers, magazines, and books. Particularly in the wake of Watergate, the media tends to regard itself as the potent critic of the presidency, a twentieth-century Paul Revere alerting the Congress and the people to the dangers of corruption and abuse of power in the highest office in the land. But that is not how presidents view the media. At times, they regard critical commentators in the press as annoying hair shirts or outrageously unfair analysts of their policies and personalities. The occasions on which presidents and their staff aides have decided not to cut some corner because their action might be discovered by the press are legion. For the most part, however, presidents regard the media as an instrument essential to developing and maintaining support for their programs and policies. The White House press corps, in particular, is perceived as the daily national amplifier of the presidential voice, the most critical link in the chain that connects the president with the millions of citizens and hundreds of interest groups he cannot converse with directly.

At some moments in their tenure, most presidents feel unfairly restricted by the media, frustrated and disturbed by their perception that the media interferes with their relationship with the people. There is no president in modern times who has not sought in anguished vain for some way to "speak directly" to the people without going through this prism of writers and broadcasters that, he feels, distorts the intended meaning of his message. The exhilaration that attends presidential forays into large, adulatory crowds, and the thousands of favorable letters and telegrams that follow a televised speech, serve to increase the frustration a president senses when he returns to communication through the reporting media.

So important is the media to a president that he often spends at least as much time trying to anticipate and manipulate its reaction to various ways of enunciating policy as he does in formulating it. It would be difficult to overestimate the measure of calculation that goes into virtually every engagement of a president with the media, whether directly, through his press secretary, or through other high administration officials. The conventional acceptance by so many of our citizens that presidents act spontaneously on matters of personal, political, or national policy significance is utterly unjustified. The syllogism of power that describes a president's relationship with the media should be constructed as follows:

—There is a heavy measure of calculation in the way the president deals with the people and their institutions.

—The media, whether television, radio, newspapers, magazines, or books, is the president's central avenue of communication, not only with the people as a whole, but often with publicly and privately institutionalized segments of them.

—Therefore, the president will be especially calculating in his relationship with the media.

If the media as a whole is the central avenue of presidential communication with the people, then surely television is the express lane down that avenue. Television is critical to the president, initially in his attempt to reach the office, then in the exercise of his power as he presents to the people his policies, programs, and interpretations of events.

Since 1960, the name of the deadly serious game of attaining and exercising national leadership has been television. The validity of this axiom has been historically demonstrated over the past fifteen years. Many commentators consider television's impact decisive in the 1960 presidential election which was dominated by the Kennedy-Nixon debates. John Kennedy perceived the power of the electronic media and gave this nation its first television presidency. The television coverage of his assassination and the tragic subsequent events turned him into an instant folk-hero president. Lyndon Johnson used television as the major forum to explain his policies in Vietnam; his opponents designed demonstrations to oppose the war, with both eyes on the ability of television to deliver their message. The American people obtained insights about Johnson's presidency from his pointed comments during Walter Cronkite's television interviews that were not available in his book, *The Vantage Point.*

Vice-President Spiro Agnew became a household word with one network television address attacking the media. George Wallace achieved national prominence during the televised confrontation on the University of Alabama campus when he stood in the doorway to block the admission of

the first black students there; he never again needed to voice
racist views to hold the "red neck" vote. Supreme Court
Chief Justice Warren Burger has concocted an annual State
of the Judiciary message in an attempt to get once-a-year
network coverage for the federal judiciary. Senator Edmund
Muskie's superb 1970 election-eve television appearance,
back to back with Richard Nixon's ineptly edited and spasti-
cally delivered speech, was credited with tipping more than
one mid-term congressional election to the Democrats.
Overnight, Muskie became the leading candidate for the
Democratic presidential nomination. So effective were Gerald Ford's swearing-in speech and his first message to the
Congress that the press instantly wiped his political slate
clean and the Democrats despaired in the summer of 1974 of
winning the presidential election in the fall of 1976.

Richard Nixon has been criticized (most sharply by the
opposition party) for his unprecedented domination of
television, dwarfing its use by every president before him.
Despite the criticism, his successors of whatever party will
almost surely exceed even Nixon's use of the television
medium. Television is without peer in its ability to mold the
minds of the masses of the electorate and to shape the appetite and will of a free country to accept, conceive, draft, and
put into effect laws and policies proposed by the administration in power. As 1968 Democratic vice-presidential candidate Edmund Muskie has testified, "Used to its fullest, television can determine the outcome not only of every political
issue, but more importantly of each and every national issue."

Richard Nixon's 1968 campaign provides the best example
of the use of television to achieve presidential power. Never
before had television been used with such shrewdly effective
calculation in a political campaign. Joe McGinnis, in his brilliant book, *The Selling of the President in 1968*, has recounted the successful marriage of television advertising and
politics to remake the image of a man to satisfy the painstak-
ingly measured visceral appetites of the electorate. Ray
Price, Nixon's top speech writer during the campaign and his
long-time political advisor, expressed it with cynical candor,

"We have to be very clear on this point: that the response is to the image, not the man. . . . It's not what's there that counts, it's what's projected. . . . It's not the man we have to change, but rather the *received* impression, and this impression often depends more on the medium and its use than it does on the candidate himself."

Nixon not only understood the importance of television during his 1968 campaign. He had the funds to use it on his own terms. His reported media costs during the campaign were more than double Hubert Humphrey's. As *Fortune* magazine pointed out in its March 1970 issue analyzing the 1968 television campaign, "From early 1967 until just before the election, Richard Nixon turned down all invitations to be interviewed on single 'free' programs like 'Meet the Press' or 'Face the Nation.' He preferred to pay for his time so that he could control content and format in his TV appearances."

The contrast between Nixon and Humphrey was sharp. Humphrey lacked the financial resources to conduct any sort of professionally controlled television campaign. He had to beg for the money and credit to make relatively few television appearances and advertisements near the end of his campaign. He was constantly groping for free television time on programs ranging from "Issues and Answers" to local interviews and late-night talk shows. Many of the formats were distinctly inappropriate for a serious discussion of the major issues facing the nation. A good number were demeaning for a presidential candidate. Only a handful were on his own terms.

The 1972 presidential campaign again demonstrated the critical importance of television to presidential aspirants. Senator George McGovern's presidential campaign was organized around "media events." McGovern and his running mate R. Sargent Shriver frenetically raced across the United States trying to get into as many media markets as possible with dramatic, picture-oriented events, early enough on each day to accommodate the technical requirements of local and national evening news shows. McGovern made charges against the Russian wheat deal in front of a silo; Shriver expressed his concern about unemployment against the backdrop of idle factory machinery. Like Democratic candidates Humphrey and Muskie in 1968, McGovern and Shriver lacked the financial resources to control their television formats and appearances. They frequently appeared on uncontrolled formats and inanely degrading local talk shows because they had no other choice. Richard Nixon campaigned almost entirely on television. As in 1968, he had the financial resources (in 1972, coupled with the power of the presidency to command television time) to control his own television appearances, a politically potent asset beyond the reach of McGovern and Shriver.

If television is important to the achievement of presidential power, it is essential to its exercise by an incumbent president. The Roper Organization's comprehensive thirteen-year survey of the media reveals that, from December 1959 to November 1972, the number of Americans who received "most of [their] news about what's going on in the world today" from television jumped from 51 to 64 percent. For millions of Americans, a presidential television appearance is often the decisive analysis, the last as well as the first political word on a national issue. The 1973 book on *Presidential Television* by former Federal Communications Chairman Newton Minow, John Bartlow Martin, and Lee Mitchell provides a forceful and accurate description of the significance of television to the exercise of presidential power.

> Presidential television means the ability to appear simultaneously on all national radio and television networks at prime, large-audience evening hours, virtually whenever and however the president wishes. It means holding a news conference before a potential audience of 60 million people. . . . Presidential television is the president's own explanation of his plans and positions to politicians, legislators, and voters—the national audience of millions. It is the carefully presented presidential "image." It is the nationally viewed justification of war, invocation of peace, praise for political allies, damnation of opponents, veto of legislation, scolding of Congress by a chief executive, commander-in-chief, party leader, and candidate.
>
> Presidential television is free use of an extremely expensive

commodity. An individual or group wishing to broadcast a half-hour program simultaneously on all three major networks during evening prime time could pay more than $250,000 [1972 dollars], exclusive of the cost of producing the program, assuming that the time could be bought—which in all probability it could not. But a president, as Senator Fulbright has noted, can "command a national audience to hear his views on controversial matters at prime time, on short notice, at whatever length he chooses, and at no expense to the Federal Government or his party." Or himself.

It is difficult to overstate the qualitative increment of power television has added to the American presidency. John Kennedy orchestrated his own television appearances, along with those of Secretary of Defense Robert McNamara and Secretary of State Dean Rusk, during the Cuban missile crisis. Each time Lyndon Johnson took to television to explain his Vietnam War policy, his popularity rating and support for the war rose. When Johnson settled a major strike in 1966, the conclusion of the negotiations and the announcement of the settlement were delayed until a few minutes before the hour. He wanted to announce the settlement on live television, with minimum disruption of the regular broadcasting schedules of the three major networks and hence minimum irritation to millions of television viewers watching their favorite shows. The dramatic, often live television of Richard Nixon's trips to China and Russia increased his popularity and the confidence Americans had in the way he was performing his job. Those exotic television shows did more to garner popular support for the policy of *détente* than all the National Security Council memoranda, presidential speeches, and thoughtful books of the last decade.

When a president has a major message or major issue that he wishes to characterize in the minds of millions of Americans, he invariably goes to television, increasingly during prime time. The State of the Union Message, which traditionally had been delivered at twelve noon on the opening day of the congressional session, became a prime-time annual special on a mid-week evening during the presidency of Lyndon Johnson. Indeed, Johnson would select the time and evening for delivery of that message after careful analysis of the regular television broadcasting schedule, ideally follow- ing the most popular programs to maximize his audience. Major announcements about economic policy (such as the wage-price freeze of August 1971), significant political an- nouncements (such as Johnson's decision to withdraw as a presidential candidate in 1968), key attempts to cool off the nation in times of crisis (such as Nixon's speech and televised press conference during the demonstrations precipitated by the 1970 Cambodian invasion) are unfolded to the American people directly through television.

Gerald Ford exhibited the presidential sense of the signifi- cance of television in unfolding his economic and energy program in January 1975. He began with a prime-time, simul- taneous three-network, fireside chat during the evening two days before he reported to the Congress. Then he delivered his State of the Union message before both Houses of the Congress to a simultaneous, three-network television audi- ence at one o'clock in the afternoon. The following Sunday, three administration spokesmen appeared on the network interview news shows: Treasury Secretary William Simon, Interior Secretary Rogers Morton, and Federal Energy Ad- ministrator Frank Zarb were interviewed on "Meet the Press" (NBC), "Face the Nation" (CBS) and "Issues and An- swers" (ABC). The next week, President Ford held a simul- taneous three-network, live press conference which began with another ten-minute prepared pitch for his economic and energy policies. The fifteen-minute opposition party re- sponses, by House Speaker Carl Albert and Senator Hubert Humphrey, at different times on the three networks were no match for the prior domination of television by the president and his spokesmen.

Television is clearly perceived—and accurately so—by presidents and those who aspire to the highest office as their most effective tool of communication directly with the peo- ple, and future presidents will act on that perception increas- ingly. Under the present system, a president can control the time, the format, the location, the make-up, the length, and the subject of a television appearance. He may make mistakes, as Gerald Ford did in his October 1974 anti-inflation pep talk; but when the White House press secretary asks the networks for presidential time, they will provide it. As long as his opponents have no such control or even remotely comparable access, television will remain a tool of maintaining and perpetuating a presidential power unparalleled in the history of this nation. Minow et al. make the point cogently: "Because he can act while his adversaries can only talk, because he can make news and draw attention to himself, and because he is the only leader elected by all the people, an incumbent president always has had an edge over his opposition in persuading public opinion. Presidential television, however, has enormously increased that edge."

Most presidents cannily use their ability to make news. Whenever the Republican National Committee was having a major meeting in Washington, John Kennedy and Lyndon Johnson would want a big news day at the White House to try and squeeze Republican criticism from the evening television news shows. In the fall of 1966, prior to the time Johnson's doctors told him he would have to undergo another operation because of a rupture of his scar from the 1965 gall bladder operation, the White House staff was planning a presidential swing across the nation to sign major legislation that the 89th Congress had passed in its last few days. These events were designed to place Johnson in several states in a nonpolitical framework (he was becoming concerned about presidential partisanship with so many powerful forces on the racial and Vietnam War issues percolating to the surface). But most importantly, they were designed to capture evening television news time. For example, White House staffer Sherwin Markman was sent out to locate "the biggest and most photogenic shopping center in the country" for the signing of the truth-in-packaging legislation (he found it in Seattle). Recognizing that it takes months and sometimes years for the impact of new legislation to be felt by individual citizens, Johnson wanted to provide visible evidence in each living room of some of the accomplishments of the 89th Congress and his administration.

Richard Nixon's Watergate appearances have demonstrated that television, at least temporarily, is also the most effective medium through which to characterize the facts as the president would like the American people to know them (e.g., his version of the March 21, 1973, hush money meeting with John Dean). For most of 1973 and 1974, it seemed almost as though Nixon did not care what inconsistencies or inaccuracies the print media later identified. He and his aides believed that, with more than 97 percent of the population in possession of at least one television set and the average set in operation seven hours each day, what counted in the consciousness of the American people was what they saw on television. Only when the other side of a presidential issue receives comparable television coverage, can the use of the electronic media as a decidedly presidential tool be effectively balanced. Such was the case when the House Judiciary Committee impeachment hearings dramatically turned the tables on Nixon in the summer of 1974.

The power of the electronic medium makes television reporters, network executives, and the seven members of the Federal Communications Commission particularly important individuals to an incumbent president. That Richard Nixon recognized this is evidenced by his appointment of Dean Burch, a singularly partisan Republican party professional and former Republican National Committee chairman, to be FCC chairman during most of his presidency. Through the men Nixon considered the most ruthless and unscrupulous on his staff, he brought the use of White House power to bear on the networks with unprecedented pressure.

Although the activities of White House aides like Charles Colson were uniquely ruthless, Nixon was not the first president to raise hell with ABC, CBS, and NBC. Both Kennedy and Johnson (and their aides) placed their share of phone calls to network correspondents and executives to complain about biased news coverage. The first three television-era presidents were all acutely aware of the importance of FCC appointments, because of its regulatory power over television. Johnson was so concerned with the power of television in the hands of a partisan or unscrupulous network president that on more than one occasion he discussed the possibility of framing legislation to break up the networks, change their relationship to the FCC, or create new broadcast networks. He once corrected the draft of a congressional message I submitted to him by changing "the public airwaves" to "the public's airwaves," to emphasize, he said, that "the airwaves belong to the people, not to three New York executives." While Johnson never proposed any such legislation, he did put his unrelated namesake Nicholas Johnson on the FCC with the deliberate intention of "shaking up the networks."

The attention paid to television does not mean that a president is unaware of the importance of the printed word. Any man who occupies the White House will be conscious of the written word, particularly the Associated Press and United Press International wires, the Washington *Post*, the New York *Times, Time* and *Newsweek* magazines, and the widely syndicated columnists. Presidents are aware of the importance of the trend-setting news organizations and writers. At the time of the Cuban missile crisis, during a meeting with President Kennedy, a White House aide took the time to write, "Is there a plan to brief and brainwash key press within twelve hours or so?" His list included columnists with views as divergent as Joseph Alsop and Marquis Childs. When Walter Lippmann was suggested for a major ambassadorial post, Arthur Schlesinger argued that Lippmann was more important to the Kennedy administration as a syndicated Washington *Post* columnist.

Presidents understand that a column by James Reston or Joseph Kraft often has follow-the-leader reverberations throughout the inbred Washington press corps, as well as around the nation in a host of newspaper editorial offices. They know that local politicians and members of the House and Senate respect David Broder's extraordinary political savvy. Even though presidents rarely see top-flight economic writers personally, they appreciate the impact of a favorable (or unfavorable) analysis by Edwin Dale or Eileen Shanahan of the New York *Times* or Hobart Rowan of the Washington *Post*. Painfully aware of the truth of Richard Neustadt's observation in his extraordinary classic on *Presidential Power* that "presidential power is the power to persuade" in many areas of national concern, presidents and their aides have a far more sophisticated understanding of the way the press operates than much of the press is willing to credit them with. As reporter Carl Bernstein of the Washington *Post* once remarked to me, "The White House knows how we conduct our business but the press doesn't know how they conduct their business."

It is understandable, then, that every recent president has tried to manage the news and every future president will make similar efforts. Attempting to manipulate the news is as natural for presidents as attempting to get the true facts is for good reporters. Managing the news was a major issue during the presidency of John Kennedy. Indeed, shortly before his assassination, there were numerous articles in national magazines and major newspapers criticizing Kennedy and his press secretary, Pierre Salinger, for their attempts to manipulate the news. President Kennedy himself admitted to his manipulation of the news media in the interest of national security during the Bay of Pigs invasion and the Cuban missile crisis. He so effectively charmed the bulk of the Washington press corps that many of them have since suffered agonizing second thoughts about the rose-colored glasses through which they viewed his administration at the time.

When Lyndon Johnson characterized Richard Nixon as a "chronic campaigner" in 1966, there were several commentaries about Johnson inadvertently permitting his disdain for Nixon to slip out during a press conference. Actually it was a deliberate characterization, discussed in advance of the press conference and designed in part to put Nixon at the forefront of Republican presidential possibilities, because Johnson regarded him as the easiest to defeat. President Ford's "spontaneous" publicized phone calls to congratulate celebrities like Hank Aaron and Al Kaline stemmed from a systematic White House staff effort to obtain "at least one telephone recommendation . . . every Friday" from each cabinet officer and other top administration officials for calls the president should place for public-image purposes.

Presidents also are aware of the mix of news that issues from the White House. Johnson decided in July 1965 sharply to increase the level of American involvement in Vietnam. On the morning of the press conference scheduled to announce the troop build-up, Johnson and Press Secretary Bill Moyers discussed other news that could run with the bad Vietnam news. Driving back from a Pentagon cost-reduction awards ceremony (to which I had accompanied them), they decided to announce that John Chancellor would become the new head of the Voice of America and that Abe Fortas would be nominated to fill the vacancy on the Supreme Court at the same press conference at which the build-up was announced. The hope was to put some pleasing, or at least neutral, news on the front pages the next morning. They thought the Chancellor appointment would be popular with the White House press corps and the Fortas nomination would be especially well received by liberals likely to be concerned about the troop build-up.

Richard Nixon blantantly manipulated the public release of his April 30, 1974, "Submission of Recorded Presidential Conversations to the Committee on the Judiciary of the House of Representatives" during the early stages of the House committee's impeachment investigation. Framed by deceptively high stacks of leather binders, Nixon went on television on the evening of April 29 to announce his decision and explain his version of certain conversations. He then released to the press his lawyer's brief in support of his interpretation of the recorded conversations early the following day. But he held back the public release of the edited transcripts themselves that day until a couple of hours before the evening news broadcasts, in order to make it difficult, if not impossible, for the network news shows and evening papers to digest the material prior to broadcast and publication. Through this manipulation, Nixon's side of the story was able to dominate the news from his televised speech on the evening of April 29 through the early evening news shows of the following day. This Nixon release of edited transcripts in April 1974 is perhaps the crudest attempt at news manipulation in recent years. As the subsequent release of the House Judiciary Committee transcripts demonstrated, outright tampering and dissembling were involved.

Whatever the incantation of First Amendment values in presidential messages and policy statements, and however sincerely issued, any man who occupies the Oval Office will regard the press as a legitimate means of exercising presidential power and he will reserve for it a special measure of calculation. Indeed, most editors and commentators in the press would consider him a fool to do otherwise. On more than one occasion during the Johnson administration, the announcement of a progressive program with great appeal to the liberal press would be made at a time that would permit the Washington *Post* to break this story in the morning, rather than the more conservative Washington *Star* in the afternoon.

Selected leaks will always be made to sympathetic newsmen. John Kennedy was just as generous in leaking to friendly reporters like Benjamin Bradlee, then *Newsweek* Washington bureau chief, as Richard Nixon was in granting exclusives to Garrett (Jack) Horner, then White House correspondent writing in the hospitable pages of the Washington *Star*. If, for example, a president concluded that Tom Wicker was particularly interested in some civil rights program and the president and his staff believed it would serve their purposes, they would leak a story about that program to him, just as they would give a Vietnam tip to Joseph Alsop. Presidents realize that an experienced columnist will not simply repeat what he hears, but they also know he wants to print news before one of his colleagues does. To do other than try to manipulate the news in this manner would be for a president to operate in Washington with one hand tied behind his back. The forces on the other side of any particular issue will also be trying to tell their story to favorably disposed key reporters and news organizations. What gives the president and his branch the extra spin is their control of so much information and their ability to determine the timing of the announcement of so many policy decisions.

In this Washington environment, the function of a good reporter, like a Max Frankel at the White House or a Daniel

Schorr on Watergate, is to know when there is an attempt to
use him and to sift out the accurate facts for the public he
informs. No good newsman likes to parrot spoon-fed leaks,
but even the most sophisticated Washington columnists and
reporters can be used by the president to the extent he
provides them information sufficiently newsworthy and
timely to be printed promptly. (There are, of course, mav-
ericks. Johnson repeatedly asked, "Why can't Mary McGrory
write something nice about us. She's the best damn writer in
Washington and she gets better and better at my expense!"
And, confronted three times a week with the deadly political
satire of Art Buchwald, Nixon speechwriter Bill Safire once
told me, "What we need is a conservative Art Buchwald.")

Newspapers and magazines also provide an opportunity
for presidents to "float" ideas in order to solicit some public
reaction, as well as obtain a sense of the attitudes of the
various constituent groups. Given an outline of a possible
new higher-education program by a presidential aide, with
the assurance that he has an exclusive (so that he has some
relief from the time pressures of daily journalism), a good
reporter will go to state universities, private colleges, key
congressional staff members, and other interested parties to
get their reactions. In this circumstance, the president and
his staff perceive the reporter as a means of obtaining feed-
back on controversial proposals, while retaining some insulation from assuming public responsibility for them. When a
paper like the New York *Times* or Washington *Post* prints
the story, some of those reactions will be reported; others will
flow to the White House as a result of the news story. Such
action and reaction provide the policy maker on the White
House staff an invaluable insight into the forces he will face
should an attempt be made to put the program into effect or
to submit it to the Congress.

There are important benefits to the operation of the democratic system from such leaks. Information made available to
the people through confidential and protected government
sources can be significant to the understanding and development of public policy. As Richard Neustadt has observed
about the Truman administration,

During the formative period of President Truman's foreign policy and again during the Korean War a great deal of illuminating detail, anticipating or clarifying governmental actions, reached the press in this fashion, as for example, the minutes of the Wake Island meeting between the President and General MacArthur. The same thing can be said, to my knowledge, of various domestic affairs, including labor relations and the conduct of economic controls during the Korean War.

To the president, the assistance such information provides to the public's understanding of national issues is often incidental to his central purpose of furthering his public policy objectives. The fact that such leaks serve not only the press and the public, but the president, and that all three perceive the service, makes them an integral part of the exercise of presidential power.

For the president, one of the key functions of the print media in the nation's capital is to serve as a major, if not paramount means of communication with the Congress and the federal bureaucracy. In a government of divided power at the national level, as well as at the state and local level, where authority is often widely dispersed within politically autonomous institutions, newspaper reportage is a critically important medium of internal communications between the White House and agencies, between executive and legislative officials, and between the president and the lesser institutions of state and local government.

Any poll of the 435 members of the House of Representatives and the 100 senators on Capitol Hill would likely reveal that, at best, only a handful ever read most presidential messages to the Congress. Except for a few hard-working committee members who study particular legislation in detail, representatives and senators rely on the Washington *Post* and New York *Times* reporting of those messages, and perhaps read whatever verbatim excerpts those newspapers print.

It is not possible for a president to speak to every policy maker in the federal bureaucracy. There are several thousand division, bureau, and branch chiefs in Washington alone, to say nothing of the regional and local office directors scattered throughout the nation. The print media particularly provides a convenient and effective means of communicating presidential policy to these key people who work in the executive branch and are responsible for the day-to-day implementation of that policy. This is one of the central reasons why presidents become so frustrated and angered when they perceive misconstructions of presidential statements and policies in the press.

Harry Truman can write John Kennedy, as he did on August 11, 1962, "Mr. President don't let those damned columnists and editorial writers discourage you. . . . you meet 'em, cuss 'em and give 'em hell and you'll win in 1964." As bravado encouragement, the note is fine. But it ignores the reality of presidential communication in the 1960s and 1970s. Those "damned columnists and editorial writers" are important mouthpieces for the communication of presidential policies. Where presidents perceive them as accurately (i.e., helpfully) communicating those policies, they will provide insights and special courtesies to them. Where presidents perceive them as "obfuscating" the communication of their policies, they will "give 'em hell" as Truman suggested to Kennedy in 1962, but usually with calculated subtlety. This is true whether it is John Kennedy pressuring New York *Times* executives to pull David Halberstam out of Vietnam, Lyndon Johnson attempting to replace a wire service correspondent there, or Richard Nixon trying to discredit CBS White House correspondent Dan Rather. The Nixon-ordered FBI investigation of Daniel Schorr and his apparent instigation of the license challenges to two *Post-Newsweek* television stations provide extreme examples of the abuse of presidential power in this area.

But giving the press hell is a chronic characteristic of presidential conduct. Thomas Jefferson said that "nothing can now be believed which is seen in a newspaper." Woodrow Wilson wrote scathingly to a friend about the press, "Do not believe anything you read in the newspapers. If you read the papers I see, they are utterly untrustworthy. . . . the lying is shameless and colossal." And, as New York attorney Floyd

Abrams has pointed out, it was not Richard Nixon and John Mitchell who answered harsh press criticism with an attempt to twist a law relating to the protection of harbor defenses from malicious injury into a federal criminal libel law for the purpose of jailing a prominent publisher. That questionable distinction belongs to Theodore Roosevelt.

The president also perceives the press as a useful means of communication with major economic interests and foreign nations. Presidents are (and should be) acutely conscious of the impact of what they say to reporters in the context of the Dow Jones ticker and the stock market. For instance, presidential comments during a Mid-East oil crisis can have a significant impact on the stock market. The tone and timing of economic news emanating from the White House and departments under its control affect industrial averages, interest rates, capital investment, and labor negotiations. John Kennedy and Lyndon Johnson were very much aware of the impact of various news stories emanating from the White House on the stock market and, on more than one occasion, used the press to hold or boost the market. During the Johnson economic jawboning days, some of the most important signals in attempts to drive back price increases were sent through the press. When he decided to sell sufficient aluminum from the stockpile to break the price increase announced by the aluminum companies, Johnson asked me to communicate that decision through a leak to the New York *Times*. But there must be substance behind the statements. Gerald Ford's threat to the Arab oil-producing countries in September 1974 failed to stem the market decline because it then appeared to have only the teeth of a paper tiger.

In the foreign policy area, presidents often speak to other nations, friend and foe alike, through the press. More than one story has been leaked by Henry Kissinger (undoubtedly at Nixon's direction), McGeorge Bundy, and Walt Rostow (undoubtedly at the direction of Kennedy and Johnson), designed to "send a message" to the Russians, or the Chinese, or the French, as the case might be, and retain some personal distance to preserve what has become pejoratively known as "presidential deniability." Kennedy meticulously orchestrated public announcements during the Cuban missile crisis because so many of those announcements were messages primarily designed for Russian consumption. Johnson carefully controlled all statements to the press during the 1967 Six-Day War in the Middle East because so many of them were designed for Russian and Arab ears. When Johnson assessed Charles DeGaulle as more a personal ego problem than a national ego problem, he ordered that no comments be made by U.S. officials that expressed or implied any personal criticism of the French general. To assure that DeGaulle understood Johnson's position, his directive was dutifully leaked to the press since this was hardly the type of message that could be transmitted directly from one chief executive to another.

The corollary of the presidential power to release information is the power to withhold it or release it selectively. The enormity of the president's advantage in modern times is in large measure a function of his access to and control of information. The importance presidents attach to such power was evidenced by Gerald Ford's unsuccessful veto, early in his administration when he was seeking an accommodation with the Congress, of amendments to the 1966 Freedom of Information Act because the virtually uninhibited power of the president's branch to classify (and hence withhold) information would have been subjected to prompt judicial review, with the final word on its release vested in the independent judiciary. Presidents have used that power not only to achieve what they perceived to be the best interests of the nation, but also to avoid or minimize political or personal embarrassment.

This is why the relationship of the press corps in Washington is always likely to be adversary and antagonistic to the occupant of the Oval Office. The calculation with which a president views the press must be matched by the skepticism with which the press views the president. When we realize that the press may be the last true adversary of presidential power, we can have some appreciation of what phenomenally precocious political seers the framers of the First Amendment were. In a capitalist society, we should understand the importance of maintaining a viable economic framework for the exercise of First Amendment rights by the nation's media.

There is little point in rendering moral, social, or political judgments on the calculated use of the press by the president. Like original sin, we must simply learn to live with it. The press is increasingly conscious of attempts to use it. What the average American citizen should understand is that White House attempts to manage the news and manipulate the press are endemic attendants to the exercise of presidential power. They must measure what the presidents say in this context. Like the criminal conduct that marked his presidency, Nixon's evasion and deceit on Watergate stand as an aberration in an amoral class by themselves. But at their most expedient, most presidents will occasionally mislead and evade, at least as a temporary diversonary tactic.

Those instances are infrequent, however. What Americans must recognize is that, in every statement, presidents will put their best foot forward. They will rarely make reference to the fallen arch or the callused heel. Presidents would rather have good news break during the week when the evening network news shows and morning newspapers have their peak audiences, leaving the bad news until late Friday afternoon in time for the low-circulation Saturday newspapers.

Presidents are most immediately and acutely aware of the day-to-day impact of the press on their activities and their ability to lead the nation and to achieve their policy objectives. But they also realize that the first draft of history is written in the pages of our major newspapers and, increasingly, in the audiovisual tapes of the major television newscasts. The longer presidents are in office and the closer they get to the end of their final term, the more conscious they become of the importance of the press in terms of the ultimate judgments of history about their administration. This presidential conviction that the judgment of history is what counts in the long run makes them acutely sensitive to papers like the New York *Times* and the Washington *Post* which so often provide basic reference material to future historians. Those presidents who survive long enough after leaving office write their own version of history; but they know that their version will be discounted as self-serving when measured against the contemporary analyses of the major newspaper, magazine, and book writers.

VI

LEVERAGING THE SPECIAL INTERESTS

The Congress, the states and cities, and the press, each in its own way, have been constitutionally enshrined as counterpoints to presidential power. They represent the deliberate fragmentation of public power, governmental and independent, to preserve individual freedom. The extent to which they share power is of practical as well as constitutional significance in achieving a perspective on the exercise of presidential power.

There are other groups whose relationship to the presidency in the last quarter of the twentieth century must be considered in any attempt to put presidential power in perspective. Economic power is distributed among business and labor interests as well as governmental institutions. There are any number of other constituencies in the private sector; civil rights organizations, educators, professional societies. Of these, big business and big labor are the most important to a president. They can add a special dimension to the exercise of presidential power.

Perhaps nowhere is the ripple effect of presidential power more keenly apparent than in the American business community. Big business, particularly, is of immense salience to any president, whether Republican or Democrat, conserva-

tive or liberal. Business is, after all, the economic engine of
American society. The managers of large corporate and
banking interests are the industrial and financial mechanics
who, in the first instance, have the responsibility for keeping
that engine tuned. When business profits are up, sales are
increasing and capital investment is high, there are more
jobs and better incomes for most Americans, and more tax
revenues for government social programs. In an analysis designed to help select relatively discreet areas of intervention
for Great Society programs in the 1960s, we once calculated
that a sound economy would take care of the material needs
of at least 75 percent of the American people. It was to the
remaining 25 percent that the bulk of the Great Society
programs were directed. More conservative political economists and analysts would probably consider the 75 percent
figure too low.

Whatever the percentage, the overwhelming majority of
the American people are well served materially by the
proper and profitable operation of American business. That
every president since Franklin Roosevelt has recognized this
is reflected in the special attention they have reserved for
American business, particularly the economic pace-setting
corporations that control growing concentrations of aggregate wealth. It is natural for any president to desire and sense
a need for some power over the men and institutions that
manage this wealth. For the good of society as a whole, it is
essential not only to place some restraints on the use of aggregate wealth for private profit, but also to encourage and
channel the investment of such wealth in certain areas.
Scientific and technological advances in every field, from
health care to communications, have led to government intervention to help assure, for example, the safe manufacture
of pharmaceuticals and the fair allocation of a limited number of radio and television communication bands. The desire
to develop energy resources and maintain transportation systems has led to preferential tax treatment and government
subsidies. The patent system guarantees monopoly profits to
the ingenious innovator.

For a progressive president, business presents an opportunity to achieve liberal goals. The National Alliance of Businessmen, which conducted the most effective job-training program of the Johnson administration, was dependent upon the wholehearted cooperation of American industry. But in that public-interest partnership, the president held the controlling shares. He established the goals and timetables; he designated the cities in which the program was to operate; he set the level of federal support and its relation to the level of private financial commitment. In effect, the president was able to commit to the hard-core unemployment problems of major urban centers hundreds of millions of dollars and talented human resources from the private sector. The benevolent objectives of the program eased the task of a president, inclined to use his implied as well as express powers, in procuring and committing those resources from American business. But the motives of business were a complex mixture not only of patriotism, but of fear and self-interest as well. They loved their country and wanted to help eliminate the persistent pockets of urban poverty amid unprecedented affluence. They feared the economic consequences of the violent wrath of large numbers of Blacks rampaging through the streets of major cities. The self-interest of American businessmen in "staying on the good side" of the president by supporting one of his pet programs left them no choice but to respond to his request for assistance. Moreover, the shortage of skilled and semiskilled labor in the overheated economy of 1968 made it imperative to train the under- and unemployed.

Pressed by the agents of an unscrupulous president, businessmen can be driven to less benevolent activity. The fund raising in 1971 and 1972 for Nixon's re-election campaign shows how easily presidential power over business can be illegitimately used to achieve personal political objectives. Scores of businessmen and corporations violated federal criminal statutes because of their concern that the president and his men either would not treat them fairly or would deliberately damage their financial interests if they failed to produce the requested tribute. It is no accident that elements of industries most intimately regulated by the government (like the airlines) and those most dependent on special tax treatment (like the oil companies) were high on the list of fund-raiser Maurice Stans and among the first to plead guilty to the illegal contribution of corporate funds to the Nixon campaign. Here the malignant objectives of the White House were achieved, at least temporarily, because of their willingness to use the array of weapons, express and implied, at the president's disposal for targeting at big business.

To understand the explosion of opportunities to exercise presidential power over American business, it is helpful to review the extent of the change in the relationship between the presidency and the American business community. Particularly during the past fifty years, American business has declined as an effective counterpoint to presidential power. The potency of large American corporations—for example, the enormous aggregates of economic power managed by the oil, automobile, and steel companies, and the major banks—should not be underestimated. But it is essential to recognize that our national commitment to control the exercise of such private economic might has led to the vesting of significant powers in the president and the central executive branch over which he presides.

One hundred years ago, sophisticated central government regulation of American business was unnecessary. Most products were locally produced and there was a close, usually personal and roughly equal relationship between seller and buyer, at the local level, in the retail store, and even at the wholesale level, with some notable exceptions. Those notable exceptions, such as the railroads and the oil interests, eventually precipitated the establishment of the Interstate Commerce Commission regulatory apparatus and the enactment of antitrust laws near the end of the nineteenth and beginning of the twentieth centuries. As the avarice of the robber barons reached serious antisocial proportions, the national government moved to curb the abuses of aggregate wealth and preserve the benefits of the free-enterprise system. But the movement was essentially a negative one. The government was given power to break up monopolies, to restrain concentrations of economic wealth from denying to the public the benefits of competitive American capitalism, and to prevent the abuse of the monopoly transportation power of the railroads.

Today, modern technology, marketing methods, and corporate institutions and managements have precipitated a different response from the central government. Merchandise, even foods, are much more complicated and it is no longer an easy matter to distinguish between a good product and a bad product, a good company and a bad company. In the early stages of our economic development, the impetus for consumer protection laws was inspired by the increasing lack of a personal relationship between the seller and the buyer. The 42nd Congress enacted legislation directed at this problem and to provide protection against abuse of a traditional government service by sellers of goods. It prohibited the fraudulent use of the mails. Then, in 1906, during President Theodore Roosevelt's administration, the Pure Food and Drug Act authorized the central government to establish and enforce minimal standards of safety in the processing and sale of foods and drugs. The Federal Trade Commission Act, designed to give the government power to eliminate "unfair trade practices," came during the administration of Woodrow Wilson.

But not until the 1930s did the Congress vest the federal executive and the new administrative agencies with broad power to regulate the American business community. During the 1930s, Franklin Roosevelt proposed and the Congress swiftly enacted a variety of laws directed essentially at problems of fraud and lack of full disclosure. Among the most familiar examples persisting to this day are the bank holding company and securities and exchange statutes. Other regulatory commissions such as the Federal Communications Commission, the Civil Aeronautics Board, and the Interstate Commerce Commission, were created, or strengthened, during the New Deal years. In the Roosevelt administration, the powers over American business were for the most part bestowed by the Congress upon independent regulatory agencies. The president had the power to appoint commission members, but the terms were for a fixed period of years, limits were placed on the number of members that could hold allegiance to any one political party, and the agencies themselves were deliberately positioned somewhat outside the executive branch. These were considered safeguards essential to limit the president's exercise of power and to create a quasi-judicial environment for the selective deployment of broad grants of power from the Congress. It remained for the next great wave of liberal legislation, and the giant steps of American technology and the financial risks entailed in taking advantage of that technology, to place significant power over American business directly in the hands of the president and the executive branch.

In 1962, President Kennedy sent to the Congress the first presidential message devoted entirely to the American consumer. Even in that message, the emphasis was on conventional theories of competition, monopoly, and fraud. To be sure, truth-in-lending (which would eventually give the Treasury Department and the Federal Reserve Board wide power to regulate the dissemination of credit information) and truth-in-packaging (which would eventually give the Department of Commerce power over product labeling) were mentioned, but no one thought there was any serious hope of enactment into law. In 1964 and 1965 Lyndon Johnson reiterated the Kennedy requests for truth-in-lending and truth-in-packaging legislation, but no action was taken; the Congress and the executive exhibited little foresight of the barrage of consumer-oriented legislation and activity that was to begin in 1966 and continue through the early 1970s.

It is important to understand the consumer movement, for it provided the motivation, and often decisive political clout, for reposing in the president's branch so much of the power it now exercises over American business. These consumer protection authorities were not vested in the central executive with the view toward reducing the power of American business vis-à-vis the president. They were lodged there to protect the individual American citizen in his dealings with the American corporation. But legislation often has unintended effects and one such effect of consumer protection laws has been to tilt the scales of economic power decidedly in favor of the American presidency.

What happened in 1966? Conceptually and politically,

three ideas coincided to ignite the flurry of consumer legislation and activity and to give the president and his branch broad power to intervene in the activities of American business. First, there was a change in the primary focus of legislative concern, from fraud and full disclosure to what might be described as balance or equalization. The objective was to put the individual purchaser on something of an equal footing with the sophisticated seller. The policy makers looked at the housewife in the supermarket, the college student or the serviceman buying a car, the husband borrowing money, and the family buying a large appliance and saw them pitted against a combination of sophisticated talent that appeared to make it almost impossible for them to get a fair shake in the market place without government assistance. They saw the seller in the modern market place supported by psychologists, accounting and marketing experts, lawyers, commercial artists, brilliant scientists, and able corporate staffs whose primary purpose was to sell the most cereal or soap powder, the largest number of cars or color TV sets, or lend the greatest amount of money at the highest rate of interest.

Television, radio, magazines, and newspapers carry advertisements designed by some of the most talented men and women in our nation. Not surprisingly, government policy makers looked at this situation and concluded that fraud in the conventional sense was not the major problem the average American consumer faced, and that full disclosure alone, whether of securities, insurance coverage, or the operation of washing machines, could often be as confusing and misleading as the best psychologists, marketing experts, and lawyers could make it in their quest to increase sales.

The government moved to write laws and regulations designed to provide clear and relevant information about products: what they will do, how long they will last, how simple or difficult they are to repair, as well as information permitting the average American to make some reasonable comparison (as Betty Furness used to say, "without a slide rule") among similar products. The quality, nutritional value, and obesity effect of food became increasingly relevant to government regulators.

The difference between an antifraud, full-disclosure rationale for government policy and a rationale designed to place the individual consumer on relatively equal footing may seem subtle. It is, however, critical that this difference be recognized in evaluating the rapidly changing relationship of the executive branch of the federal government to American business, as well as to the American consumer. The equalization rationale supports a depth of government intervention far beyond that required for the effective enforcement of antifraud and full-disclosure statutes. Under typical fraud and full-disclosure laws, the power of the government is essentially limited to assuring that sellers did not intentionally deceive consumers about their products and that materials designed to induce the purchase of stocks and bonds revealed all the relevant (largely financial) facts when securities were marketed.

The consumer legislation of the late 1960s and early 1970s jibed on a different tack. It impowered the central executive to determine whether products, like children's toys and flammable materials, were so dangerous that they should not be marketed, to review the methods by which credit was extended to borrowers, to impose specific requirements on the manufacture of automobiles. In effect, that legislation embodied a national judgment that the market place so decidedly favored aggregate wealth that the individual consumer, through his purchasing power alone, was unable to impose elementary demands of safety and value received for money paid to the seller.

Prior to this wave of consumer legislation, power had been vested largely in independent agencies and then only to regulate monopolistic segments of American business, like telephone communications and the railroads; to preserve through the antitrust laws competition in essentially unregulated markets; and, with the exception of the Food and Drug Act, to require full disclosure or outlaw false claims. During the 1960s and early 1970s, beginning with the 1963 Food and Drug Act amendments, power over American business was lodged in the president's branch itself and then to mandate the contents of various products, like automo-

biles (safety belts) and children's toys (no cutting edges), and
to remove from the market products that failed to comply
with such mandates. The consumer legislation of this era
essentially changed the character of the power lodged in the
president's branch from simply telling American business
what it could say about products or what share of the market
an individual company could acquire to determining how
certain products should be manufactured as a precondition
to market entry.

The second concept which gained widespread acceptance
in academic and Washington circles during the middle and
late sixties was that, no matter how well-intentioned corporations or the executive or legislative branches may be, they
are in many ways inhibited by their very nature in their
ability to protect the interest of individual consumers. Corporations are by law and instinct profit motivated. Traditionally, they serve the public interest most immediately by their
contribution to economic growth and the taxes they pay to
help provide public services for our citizens. Government,
particularly at the top policy-making level, is essentially big-
issue-oriented; concerned about unemployment statistics,
housing starts, capital investment, war, and peace.

As a result, the government began directly (through the
Office of Economic Opportunity and its legal services programs) and indirectly (by encouraging various foundations to
make grants) to move public-interest corporations and law
firms into the consumer vacuum. Particularly in Washington,
these firms began to press for further legislative changes.
They urged administrative agencies like the Food and Drug
Administration and the Federal Trade Commission to
toughen their regulatory posture. They intervened in individual cases involving the relationship of large corporations
to the individual and the government. The customarily
stated purposes of these groups were to hold the profit-mak-
ing corporations to a standard of accountability far beyond
their shareholders' concern for profits and to press government agencies to look at the individual trees in their statistical forests. They are recognized and highly thought of by
three of their major sources of power: the press, the congres-

sional committee staffs, and the liberal young lawyers and administrators in the government.

As Simon Lazarus points out in his perceptive book, *The Genteel Populists,* they pressed the Congress to enact legislation giving additional power to the federal government. There were occasional grants of power to independent agencies like the Federal Trade Commission (which was granted special injunctive and investigatory power in the early 1970s) and the semi-independent Product Safety Commission. For the most part, however, these groups sought to vest power in the executive branch itself. The most effective self-appointed representatives of the consumers, the Ralph Naders of the nation, often expressed skepticism about overreliance on government to represent consumer interests. Nevertheless, they looked largely to the central executive for assistance in harnessing corporate America, and the fruits of their work served to increase presidential power over American business.

The third element of the consumer revolution was essential for its success and critical to the decisions to lodge such potent economic leverage in the president's branch: The politicians of America recognized that consumerism had become a broad-based and popular political issue. Early in the Johnson administration, for example, there was substantial reluctance to identify consumer legislation as such because of a conviction that the label itself increased the difficulty of enactment. The traffic safety bill was first included in the 1966 transportation program of the president, not in his consumer program. Within one year, however, the pendulum had swung. By January 1967, it became a distinct plus, worth scores of votes in the Congress and widespread favorable press, to characterize a program as consumer legislation. As a result, in that year, Johnson unfurled the banner of consumerism and, as the Congress cheered, raised it high on the executive branch flagpole.

At the federal level it makes little difference whether the administration is Republican or Democrat, conservative or liberal. For Republicans, consumerism is a solid middle-class program with significant attraction for the poor and the

Black constituencies for which Republicans traditionally
have few, if any, appealing programs. For Democrats, the
middle-class nature of consumer programs takes some of the
edge off the traditional Democratic emphasis on the poor
and the Black as far as the affluent majority is concerned.
Both parties sensed the profound frustration of individuals
over their inabilities to affect everyday events in their own
lives—the "psychology of being powerless" that Paul Good-
man essayed so well—and rightly perceived in that frustration a deeply rooted psychological base for the consumer
movement across every strata of American social and economic life.

The political attraction of consumer programs is enhanced
because so often they have virtually no budgetary impact. In
a federal budget that, in fiscal 1976, is set at some $350 billion
and is projected to increase to some $480 billion by fiscal
1980, the few million dollars it costs to launch and administer
a consumer protection program is hardly noticeable. For the
foreseeable future, even with increased tax revenues, the
viselike squeeze on the federal budget will persist, with
tighter restrictions on government spending and intensified
constituent pressures for what relatively small amounts of
increased public funds are likely to be available. Consumer
legislation provides a president and his administration, as
well as the Congress with a highly visible record of "protecting the public" at little or no cost to the taxpayer. The enactment and operation of consumer programs provide a series
of opportunities to take broadly popular regulatory actions
that are likely to be politically beneficial. With both eyes
fixed on the immediate political benefits of such programs
and the need for consumer protection in the 1960s and early
1970s, only a few consumer lobbyists and even fewer in the
Congress looked over their shoulders to see how mightily
their proposals were increasing the power of the presidency
over the manufacture, distribution, and marketing of goods
in our society.

By the end of 1966, President Johnson called the 89th Congress "a consumer's Congress." It had passed the Truth-in-
Packaging Act, which gave the Department of Commerce

power over nonfood packaging; the Child Protection Act, which gave power over children's toys initially to the Department of Health, Education and Welfare; the Traffic and Highway Safety Acts, which gave special powers to the Department of Transportation. The 90th Congress continued the momentum, passing legislation that gave the executive branch power to deal with hazardous appliances, unsafe tires, substandard clinical laboratories, lending practices, and a number of related consumer matters. The conservative Nixon administration continued to fuel the consumer bandwagon. With an enthusiastic assist from a liberal Democratic Congress, consumer protection power continued to flow to the executive branch in the closing years of the 1960s and early 1970s.

While the Congress was granting the president expanded power over business to aid the American consumer, the giant advances in technology and the unprecedented financial risks of taking advantage of that technology led to new partnerships between the executive branch and American business.

In the mid-1950s following World War II, in order to obtain essential skills that its own arsenals and laboratories lacked, the government spawned new private profit and nonprofit organizations, literally self-extensions, to help develop strategic ballistic missiles and strategy itself. During the tense years of the hot and cold war race for survival, some of the traditional barriers between government and the private sector gave way to a series of a financially and militarily comfortable joint ventures. These skill partnerships not only developed the military hardware and weapons systems of deterrence, they also provided ample precedent for the government-controlled joint effort with business that launched our space program. The technological fallout from these partnerships helped make life easier and better for most Americans and helped to increase corporate profits with jet transports, television, transistor radios, and teflon frying pans.

Those skill partnerships set the stage for the next step in the relationship between the president's branch and American business. What would happen if the time were ripe for commercial development of a major technological advance that was far beyond the ability of private industry to finance? How would the democratic, free-enterprise system respond to a situation where military need did not justify the expenditure of defense funds, but where perceived national need and opportunity inspired risks beyond the capability of private industry to finance? By forming risk partnerships between American business and the federal government. Through such partnerships, the federal government would undertake to fund or guarantee the financial risks of projects deemed to be of sufficient national interest to provide the protection against loss needed to attract private-sector investment of talent and technical skill. In a sense, special tax benefits for certain industries, like oil and housing, had established a precedent for such action by the government. But these risk partnerships were distinct; once undertaken, they engaged the government as a partner with the decisive voice in the board room of corporate management.

The most controversial risk partnership of the 1960s involved the supersonic transport. The development of a supersonic transport was considered beyond the financial capability of any commercial firm. The generation of technology to be leapfrogged imposed extraordinary economic risks. Unlike most prior commercial aviation advances, the supersonic transport did not have the bonus of extensive military technology at the taxpayer's expense. The Defense Department foresaw no military requirement for such a plane. Nevertheless, the promise of thousands of new jobs for American workers, millions of dollars of new orders for our factories, and the desire to maintain world leadership in commercial aviation in the face of foreign competition, led the government to join in a new, albeit eventually aborted, venture with the private sector. The government selected the engine and air frame manufacturers and the Congress appropriated the funds to help finance the development of a supersonic transport.

The Communications Satellite Corporation (COMSAT), formed to launch and operate commercial communications satellites, is another example of the kind of skill and risk partnerships that increasingly marked the relationship of the central government and American business in the 1960s. The immediately relevant common characteristic of these partnerships has been that the president's branch, which provides the bulk of the resources, maintains the controlling interest.

American businesses continue to remain a powerful and significant economic and social force in American life. But the unintended result of the consumer legislation and the skill and risk partnerships of the last thirty years has been to tilt the power decisively to the president's branch of the federal government in its relationship with American business. The probusiness posture of a particular administration in its exercise of executive power may temporarily render the vesting of that power more palatable to the business community and more suspect to a Ralph Nader. But in the longer run, what is most significant to the exercise of presidential power over business is the fact that the institutional capabilities are built into the executive branch. In this regard, the jawboning of Lyndon Johnson in his attempt to hold down prices and allocate resources in certain basic industries without imposing price controls was less debilitating to the role of business as a counterpoint of presidential power (although undoubtedly more aggravating personally to American businessmen) than the formal imposition of wage and price controls in 1971 or the creation of the Federal Energy Administration in 1974. The lethargy of legislated bureaucracy informs institutionalized power with a continuing potency that does not attend the assumption of *ad hoc* power. Appreciation of this political axiom was largely responsible for Johnson's refusal to institute fair housing by executive order and his insistence on authorizing legislation.

Institutionalized powers do provide a strong president with an often decisive degree of leverage over American business. Presidents will use that leverage where they believe necessary. John Kennedy did not hesitate to threaten the use of tax laws against the steel executives and antitrust

laws against their companies. Lyndon Johnson did not hesitate to use the government stockpiles against the aluminum
and molybdenum industries when he felt their prices moved
out of line. Richard Nixon did not want wage and price control authority; it was pressed on him by a Democratic Congress. Once vested with that power, however, he used it
when he thought it might stem inflation. All three presidents
have used the government's leverage as a contractor to
achieve economic and political objectives. The same government contracts that can be used to force corporations to hire
minorities and women can be used to help roll back price
increases, enhance economic development in certain sections of the nation, or, in the hands of a corrupt president, to
assist "friends" of his administration. Whether business
becomes a corrupting partner of federal regulation, subservient to the regulators, or dependent on government contracts, it loses much of its potential as an effective institutional counterpoint to the president and the branch over
which he presides.

For a president, business is a key to economic prosperity
and taxes on its profits are essential to the funding of public
programs. This was why economic policy was of such importance to Lyndon Johnson during the Great Society years. The
success of this policy was essential to provide directly for the
material needs of the vast majority of the American people
in the first instance, and indirectly to provide, through taxes
on profits and wages, the funds necessary to take care of their
less fortunate population, those who needed health care,
education, or job training to rise above poverty and share in
the material prosperity of the nation, and those like the aged,
the totally disabled, and the very young, who must look to
their fellow men for the goods and services essential to live
at some minimal level of human dignity.

To a degree he rarely admits to himself, the president
regards American corporate power as very much an extension of the state. Businessmen themselves have come increasingly to accept this role. They collect social security and
income taxes, train the hard-core unemployed, fight discrimination, supply the Defense Department, perform government research, and support all manner of presidential

health, athletic, and social objectives. Symptomatic of this relationship is the increasing frequency and ease with which top corporate executives move in and out of the executive branch. John Kenneth Galbraith, in his extraordinary analysis in *The New Industrial State*, has captured this point:

> The instinct which warns of dangers in this association of economic and public power is sound. . . . But conservatives have looked in the wrong direction for the danger. They have feared that the state might reach out and destroy the vigorous, money-making entrepreneur. They have not noticed that, all the while, the successors to the entrepreneur were uniting themselves ever more closely with the state and rejoicing in the result. They were also, and with enthusiasm, accepting abridgement of their freedom. Part of this is implicit in the subordination of individual personality to the needs of organization. Some of it is in the exact pattern of the classical business expectation. The president of Republic Aviation is not much more likely in public to speak critically, or even candidly, of the Air Force than is the head of a Soviet combinat of the ministry to which he reports. No modern head of the Ford Motor Company will ever react with the same pristine vigor to the presumed foolishness of Washington as did its founder. No head of Montgomery Ward will ever again breathe defiance of a President as did Sewell Avery. Manners may be involved. But it would also be conceded that "too much is at stake."

If business has lost much of its force as a counterpoint to presidential power, labor has managed to retain a remarkable degree of independence, ironically by co-opting the instruments of presidential power. The Federal Trade Commission and the Securities and Exchange Commission, as well as the executive departments of the federal government charged with regulating American business, are not controlled by American business. They may be more or less pro- or antibusiness depending upon their membership at any given time and the attitude of the administration in power. But, unlike the single-industry regulatory commissions and the Department of Commerce, they are not myopically responsive to the corporate community.

The situation with respect to the American labor movement provides a striking contrast. Even in big-business-oriented administrations, the Department of Labor has been generally manned at the top policy-making levels by individuals favorably disposed toward the labor movement. During the Kennedy and Johnson administrations, the secretaries of labor were Arthur Goldberg and Willard Wirtz. Goldberg had been general counsel to the United Steelworkers. Wirtz, a former law partner of Adlai Stevenson, was a well-known friend of the labor movement before he assumed office. During the Nixon administration, the secretaries of labor were initially George Shultz and James D. Hodgson, both of whom were unsympathetic to the labor movement. Finally, President Nixon bowed to the intense interest of big labor in the department and appointed Peter Brennan, former head of the New York State Building and Construction Trades Council, a man who had spent his entire adult life in the labor movement, to be secretary of labor. Brennan did not seem to share the more liberal and socially progressive views of George Meany and Lane Kirkland of the AFL-CIO. But that was less to the point than the fact that he did share their views on the rights and needs of the labor movement on labor matters and their concept of the role of the federal executive in administering the laws and regulations that affect the day-to-day operation of American unions. For, to a significantly greater degree than the Commerce Department, the Labor Department has the statutory responsibility to regulate many activities of organized labor.

The other major segment of the national government that deeply touches the American labor movement is the National Labor Relations Board. Traditionally, appointments to that board, whether by Republican or Democratic presidents, are cleared either directly or indirectly with the AFL-CIO offices on 16th Street in Northwest Washington. The American labor movement has many government interests (over which it has little control) besides its narrow ones, but its influence over the Department of Labor and the National Labor Relations Board inhibits the exercise of presidential power over the labor movement.

There are, of course, socially and politically disturbing

consequences whenever the regulated private sector controls or exercises excessive influence over the regulating public sector. It is also true that, to the extent labor relies on co-opting segments of the executive branch, the ultimate ability to tip the scales in favor of the White House remains in the president's hands. But there are other sources of labor influence over the exercise of presidential power.

Both big labor and big business have money that can be spent to achieve their political objectives. But the labor movement also has national political organizations with effective local branches, such as the Committee for Political Education (COPE), which can be deployed to provide favored candidates with workers in political campaigns. The combination of money and campaign workers has been of immense political importance to any aspiring presidential or congressional candidate. While it is clear that George McGovern would not have defeated Richard Nixon even if he had obtained broad labor support, he would have accumulated millions of additional votes had the labor movement backed him wholeheartedly. Labor's negative neutrality during the 1972 presidential campaign denied McGovern a legitimacy within its own constituency that was costly to the Democratic candidate.

The impact of organized labor on the exercise of presidential power is also felt through the Congress. The vast majority of the American people are "working people" and on legislative matters they are sufficiently responsive to the characterization of their interests by union leaders to give these men potent voices on Capitol Hill. President Johnson used to say (and it is still true in Washington today) that there was no way to pass an antilabor bill in the Congress. In 1966 during a major legislative battle on the House floor over the bill to establish the Department of Transportation, the central issue focused on whether the House would vote to maintain the Maritime Administration as a Commerce Department agency outside the proposed new department. The issue was razor close until the morning of the vote when George Meany sent a telegram to each House member, signaling that a vote to put the Maritime Administration in the Department of Transportation would be regarded as an antilabor vote. As indicated in Chapter II, the House voted decisively to leave the Maritime Administration in the Commerce Department.

In 1967, when Johnson was trying to pass legislation to end a railroad strike, there were problems with the Senate Labor Committee, of which Robert and Edward Kennedy were members. I recall Johnson and Larry O'Brien, then both postmaster general and the president's chief legislative advisor, concluding that there was no way to get the Kennedy brothers to help us because "no Democrat with national political ambitions can afford to cast an antilabor vote, particularly one breaking a strike."

The labor movement is likely to remain an effective counterforce to the exercise of presidential power in those areas of its most intimate concern, even with public financing of presidential campaigns. Its influence, political funds for presidential primaries, and well-organized political action cadres all contribute to its ability to deter exercises of presidential power perceived as inimical to its interests. Organized labor represents perhaps the only constituency of the private sector that has derived strength and independence from the prounion legislation of the New Deal and interventionist job-training programs of the Great Society. While each private-sector constituency has a special relationship to the use of presidential power in matters of parochial concern, none has the independent strength of the labor movement.

Business and labor are broad-based forces in American society of wide relevance in putting presidential power in perspective. But there are other forces and constituencies against which presidential power must be measured. Most presidents visualize themselves as representing the national constituency, often stating publicly and privately that they are the only officials in the United States government elected by all the people. While most chief executives believe that they act for the good of the nation as a whole, on particular issues they sometimes represent more limited constituencies.

A brief examination of some aspects of the presidency of Lyndon Johnson illustrates the point. Johnson was firmly allied with the American Black community. Some of his most effective and controversial legislative programs were directed in very specific terms at helping Blacks: the Civil Rights Act of 1964, which established the Equal Employment Opportunity Commission; the Voting Rights Act of 1965; and the Fair Housing Act of 1968. In addition, many other legislative proposals that Johnson sent to the Congress were aimed in large measure at assisting the Black community. The war on poverty was the most controversial and visible example, but numerous job-training, health, and education programs were also targeted at Black America. Johnson also used his executive, administrative, and appointive powers to assist the Black community and its leaders. He took these actions because he considered them important to all Americans; but he expected and received the overwhelming political support of Black Americans.

When presidents act to support and assist relatively narrow constituencies of American life, they usually consider their actions to be in the interest of the American nation as a whole. While their motivations are often politically altruistic, their expectations are invariably politically pragmatic. They expect a favorable response from the constituencies which they are helping (as well as an unfavorable one from those whose narrow interests they hurt). They do not just expect a response at the polls. They expect assistance in passing legislative programs, in obtaining the funds necessary to operate programs, and in political support for future programs.

Presidents are deeply conscious of these special constituencies: home builders, defense contractors, the aerospace industry, the banks, the scientific and education communities, the health professions, and the senior citizens. To the president, these groups are helpful allies in achieving what he considers to be worthy national goals. To those constituencies who are his allies, the goals represent a satisfying confluence of their own self-interest with the public interest. The academic, scientific, and education communities join with the president to obtain elementary, secondary, and higher-education programs, and funds for research for the National Science Foundation and the National Institutes of Health. If the joint effort is successful, funds begin to flow to local schools and to universities for education and research projects.

Over time, as federal funds continue to flow to constituencies such as these, they become increasingly dependent upon the president and the executive branch of the federal government for assistance. As a result, many constituencies support administration programs unrelated to their narrow interests because they are dependent on the president for assistance through programs his branch controls. One constituency can be leveraged by a president to assist him in dealing with another. So can the congressmen who support those constituencies or hold powerful committee chairmanships. When Carl Vinson and Richard Russell chaired the House and Senate Armed Services Committees during the presidencies of Eisenhower, Kennedy, and Johnson, Washington bureaucrats quipped that their home state of Georgia might sink under the weight of federal grants and installations placed there (often to achieve unrelated presidential and Pentagon objectives). In a few cases, federal programs create independent constituencies capable of moving the Congress. But, aside from maintaining the programmatic *status quo* by capitalizing on bureaucratic entrenchment, rarely are such constituencies able to move the Congress to new commitments over the opposition of the president, particularly (as Eisenhower and Nixon have demonstrated) where he is willing to use his veto power.

The potential for the exercise of power inherent in constituency-oriented programs raises the most serious issues for American liberals and for progressive presidents who tend to favor them. As presidents acquire more power through grant-in-aid programs, troubling questions surface concerning the extent to which those programs should be permanently authorized, the discretion which should be lodged in the president's branch to determine those within the targeted constituency to receive the most benefits, and the manner in which the chief executive and the branch he heads can best be held accountable for the administration of these programs.

Dominating the power relationship between the president and the various constituencies interested in specific grant-in-aid programs is the power of the president and the appointees who serve at his pleasure to control the timing and the recipients of federal grants. Ordinarily, when the Congress appropriates in support of legislative authorizations, it releases hundreds of millions of dollars to the executive branch. The selection of the states, cities, communities, universities, hospitals, scientific researchers, and poverty workers to receive that money is a matter normally left to the discretion of the program administrators. The Department of Housing and Urban Development is perpetually in the process of selecting one home builder over another, one city over another, as it establishes priorities for its housing programs. The Department of Health, Education and Welfare processes thousands of requests for federal funds from universities and local schools. Any mayor, educator, or home builder, who has applied to the federal executive for funds for an institution he represents, knows how decisively these grant-in-aid programs can tilt the balance of power between relatively narrow constituencies and the president. The power of the president's branch to decide whom to assist and when to provide such assistance can assume political and financial life-or-death dimensions.

One of the more persuasive arguments for pure revenue-sharing programs that operate on automatic formulas is the extent to which they remove discretionary power from the executive branch of the government. In effect, some of the pure revenue-sharing proposals would have the Congress appropriate certain amounts of money for broad areas of interest—education, health, urban development—and allocate that money under a statutory formula enacted by the Congress. Under such a system, the executive branch would play a role analogous to the Social Security Administration. With some minimal objective standards of age and disability, social security funds are automatically paid, with no discretion vested in the administration of the program.

The point here is not to argue the social and programmatic advantages and disadvantages of automatic payment programs like social security as compared with discretionary categorical grant programs such as those in the health and education areas. It is rather to note that the federal executive operates some five hundred categorical grant-in-aid programs and that, through his appointees, the president has substantial power to determine the grantees among eligible recipients. What is needed, of course, is some balance between automatic payments and discretionary grant-in-aid programs. Where broad discretion is vested in the president's branch, objective standards must be developed against which the president's performance can be evaluated. In this way, the president and his executive branch can fairly be held accountable for the manner in which they conduct such programs.

In some cases, it is relatively easy to establish an objective standard. In the housing area, for example, if the Congress determined that the housing gap should be closed within ten years (as it did in 1968) and that this would require that a certain number of units be built each of those ten years, the executive could be required to report as to whether that number of units had been built, the relationship of the location of those units to demographic trends, what the shortfall was and the reasons for the shortfall. But such standards are not always so readily available. If the national objective is to work toward the elimination of poverty among the 15 percent of the American population persistently in that condition, it is difficult to measure success except in the macroeconomic sense. One can note the economic progress of Blacks during the years of Lyndon Johnson's presidency and the marked increase in the proportion of Black males from 20 to 29 years of age who are completing high school (from 38 percent in 1960 to 64 percent in 1972) and Black males in the 24 to 34 age group who are completing college (from 4.1 percent in 1960 to 7.0 percent in 1972), as former Federal Reserve Board Governor Andrew Brimmer has. But who can say with any precision which of the federal programs contributed most effectively toward these educational and economic improvements. Or whether and how the exercise of discretion over grant-in-aid power by the federal executive helped achieve or impede them.

Complex and elusive as the task may be, the development of standards by which presidential performance can be measured is essential to the intelligent deployment of our resources to the solution of domestic problems. Such standards can also provide a significant restraint on the potential for abuse of presidential power through the manipulation of discretionary grant-in-aid programs. Relatively narrow constituencies, which have the potential to exercise real influence on the president and his executive branch, diminish their power vis-à-vis his each time they increase their financial dependency on the federal government. The weakness is more serious when that dependency assumes a measure of permanence and the president and his appointees are given wide discretion in dispensing needed support. Few, if any, presidents and White House aides will be as corrupt as Richard Nixon and members of his staff, blatantly trading federal programs for political support. But the temptation to leverage such programs to achieve broad public policy objectives or unrelated goals has been found irresistible by every recent president.

VII

THE APARTISAN PRESIDENCY

The two-party system has been taught as the sacred scripture of American democracy in the elementary and secondary schools of our nation for the better part of this century. There have been aberrations, like Theodore Roosevelt's Bull Moose party and Henry Wallace's unsuccessful run with the Progressive party in 1944. But they were exceptions that proved the point for the schoolteachers of America. Each American school child learned that, to be elected president, one had best choose between the Democratic and Republican parties. As a matter of practical politics, the lesson has been well taken to this day.

What the American school child has not been taught is that, once president, the political party is at best of marginal relevance to the performance of the duties of the Oval Office. The partisan political allegiance essential to those who aspire to nomination as presidential candidates often becomes an impediment to those incumbents who aspire to conduct a great presidency. Once the presidential brass ring is grasped, the political party machinery—the national committee, the state chairmen, and the local party organizations—becomes irrelevant as an ideological boundary marker for policies and ineffective as an instrument to extend the reach of presidential power. The dramatic change in the role of the federal executive, the impact of television, and the complexity of the international role of the United States have established an apartisan political environment for the exercise of presidential power in the last quarter of the twentieth century. The pragmatic realities of the importance of political party machinery to the presidential aspirant, its only marginal relevance to the presidential incumbent, and the forces that have occasioned this political condition have put a severe strain on the two-party system in the United States. While the full impact of public financing will not be known for some time, the constitutional requirement to provide some such funds for the lesser political parties is likely to add to that strain.

The relationship of the aspirant to presidential nomination with the national committee and the local apparatus of his party, whether Republican or Democratic, can be of decisive significance to his venture into national politics. The Democratic and Republican National Committees are moving toward the establishment of procedures to govern combatants for party nomination that make control over those committees, or at least their neutralization, important to presidential nomination by either major political party.

The 1972 Democratic Convention confirmed the importance of partisan political machinery to presidential aspirants of that party. Out of the political ashes of the 1968 Democratic Convention in Chicago rose the seductive phoenix of party reform. For the most part, all candidates except Senator George McGovern and congressional and state and local elected and political officials ignored the party rules formulation process.

The attitude of congressmen and senators was traditional and understandable. Unless they sought the presidential or vice-presidential nomination for themselves or some close political colleague, their interest in their national party convention tended to be much like that of any other conventioneer. They looked forward to a reunion with old friends, parties filled with political gossip, spending a few days in the sun, and getting free national television time on the floor of the

convention. State and local elected and party officials traditionally controlled their delegations and that was fine with
most congressmen and senators.

But even those Democratic party leaders involved in the
presidential quest believed that the newly established
McGovern-Fraser Commission procedures would be of little
significance. They assumed that the rules of the presidential
nomination game would be basically the same. The presidential nomination, they believed, would go to the man who won
the most primaries, or at least the key ones, and who obtained commitments from state and local political leaders
with wide national impact as far in advance as the shrewd
political instincts of those leaders would permit. Their failure
to appreciate the depth of the procedural revolution reflected in the new rules left them standing, mouths open,
shocked into political impotency during the preconvention
and convention rites both in Washington and Miami Beach
in 1972. As a result, the McGovern forces, well armed with
detailed knowledge of the intricate rules, dominated the
platform hearings, the credentials committee, the convention itself, and the formulation of the mandates for the reform commissions established by the 1972 Democratic Convention.

The rules were too intricate, but many of them made abundant good sense and are likely to survive future Democratic
conventions and be adopted by the Republican party as well.
Among the rules likely to survive, for example, are those
requiring the advance public announcement of state and
local meetings concerning the selection of national convention delegates and those imposing restrictions on the use of
entrenched power by local political machines to deter entry
by newcomers. Others, like the virtual quota system for
minorities, youths, and women, were seen as overreactions
to perceived past wrongs and have been softened.

The 1972 Democratic Convention demonstrated the importance of the national party machinery for the aspiring
Democratic presidential candidate. The commissions it authorized have drafted another set of intricate rules and
procedures for the future presidential aspirants. Some of

them may have a decisive impact on the 1976 Democratic Convention, such as eliminating the winner-take-all primary and granting proportional representation to any candidate with 15 percent of the vote in a state-wide primary. Most significantly, the Democratic party has now clearly asserted the power under the First Amendment "right of the people peaceably to assemble" to pre-empt state and local law with respect to the selection of delegates to its presidential nominating convention. And, in January 1975, the Supreme Court blessed that position. As a result, the Democratic National Committee and the various commissions it and the quadrennial convention create will keep the attention of aspiring presidential candidates focused on national party machinery.

In a distinctly more measured beat, the Republican party has begun to play the same political tune. Republicans have created their own reform commission to allocate delegates among the states as well as to draft rules for delegate selection within each state. While Republicans are not nearly as likely to go down the road of proportional representation or to establish detailed rules or affirmative action programs to assure minority, youth, and female representation at their national conventions, they are, nevertheless, considering modifications of their national candidate selection procedures that would make the Republican National Committee and its quadrennial convention the center of attention for nonincumbent candidates seeking the Republican presidential nomination.

While the national machinery of each major party is of increasing importance to any nonincumbent candidate for the presidential nomination of that party, its significance to an incumbent president is more rhetorical than real. The national committee of a given party is of importance when an incumbent seeks to run for a second term only if he chooses to make that committee the instrument by which he mounts his re-election campaign. Should he decide not to use his party's national committee, it becomes essentially irrelevant to the incumbent president in his quest for a second term.

Four recent presidents essentially made decisions to ig-

nore their national committees. Early during his first term in
office, Richard Nixon chose to render impotent the Republican National Committee. Nixon chose to conduct his 1972
re-election campaign through the specially created Committee for the Re-election of the President. Chaired first by
former Attorney General John Mitchell and then by former
Congressman Clark MacGregor, that committee was where
the action was for the Republicans during the 1972 presidential campaign. The Republican National Committee could
easily have closed its offices for what it contributed to the
Republican presidential re-election effort. Gerald Ford's
pointed criticism of CREEP was designed to put some political distance between its criminal and immoral activities and
the Republican party, not to deny an incumbent president
the right to organize his re-election campaign as he sees fit.
The problem was people, not organization; had the Mitch-
ells, Magruders, and Haldemans chosen the Republican National Committee as their instrument, their campaign activities would have been no less grotesque.

Eisenhower had little use for the Republican National
Committee or party machinery as he strove to conduct an
apartisan presidency. John Kennedy wasted little time after
his nomination and election in ending the active role of
Democratic National Committee Chairman Paul Butler and
the Democratic Advisory Council he created in the 1950s.
During the Eisenhower administration, when the Democrats
controlled the Congress, the Democratic National Committee became an irritant of serious proportions to congressional
leaders Lyndon Johnson and Sam Rayburn in their relationship to the White House. Johnson and Rayburn saw the committee and the council as a group of people who did not have
to be elected and who were creating unnecessary friction in
their relations with Eisenhower and placing political pot-
holes on the road to a Democratic White House victory in
1960. Once nominated, Kennedy acted in agreement with
that perception. The advisory council established by Butler
may have provided several ideas that were useful to presidential candidate John Kennedy, but the council and an independently vocal national committee were seen as poten-

tial problems by presidential incumbent John Kennedy. As a result, he placed its more talented members, like John Kenneth Galbraith, in his administration and proceeded to defuse the Democratic National Committee and dismantle its advisory council.

Lyndon Johnson, once he had won overhwelming election in 1964, continued John Bailey in office as the national chairman, not to use his expert political talents, but rather to display public political continuity with John F. Kennedy. Shortly after his 1964 election it became clear that Johnson regarded the Democratic National Committee as a debt-ridden, and presidentially irritating and irrelevant encumbrance.

Unless a first-term president decides to use the national committee of his party as the organizational instrument for his re-election campaign, he is likely to perceive his interest as being better served by the elimination of that committee as a factor in his political maneuvering. It is difficult to staff the national committee of an incumbent president with first-rate people. The most talented men and women in party politics at the national level are likely to prefer to be part of the executive branch of the government. An incumbent president has no interest in having any independent political power base built up at the national level that he can avoid, much less one staffed with mediocre people he sees as likely to make mistakes.

The steps by which an incumbent president eliminates the danger of his party's national committee becoming an independent political base are familiar to sophisticated Washington observers. Leaving the national committee superficially in place, he first reduces it to a political eunuch by sharply cutting the staff, raising money through independent committees (like president's clubs), and making it clear to the professionals that political problems will be handled by someone on his own White House staff. Then he places the national committee shell that remains under the control of a man who may or may not be designated chairman, but whose paramount dedication is to the president, as distinguished (where necessary) from the party. The shell is important to a president because it can issue the occasional nasty partisan jibes considered inappropriate for a president or member of his administration, raise funds for the purchase of political paraphernalia (tie clasps, cuff links, etc.), and pick up the political pieces, notably including the debts of unsuccessful candidates.

To the extent private financing is needed for presidential politicking, the national committee party machinery can become a source of particular irritation and annoyance to a president. Lyndon Johnson believed that most money spent by the Democratic National Committee was wasted. The Democratic party was in debt when Johnson was re-elected in 1964 and, in order to defray that debt, he found it necessary to attend a series of dinners during the course of his presidency. He invariably found those dinners demeaning. Often he would say, "It is insulting to the presidency and wrong for a president to go hat in hand asking for money from the wealthy few. Particularly in time of war and racial crisis, he must be president of all the people, and the people must perceive him as such." Whatever public financing plan for presidential candidates eventually survives constitutional muster, it is likely to render national party machinery even less relevant to presidential incumbents. It will permit them to remove themselves even further from the fund-raising roles often performed by national committees.

The incumbent president has strong allies in any move to eliminate his party's national committee and its machinery as a meaningful political force. The White House staff is perhaps his most enthusiastic ally, but it is closely followed by his congressional party. Once in office, men like Kenneth O'Donnell under Kennedy, Marvin Watson under Johnson, or Bob Haldeman under Nixon, quite naturally want to control the political machinery of their president's party. With their daily access to the president on political matters, no national party chairman is a match for them. Most party chairmen take their orders from the O'Donnells, Watsons, and Haldemans, and come to the White House only after repeated pleas that they will have no credibility even as a partisan spokesman unless they are occasionally seen there.

As DNC chairman Robert Strauss bluntly put it, "If you're Democratic party chairman when a Democrat is president, you're a Goddamn clerk." This is exactly the way the other White House aides involved in developing and coordinating domestic and foreign policy want it. In short order, they conclude that they need to control all the political (and other) power available to move the legislative and executive branches to support and implement presidential policies.

At one time, national committees performed important patronage functions for their presidents. This was true prior to and during the early years of FDR's administration. In more recent times, however, the patronage function has been performed by the executive branch itself. The grants-in-aid, jobs, advisory commission seats, and coveted social invitations now come from executive branch programs and the presidential staff. Here, the national committee has nothing to offer when its own party occupies the White House.

The Congress—whether its majority members are of the incumbent party or the opposition—prefers to deal with the White House directly and to ignore the national committees. An incumbent president must on a day-to-day basis work with the Congress. Both he and the congressional leaders, committee chairmen, and ranking minority committee members know that. An active president, like Lyndon Johnson, who proposes to the Congress more than a hundred bills each year of his presidency, must make and keep peace with the Congress. But even a passive president, like Dwight Eisenhower, needs the support of the Congress on many international matters (the Korean peace negotiations or the Quemoy and Matsu crisis), domestic crises (like the integration of the high school in Little Rock, Arkansas), and to support his vetoes. The congressional leaders recognize the delicate complexity of their relationship to the White House and the states, they enjoy the national publicity that attends that relationship, and they prefer not to have any third parties, including the national party committees, involved.

From the presidential vantage point, it is not simply that he considers partisanship in its narrow sense unbecoming in his dealings with the Congress. Partisanship in dealing with the Congress is counterproductive for a president. Presidents need liberal, conservative, or *ad hoc* majorities, more than they need either Republican or Democratic majorities. They need shrewd and well-respected floor managers for their major legislative proposals, from either (or both) sides of the aisle. Life is, of course, much easier for a president if the Congress is in the hands of his own political party. But this is as much because they are more likely, on the whole, to share somewhat similar ideological positions as it is because they are likely to share any party loyalty. Would John Kennedy or Lyndon Johnson prefer two liberal Republican senators, like Jacob Javits and Charles Percy, or would he rather have two conservative Democrats like James Eastland and John Stennis? And what would be the private preference of Richard Nixon or Gerald Ford?

For a generation, this nation, often to its detriment, has largely adhered to the principle that partisan politics stops at the water's edge. As David Broder has pointed out, there are historical justifications for this principle. Roosevelt felt the need to make his cabinet bipartisan during the World War II years. Truman had to deal with a Republican Congress when he put the Marshall Plan into effect. Eisenhower was faced with a Democratic Congress throughout his presidency. The youthful Kennedy turned to nonpartisan members of the establishment like Dean Rusk, Robert McNamara, and McGeorge Bundy for the top foreign policy posts in his administration. Particularly in the latter years of his administration, Lyndon Johnson needed Republican congressional support for his Vietnam policy. Nixon turned to Nelson Rockefeller's Henry Kissinger who, in turn, had to reach an accommodation with Democratic Foreign Relations Committee Chairman William Fulbright. Gerald Ford felt obliged to announce that he was retaining Kissinger as secretary of state before he took the presidential oath of office. Partisan politics have thus had little relevance to the conduct of foreign policy for more than thirty years.

What has been less fully appreciated is that, since the presidency of Dwight Eisenhower, party politics had little to do with the pursuit and achievement of domestic policy objectives. Lyndon Johnson concluded from the day he stepped into the Oval Office that a progressive president needed leaders of both parties to obtain the necessary votes for his domestic programs.

For an active president, partisan party politics are much less important in legislative terms than congressional politics. Once a majority of the Congress is in the hands of the party of the incumbent president, the committees and their staffs will be in his party's hands, as will the power to schedule legislation for consideration on the floors of the House and Senate. Beyond that, the president is much more interested in congressional politics, regardless of party, than he is in any partisan politics. For a progressive president to achieve his goals, he must have a liberal majority in the House and be able to muster the sixty votes in the Senate necessary to terminate a conservative filibuster. But even a negative, conservative president like Nixon, needs bipartisan support. Critical votes necessary to sustain more than one of his vetoes came from conservative, Southern Democrats. Gerald Ford has placed similar reliance on conservative Democrats in the House and Senate in his attempts to sustain vetoes. An examination of presidential-congressional relations since Harry Truman left office illustrates why, as David Broder concluded in his superb analysis of the decline of the two party system, *The Party's Over,* "the instrument of responsible party government" has been so little used over the past twenty years.

The remarkable legislative achievements of the 89th Congress during the Johnson administration were attributable not merely to the fact that a Democratic majority ruled both Houses of the Congress. They were attributable to the fact that the House of Representatives, for the first time since the initial years of the Roosevelt administration, was controlled by a liberal majority, not merely a Democratic majority. On the Senate side of the 89th Congress, it was imperative for Johnson to have Republican support for his most controversial legislation. The intimate, one-on-one conferences with Republican leader Everett Dirksen and the meeting of the Johnson and Dirksen minds were essential for the passage of the Civil Rights Act of 1964, the Voting Rights Act of 1965, and the Fair Housing Act of 1968. Without the support of Senate Minority Leader Dirksen, those presidential proposals would have been killed by Senate filibuster. Johnson's recognition of that political reality assured Republican Senate Leader Dirksen of the same preferred treatment from the president and his staff that was accorded Senator Mike Mansfield of Montana, the Democratic majority leader.

There are other party elements of presidential interest around the nation: the state and local party organizations, the governors, and the mayors. It is, of course, of benefit to a president to have governors and mayors of his own political party in political control of major states and cities. Such elected officials can bolster party morale and assist an incumbent president running for re-election. But they are of distinctly greater significance to the aspiring presidential candidate than to the incumbent president. The aspiring presidential candidate, in most cases, needs to build on state, city, and county political organizations in order to achieve his goal. The more state houses and city halls that are in control of his own party at the time of his nomination, the easier this task may be.

Once the aspiring candidate has become president, however, the state houses and the city halls are of less relevance to him. Two dramatic changes in recent years have precipitated this condition: (1) the unfettered access of an incumbent president to national television (largely on his own terms) discussed in Chapter V, and (2) the decline of the state and local political dynasties. The electorate is becoming more sophisticated, less often voting straight party lines. Instances where governors and mayors are so phenomenally popular within their own jurisdictions that they can help an incumbent president are rare. Such popularity and its ability to build and sustain crack political organizations are relics of another political age. With the resignation of New York Governor Nelson Rockefeller and the debilitating stroke of Chicago Mayor Richard Daley (as well as the scandals surrounding his administration), it is difficult to identify a gover-

nor or mayor of either party who is likely to enjoy such
sustained popularity over any extended period, even predictably three or four years hence, and thus be useful to an
incumbent president seeking re-election to a second term.

The problems that plague city halls and state houses have,
in recent years, destroyed more politicians and political organizations, Republican and Democratic, than anyone imag-
ined possible a generation ago. In this age of relentless taxation and seemingly intransigent urban decay, it is a major
achievement for a man to survive more than one or, at most,
two terms as governor or big-city mayor. Where a governor
or a mayor does survive for an extended period of time or
where he has been singularly popular, as in the case of Nelson
Rockefeller and Ronald Reagan in the Republican party, his
personal ambition is likely to lead to political antagonisms
with the incumbent president of the same party.

Even where such antagonisms do not arise, state and local
coattails are rarely, if ever, perceived by the incumbent
president seeking re-election as long or strong enough to
provide any reliable assistance. As the analysis in Chapter IV
demonstrates, most major projects of states and cities today
require substantial federal support, whether they are new
hospitals, universities, elementary schools, or mass transit
systems. An incumbent president can make it politically
clear that "his" federal funds, not the "governor's" or
"mayor's" funds, are building the new mass transit system in
San Francisco, the new hospital complex in New York City,
or the new low- or moderate-income housing project in At-
lanta; that "his" Model Cities funds are helping rebuild Watts
in Los Angeles or Hough in Cleveland. Even the most ardent
presidential advocates of revenue sharing, like Gerald Ford,
have not displayed any inclination to let the governors and
mayors take credit for the projects such funds support.

The inability of the major parties to provide ideological or
often even politically pragmatic bearings for the exercise of
presidential power, much less restrain its abuse, except perhaps in the most egregious circumstances, is a condition of
political impotence likely to continue for the foreseeable

future. There are, of course, elements within each political party that do have an impact on the exercise of presidential power, at least with respect to certain issues. Often these elements exist in both parties. The political activism of the potent oil and farm lobbies have, for example, influenced the policies of both Republican and Democratic presidents. Some segments of society, like organized labor, are influentially present largely in one party. Since the time of Franklin Roosevelt, the Blacks have been predominately Democratic and, after Lyndon Johnson (followed in sharp contrast by Richard Nixon and Gerald Ford), it would take a revolutionary change for them to switch to Republican allegiance. Similarly, the profitability of big business during every Democratic administration since Franklin Roosevelt has not eased the anxiety of corporate executives about the socially liberal bent of the Democratic party or loosened their ties to the Republicans.

Both major parties contain distinctly conservative and liberal elements. This diverse ideological ambiance inhibits their ability to provide consistent ideological restraints on the exercise of power by an incumbent president of the same party. There are, however, situations in which the opposition party can restrain the exercise of presidential power. Certain leadership elements of the opposition party may be attractive targets for co-option by an incumbent president. A conservative Republican president will seek out Southern Democrats; a liberal Democratic president will seek out some Northern Republicans. Opposition party congressional leaders, like Everett Dirksen during the Kennedy and Johnson administrations or Johnson during the Eisenhower administration, can have a major impact on certain presidential policies. The level of their influence, however, will depend more on the number of seats their party holds in the House and Senate and the specific issues involved than on any national party organization.

Citizen skepticism about the motivations of politicians and political parties is perhaps the most debilitating factor in rendering both the president's party and that of the loyal opposition such ineffectual instruments to restrain the exercise of presidential power. The 1974 House Judiciary Committee impeachment proceedings tellingly made this point. The central concern of the House Democratic leadership and most thoughtful commentators in the press was that the American people would regard a Democratic vote recommending impeachment as an unwarranted partisan vendetta unless it was accompanied by broad Republican support. In the face of overwhelming evidence that Nixon had obstructed justice and abused his power, it was widely accepted that American distrust of political parties was so deeply rooted that the loyal opposition could not hope to convince the people it had acted out of a sincere desire to perform its constitutional function unless it could produce widespread bipartisan agreement. As a result, the committee proceedings were prolonged for months to muster such agreement, despite the facts that Nixon had been named an unindicted coconspirator by the Watergate cover up grand jury and that the committee had tapes which convincingly implicated the president in his own words.

The most significant and profoundly disturbing aspect of an analysis of presidential power in partisan political perspective is that incumbent presidents in the last quarter of the twentieth century are not likely to have much interest in or incentive to build their political parties for the future. In my years on Lyndon Johnson's White House staff, never once did I hear him say that he wanted to leave behind a strengthened Democratic party. The legacies he sought for the American people were peace, racial equality and harmony, the elimination of poverty, economic stability, and equality of educational opportunity. In all the books written about John Kennedy, not once is such an interest revealed. I doubt that any recent president has set much priority on strengthening his political party except for his own short-term purposes, however vigorously partisan his campaign or after-political-dinner rhetoric. The problems of incumbency tend to focus presidential attention on congressional and special-interest politics, not partisan party politics.

Since the administration of Franklin Roosevelt, American presidents have been consumed with apparently intractable problems at home and abroad: recurring inflation, poverty amid unprecedented affluence, the decline of Europe, the rise of Communist China and Soviet Russia, war in the Middle East, racial tension, world hunger. Faced with problems of such human and historical significance, no president is going to expend much time or energy in building his own political party or in deferring to it in the exercise of his power. The incumbent years of a president are aimed at the stuff of history—winning wars, achieving peace, ending depression, harnessing inflation, or wiping out poverty—and reinvigorating partisan political parties is not presidentially perceived as historically momentus. Historians pay reverent homage to the strength Andrew Jackson vested in the American presidency; they reserve derisive footnotes to his party patronage quip, "To the victor belong the spoils."

In 1950, a committee on political parties of the American Political Science Association described the decline of a responsible two-party system in the United States. The committee report, "Toward a More Responsible Two-Party System," predicted that one of the central dangers of the disintegration of that system would be "that the American people may go too far for the safety of constitutional government in compensating for this inadequacy by shifting excessive responsibility to the president." Even in mass psychological terms, the causal relationship between the declining effectiveness of two major parties and the increased focus of power in the presidency seems overstated. As we have seen in the course of this analysis of presidential power, a number of constitutional, political, and technological factors have combined to strengthen the presidency and debilitate the traditional sources of countervailing power envisioned by the original framers. But it is difficult to argue with the prescient conclusion of the 1950 American Political Science Association committee concerning the shift of responsibility (and authority) to the presidency during the last quarter century. And it is reasonable to conclude that, short of a smoking gun in evidence of criminality, neither the incumbent president's political party nor its loyal opposition has maintained the ability to hold presidential power in democratically healthy constitutional perspective.

VIII

———— ❧ ————

TAKING
PRESIDENTIAL
POWER INTO COURT

During the summer of 1835, when President Andrew Jackson was selecting a successor for the recently deceased and powerful Chief Justice John Marshall, John Quincy Adams confided to his diary that "the office of Chief Justice is a station of the highest trust, of the deepest responsibility and of influence far more extensive than that of the President of the United States." During the next 140 years, the Court won a few battles with the presidency, but it lost every war. Today, even after the 1974 decision upholding the right of the special prosecutor to subpoena certain Nixon tapes, no thoughtful American would make John Quincy Adams's claim.

Indeed, by the time Jackson had completed his term of office two years later, the presidency was well on its way to becoming the paramount focus of government and the moving force for change and progress in the young nation. Jackson's famous battle with Nicholas Biddle over the constitutionality of the Bank of the United States reached the Supreme Court. Predictably, the Court held the Bank of the

United States to be constitutional. That holding did not, however, deter Jackson from killing the Bank. He could have vetoed the Bank legislation on any number of policy grounds, but he chose to take on the issue of constitutionality. Putting it sharply to the Court, Jackson informed the Congress:

> The opinion of the Supreme Court ought not to control the coordinate authorities of this Government. . . . The opinion of the judges has no more authority over Congress than the opinion of the Congress has over the judges, and on that point, the President is independent of both. The authority of the Supreme Court must not therefore be permitted to control the Congress or the Executive when acting in their legislative capacities, but to have only such influence as the force of their reasoning may deserve.

The Supreme Court notwithstanding, the veto stuck and the Bank of the United States was dead. Since then, except for temporary and often dramatic victories, the court has not fared well eyeball to eyeball with the presidency.

The next direct presidential confrontation involved Abraham Lincoln. When Lincoln suspended the writ of habeas corpus, he confronted Chief Justice Roger B. Taney, the author of the Dred Scott decision. In May 1861, Chief Justice Taney was sitting in Baltimore to hear the return of a writ of habeas corpus he had issued.* An aide-de-camp in military uniform appeared and declined to obey the writ on the ground that habeas corpus had been suspended by order of the president. The chief justice described the case in *Ex Parte Merryman:*

> The case, then, is simply this: a military officer, residing in Pennsylvania issues an order to arrest a citizen of Maryland, upon vague and indefinite charges, without any proof, so far as appears; under this order, his house is entered in the night, he is seized as a prisoner, and conveyed to Fort McHenry, and there kept in close confinement; and when a habeas corpus is served on the commanding officer, requiring him to produce the prisoner before a justice of the supreme court, in order that he may examine into the legality of the imprisonment, the answer of the officer, is that he is authorized by the president

*In those days, it was common for Supreme Court justices to sit in various circuits around the country.

to suspend the writ of habeas corpus at his discretion, and in the exercise of that discretion, suspends it in this case, and on that ground refuses obedience to the writ. . . .

. . . the documents before me show, that the military authority in this case has gone far beyond the mere suspension of the privilege of the writ of habeas corpus. It has, by force of arms, thrust aside the judicial authorities and officers to whom the constitution has confided the power and duty of interpreting and administering the laws, and substituted a military government in its place, to be administered and executed by military officers.

With a confession of helplessness, the chief justice proclaimed the fundamental principles of civil freedom from military usurpation and closed his opinion: "My duty was too plain to be mistaken. I have exercised all the power which the constitution and laws confer upon me, but that power has been resisted for a force too strong for me to overcome."

Lincoln ignored the decree of the chief justice with the comment, "the candid citizen must confess that if the policy of the Government upon vital questions affecting the whole people is to be irrevocably fixed by decisions of the Supreme Court, the people will have ceased to be their own ruler, having to that extent practically resigned their Government into the hands of that eminent tribunal."

There were a number of skirmishes during the ensuing seventy-five years. But the next great confrontation between the judiciary and the presidency came during the administration of Franklin D. Roosevelt. During its first seventy years the Supreme Court set aside as unconstitutional only two acts of the Congress. Between 1920 and 1930, however, the Court became distinctly less deferential toward the legislative branch and invalidated nineteen of the laws enacted by the Congress and signed by the president. In 1935 and 1936, during the first term of Franklin Roosevelt in the depths of the Depression, the Court systematically declared central pieces of New Deal legislation unconstitutional. Roosevelt decided to take on the members of the Court directly and personally.

In a radio address to the nation five days after his second-term inauguration in 1937, the president noted that the Supreme Court used its veto power sparingly in the early years of its life. He cited with approval Mr. Justice Bushrod Washington's remark, "It is but a decent respect due to the wisdom, the integrity, and the patriotism of the legislative body, by which any law is passed, to presume in favor of its validity until its violation of the Constitution is proved beyond all reasonable doubt." Roosevelt then set the issue before the people:

> But since the rise of the modern movement for social and economic progress through legislation, the Court has more and more often and more and more boldly asserted a power to veto laws passed by the Congress and State legislatures in complete disregard of this original limitation. In the last 4 years the sound rule of giving statutes the benefit of all reasonable doubt has been cast aside. The Court has been acting not as a judicial body, but as a policy-making body.

He proposed legislation to add "a new and younger judge" to the Court automatically as a justice reached the age of seventy. "Our difficulty with the Court today rises not from the Court as an institution but from human beings within it. But we cannot yield our constitutional destiny to the personal judgment of a few men who, being fearful of the future, would deny us the necessary means of dealing with the present."

Roosevelt lost that battle. His Court-packing plan did not become law. But he dramatized the issue and won the war. The Supreme Court curtailed its intervention in the economic reordering of the nation's affairs, reread the interstate "Commerce Clause" of the Constitution, and opened the constitutional doors for the president and the central executive to move deeply into the economic regulation of our everyday lives.

Since then, with exceptions in 1952 and 1974, the Court has kept its distance from the president. In the long run of history, Harry Truman's confrontation with the Supreme Court over the federal government seizure of the steel mills in 1952 was only a skirmish lost. Whether the intrusions of post-Truman presidents have been more shrewdly subtle or recent justices more cautious, a truce, sometimes uneasy, effectively eliminated direct confrontations, until the Watergate criminal trials and the revelation by Alexander Butterfield that Richard Nixon had secretly tape-recorded most of his office and telephone conversations.

President Nixon's attitude throughout the Watergate scandals presented the courts with a unique problem. Watergate involved criminal activity by high government officials, well-supported allegations of criminal activity by the president himself, and an impeachment proceeding whose conclusion became so evident that the president resigned rather than subject himself to certain Senate conviction.

In the early stages, the courts and the president cagily took each other's measure, finessed direct conflict, and avoided issues of the sort that Taney and Lincoln had joined during the Civil War. Subpoenas of the House Judiciary Committee were defied by the president, but the issue was never placed before the courts. The House of Representatives did not recognize any jurisdiction in the courts to settle its disputes with the president. It chose to rely instead on the fact that the Constitution vested it with the "sole power of impeachment." In accord with this position, the House Judiciary Committee voted an Article of Impeachment specifically relating to Nixon's refusal to honor its subpoenas.

The courts faced a president enmeshed in impeachment proceedings and personally involved with the criminal justice system as a potential defendant, who was also in sole possession of evidence relevant to pending grand jury investigations and criminal trials of his closest aides. Initially, federal district judges like John Sirica and Gerhard Gesell expressed frustration and aggravation at President Nixon's sweeping claims of executive privilege and his recalcitrance in responding to subpoenas from Special Prosecutor Leon Jaworski and the grand juries investigating Watergate. In October 1973, the president backed down in the face of a Federal Court of Appeals decision, approving with modifications Judge Sirica's order to produce certain presidential tapes. In other cases, lower court orders to produce documents and tapes were threatened and leveled at the president, but eventually compromises were reached accommodating the interest of the judiciary and the Nixon presidency.

Then, in mid-1974, Special Prosecutor Jaworski subpoenaed several tapes, including one of a conversation between the president and his top aide, Bob Haldeman, on June 23, 1972, six days after the illegal entry into Democratic National Committee headquarters at the Watergate complex. The president unsuccessfully invoked executive privilege before Judge Sirica. When Nixon lawyer James St. Clair moved to place the issue before the Federal Court of Appeals, Special Prosecutor Jaworski persuaded the Supreme Court to take the extraordinary step of hearing the case immediately, without awaiting action by the intermediate appellate court. By a unanimous 8–0 decision,* Richard Nixon lost his case. But the power of the presidency won. The Court ordered Nixon to turn over the subpoenaed tapes, but it narrowly confined its rejection of the president's "generalized assertion of privilege . . . to the demonstrated, specific need for evidence in a pending criminal trial." The Court repeatedly indicated that it was confronted with an unusual criminal proceeding in which the president was an unindicted coconspirator—it was widely known that Nixon was unindicted only because the special prosecutor convinced the grand jury that it probably did not have the legal authority to indict a sitting president.

The Supreme Court unanimously agreed that a president did have a right to assert executive privilege, not simply in military and diplomatic affairs, but more broadly. "A President's acknowledged need for confidentiality in the communications of his office is general in nature," the Court noted, distinguishing from the case before it matters involving the need for relevant evidence in civil litigation, congressional demands for information (the District of Columbia Federal Court of Appeals had twice denied the Senate Watergate Committee access to Nixon tapes, thus upholding the president's claim of executive privilege), as well as the presi-

*Justice William Rehnquist, who had served as assistant attorney general (Office of Legal Counsel) under President Nixon, disqualified himself.

dent's interest in preserving state secrets. The Court concluded that the presidential "interest in preserving confidentiality is weighty indeed and entitled to great respect." Chief
Justice Warren Burger's opinion pointedly narrowed the impact of the Court's holding to the criminal situation before it:
"We cannot conclude that advisers will be moved to temper
the candor of their remarks by the infrequent occasions of
disclosure because of the possibility that such conversations
will be called for in the context of a criminal prosecution."

The contemporary fanfare centered on the Court's order
that a potentially criminal president had no right to deny the
United States prosecutor access to tapes relevant to criminal
proceedings. Such an order by a court to a president was
without precedent in our history. It came at a critical junc-
ture in the Nixon impeachment proceedings and, although
technically unrelated, was woven of the same political and
psychological cloth. But the enduring impact of the decision
is likely to be the judicial canonization of executive privilege
as a constitutional presidential power. The implications of
the decision for congressional and media attempts to obtain
executive office material, even under a strengthened Freedom of Information Act, are ominous.

The Nixon reaction to the Supreme Court decision provides revealing anecdotal evidence of the relationship between the president and the Court. Aware of the precedents
for presidential defiance of an adverse court ruling, by all
published accounts, Nixon's decision to obey was based less
on the enforcement power of the Court than on the politics
of his own desperate situation. Defiance was measured
against its impact on his impeachment proceedings, his perception of the judgment of history on such an action, and
perhaps, in anticipation of his resignation, his ability to obtain
the pardon which Gerald Ford gave him on September 8,
1974. For its part, the Court shrewdly timed the announcement of its decision to coincide with the critical phase of the
House Judiciary Committee impeachment deliberations,
thus exerting maximum moral and public pressure on the
president to comply. The aberrational nature of the Nixon
presidency and this case should not obscure the fact that, in

terms of lasting institutional power, the Supreme Court acknowledged and judicially sanctioned a broad range of executive privilege for the presidency. A few months later, that
same Court endorsed, in sweeping terms, essentially unlimited pardon power for the presidency.

A few modern-day Jeffersonians still tend to regard the
Court as outrageously self-important, tyrannical, irresponsible, and unaccountable. This was essentially how the Warren
Court was perceived by much of the South and numerous
law-enforcement officials during the 1950s and 1960s. Yale
Law School Professor Fred Rodell has couched the Jeffersonian argument in modern terms, extremely characterizing
the Supreme Court as a threat to self-government: "Not even
the bosses of the Kremlin, each held back by fear of losing his
head should he ever offend his fellows, wield such loose and
long-ranging and accountable-to-no-one power as do the
nine or five-out-of-nine Justices who can give orders to any
other governing official in the United States . . . and make
those orders stick. . . . there is no check at all on what the
Supreme Court does."

The power of the Court approaches such awesome proportions only when the federal executive, the president's
branch, acts in concert with it or energetically enforces its
rulings. The activities of the Justice Department Civil Rights
Division during the Kennedy and Johnson administrations is
illustrative of the combined power of the courts and the
presidency in pursuit of the same objective. Absent such
concert of action and purpose, the realities of the relationship between the federal judiciary and the executive branch,
between the Supreme Court and the presidency, offer little
justification for the fears of modern-day Jeffersonians like
Rodell.

As a separate institution, the Court is essentially passive. It
must confront a specific case or controversy before it can act.
Like the Pope, its pronouncements have moral force; but just
as the Pope's greatest impact is on Roman Catholics, the
Court's greatest impact is on those who tend to agree with
its decisions. A cynical president might well raise the same

question about the Court that Josef Stalin asked about the Pope: How many divisions does he have? Andrew Jackson once said, "The Supreme Court has stated the law. Now let them enforce it." The enforcement of its pro-civil-rights decisions is one thing in the hands of a true-believing integrationist like Lyndon Johnson, quite another in the hands of a doubting Thomas like Richard Nixon. President Ford's 1974 public criticism of the Boston school busing ordered by a federal court and his reluctance to provide federal executive enforcement assistance stands in sharp contrast to Kennedy's actions when James Meredith was ordered enrolled at the University of Mississippi. It also serves to put the entire federal judiciary on notice for the future.

The historical and moral significance of the Supreme Court should not cloud the true limits of its power as a lonely institution. In his book, *Struggle for Judicial Supremacy,* Justice Robert Jackson provided this assessment of the Court's constitutional limitations:

> [The Court] has no function except to decide "cases" and "controversies" and its very jurisdiction to do that was left largely to the control of Congress. It has no force to execute its own commands, its judgments being handed over to the Executive for enforcement. The Justices derive their offices from the favor of the other two branches by appointment and confirmation, and hold them subject to an undefined, unlimited and unreviewable Congressional power of impeachment. They depend annually for the payment of their irreducible salaries and the housing of their Court upon appropriations from Congress.

The Supreme Court does not initiate, enact, or administer legislation. It does not appropriate money, govern, or make foreign policy. The Court does not have access to television time and, except for Chief Justice Burger's annual report on the State of the Judiciary, choses for its own good reasons largely to eschew the power that comes from modern communications. The Congress passes laws and appropriates money. The president administers laws, often recommends new ones, and makes foreign policy.

Every two years, members of Congress must return to the

people to defend their records and recharge their electoral batteries. Every four years, presidential candidates tell the people how a federal executive under their leadership can best serve national interests. The Supreme Court speaks only in its opinions. It has no advocates on the hustings. Pious incantations of the majesty of the Court as the ultimate preserver of the rule of law come as often as not from those who support particular decisions or judicial trends. Recognizing that its Olympian perch is not alone sufficient to maintain the status of constitutional supremacy envisioned and articulated by Chief Justice John Marshall, the Court has paid sufficient homage to the clearly expressed views of a steady popular majority for some critics to assert that judicial supremacy is what the people say it is at the most recent election. As Robert McCloskey discovered in his research, "it is hard to find a single historical instance when the Court has stood firm for very long against a really clear wave of public demand." Justice Robert Jackson perhaps best described this posture of the Court in his observation that, "The unifying principle running through all of our constitutional litigations has been the recognition that the Constitution contemplated a really effective government."

Simmered to its essence, the role of the Court is primarily a conservative one, providing a kind of count-to-ten, stop-and-think point for checking and testing. Its power vis-à-vis the president is occasionally important, but largely negative. As constitutional scholar Judge Stephen Field wrote in optimistic overstatement on his resignation in 1897, "[The Court] carries neither the purse nor the sword. But it possesses the power of declaring the law, and in that is found the safeguard which keeps the whole mighty fabric of government from rushing to destruction. This negative power, the power of resistance, is the only safety of a popular government."

Taking the measure of presidential power in judicial perspective requires a more penetrating examination than Judge Field's rosy resignation statement provides of how the Court's power to say "no" has affected the relationship of the presidency to the other institutions of our society and to the American people. For those who look to the Court as the last bastion of protection against an excessively strong presidency, history provides some profoundly disturbing precedents. This is particularly true in terms of the Court as an institutional balance between the presidency and the major potential counterforces in our society. As Robert McCloskey wrote, "In no major conflict with the representative branches on any question of social or economic policy has time vindicated the Court."

The central political dispute of our nation's first seventy years was the issue of slavery. While economic and social considerations determined most views on the issue, the dominant ideological debate concerned the proper apportionment of power between the national government and the states. As states' rights and slavery became one and the same cause, and as a powerful presidency and popular sovereignty became closely identified, the Era of Good Feeling evaporated and the nation was divided. The Southerners were especially loath to subject their states to the power of a central government dominated by Northern interests.

The role of the Supreme Court was brief but incendiary. The same day James Buchanan was inaugurated in March 1856, the Supreme Court opted for states' rights and the South in issuing the Dred Scott decision. Soon thereafter, the Court was reversed by the Civil War, followed by Reconstruction and the Fourteenth Amendment. The combined impact of these events rendered a serious blow to the viability of the states as counterpoints to presidential power. In subjecting the states to the constitutional power of the central government to protect individual rights, the Fourteenth Amendment vested the presidency (as well as the Congress and indirectly the federal courts) with decisive power to determine a citizen's rights in terms of the actions of the several states.

The ideological debate over the apportionment of power between the federal government and the states persisted long after the North's victory in the Civil War; there are echoes to this day, most notably in the voices of proponents of revenue sharing. But throughout the twentieth century, those justices who professed the cause of states' rights against the central government have been in distinct, though occasionally distinguished, minority. Justice Oliver Wendell Holmes, widely regarded as one of the Court's great judicial liberals, often dissented in the name of state sovereignty. In a case holding unconstitutional under the Fourteenth Amendment an Arizona statute prohibiting the issuance of injunctions "in any case between an employer and employees," Holmes wrote in dissent, "There is nothing that I more deprecate than the use of the Fourteenth Amendment beyond the absolute compulsion of its words to prevent the making of social experiments that an important part of the community desires, in the insulated chambers afforded by the several States, even though the experiments may seem futile or noxious to me and to those whose judgment I most respect."

This same doctrine which, in the hands of a Holmes was a weapon for change and experimentation, provided rhetorical cover for the judicial conservatism of Felix Frankfurter, Robert Jackson, and John Harlan. Today, Justice William Rehnquist gives every indication of reinvigorating the Jeffersonian language of state sovereignty. But postindustrial America provides little hope for more than an occasional grandiloquent revival of states' rights by the federal judiciary. Modern technology, the nationalization of communications, interstate aggregations of wealth in corporations, the mobility of our society, and the functionally incoherent boundary lines of the states (and cities) render politically quixotic reliance on the Supreme Court for protection of the power of the states and cities vis-à-vis the president and the central government.

During the second seventy years of our nation's history, The Supreme Court cast its lot with entrenched private economic interests in opposition to the leveling efforts of a presidency and central government seeking to regulate and redistribute disproportionate aggregations of material wealth. Again, the Court was reversed; this time by the Depression, one of the most popular presidents in our history, world war, cold war, and irrepressible technological advances.

Between 1865 and 1937, the Supreme Court became a critical battleground between private economic freedom and private power on the one hand and public policy and governmental power on the other. The federal judiciary stood firmly for property rights and freedom of contract against the more transcendent redistributive and human objectives pursued with programs emanating from the White House. The mood of the Court was captured by a federal district judge who bluntly proclaimed from the depths of the 1930s Depression, "It should be remembered that of the three fundamental principles which underlie government, and for which government exists, the protection of life, liberty and property, the chief of these is property."

But the Court could not ignore the desperate need for a multitude of economic and social measures that only the central government could undertake in a timely and effective manner. By the end of the 1930s, with its re-examination of the "Commerce Clause," the Court discovered ample constitutional authority to justify the intervention of the federal executive across the spectrum of American economic life. Justice Louis Brandeis articulated the importance of economic data to legal and constitutional ideology and helped lay the intellectual pavement for the intrusive efforts of the presidency and the central executive to regulate economic power and redistribute economic wealth.

What Brandeis did to enhance the power of the presidency as to economic intervention, Chief Justice Earl Warren did to enhance the reach of its social intervention. Particularly with the 1954 decision in *Brown v. Board of Education*, the Warren Court gave the president and his branch not only the right but the duty to intervene deeply in domestic, social affairs to end racial discrimination. The school desegregation decision in *Brown* was the cutting edge of a judicial philosophy that recognized modern psychology, sociology, behavioral sciences, and population mobility as relevant to the interpretation of the Constitution and the powers it bestows on the president and the central government.

Then in 1964, Lyndon Johnson's Great Society moved to center stage with all the legal and constitutional props it needed. The Supreme Court's economic and social constitutional philosophy provided more than enough room for the most imaginative Great Society planners to inject the federal executive deeply into the mainstreams of everyday American life. Civil rights legislation imposed affirmative action requirements on the hiring of minorities and women, mandated nondiscrimination in the sale and rental of housing, and redefined the concept of public accommodations. The federal executive offered American families birth control programs and often encouraged the poor to use them. The grant-making power lodged in the executive branch made the president and his Department of Health, Education and Welfare *de facto* directors of research at many universities and powers to be reckoned with by every school district in the nation. Providing funds or mortgage guarantees for virtually all middle- and lower-income housing gave the central executive the power to determine where houses and apartments would be built, and when. From broad economic regulatory powers, the consumer programs moved the president's branch deeply into such business decisions as those relating to safety, pollution control, advertising, medical devices, and children's toys. Richard Nixon reluctantly took the next giant step of creating a Product Safety Commission that gave sweeping powers to the national government over the safety of products, roughly comparable to the powers of the Food and Drug Administration over foods and drugs.

The courts have not simply blessed these activities as constitutional. Often, they have broadly interpreted statutes to justify or require a measure of federal intervention in economic and social affairs hardly conceived of a generation ago. Joining forces with the presidency, the courts have upheld the exercise of central executive power to control and regulate all manner of private economic and social institutions. The benevolent use of such presidential power eased the way for the development of legal and constitutional dogma to support its profound intervention into American life.

Since the Civil War and the adoption of the Fourteenth Amendment, and with the inexorable rush of massive industrialization and national income taxation, the Supreme Court has positioned the federal judiciary solidly on the side of presidential power vis-à-vis the states and cities and private economic and social institutions. No match for the other forces in modern society, the Court has, in these areas at least, decisively joined a central executive power it could not beat. However, its stance in the power relationship between the presidency and the Congress has remained ambivalently neutral. Most often, the Court acts in this area where the president and the Congress are on the same side, to determine the constitutionality of legislation passed by the Congress and signed by the president. During the Watergate investigation, the courts refused to give the Senate Watergate Committee material the president claimed was protected by executive privilege, although the Supreme Court ordered similar material turned over to the special prosecutor. While the House Judiciary Committee, as noted earlier, stated its refusal to go to court to enforce its subpoenas for Nixon tapes in terms of its claim to the "sole power of impeachment," there were committee members concerned that the Court would refuse to decide the dispute and leave the conflicting powers of the presidency and the House in dangerously ambiguous posture.

In continuing institutional terms, the courts are of only marginal importance in the distribution of power between the president and the Congress. This conclusion stems not only from the traditional reluctance of the Supreme Court to enter the presidential-congressional fray. That reluctance is, in turn, based on the recognition by the federal judiciary that its actions are drops of water in the sea of relationships between the executive and legislative branches.

More than one federal judge, for example, ordered the continuance of the poverty program in the face of Nixon administration attempts in the early 1970s to cut some corners in closing it down. The effect of those decisions was simply to delay the termination of much of the program, not to decree its continuance.

The Congress has the appropriations power, as well as the power to legislate. House and Senate committees can investigate and harass the executive. The Senate has the power to confirm most major presidential appointees and to ratify treaties.

The president has the power of appointment. He can com-

mand wide publicity. Even when a president is relatively
unpopular, as Lyndon Johnson was in late 1967 and early
1968, there are always more congressmen of both parties
than he can accommodate who want to travel with him, sit
on the podium when he speaks, or attend bill-signing ceremonies. Perhaps most importantly, the president and the
executive departments have so much discretionary grant-
making and contracting authority that they can place such
congressionally coveted institutions as military bases, hospitals, federal office buildings, housing, schools, or day-care
centers in particular states and congressional districts and on
a politically timely basis. The courts can play a temporary
role in declaring illegal the refusal of a president to spend
appropriated funds or to allocate fuel to a particular state or
city. But over the long haul, there is little doubt as to the
response of any congressman, senator, governor, or mayor if
asked whether he would rather rely on the federal judiciary
to extract funds from a reluctant federal executive or
whether he would prefer to work it out in the political arena,
in a rough and tumble give-and-take with the president and
his aides.

The role of the federal judiciary in the relationship of the
president to the executive branch is of even less significance
than its role in the power relationship between the president
and the Congress. True, the courts can order a federal employee reinstated, declare a loyalty program unconstitutional, or impose stringent procedural requirements on the
manner in which a president exercises some of his power
vis-à-vis his own branch. But the president's ability to mold
the executive branch to his own image is likely to be inhibited more by powerful congressional committees and special-
interest groups who are constituents of particular departments and programs than by any actions the federal judiciary
can take.

What, then, is the role of the federal judiciary in putting
presidential power in perspective? Its role is critical to the
relationship of the press to the presidency and the protection
of the individual against the increasing intervention of the

federal executive in his life. The Warren Court intuitively sensed this role and acted forcefully to fulfill it. Failure to perceive the importance of protecting the press and the individual in the face of increasing presidential power could be the most costly error of the federal judiciary in the last quarter of the twentieth century.

In the 1960s, the Supreme Court moved to strengthen the posture of the press vis-à-vis the presidency and the power of the central executive. In a series of decisions, the Court protected the media from libel actions where public figures or public issues were involved, unless the plaintiffs could prove that the media acted in willful or reckless disregard of the truth. These decisions provide significant protection to the press in exposing abuses of executive power. They have made libel a difficult avenue of pursuit for public figures who desire to deter penetrating investigative reporting. They have given the press more power to investigate and publish. They have begun to recognize that the economic costs of trying libel lawsuits can have a chilling effect on the exercise of First Amendment rights by the press.

In *Branzburg v. Hayes,* the Supreme Court decided that the confidential sources of reporters were not protected where reporters had witnessed a crime and were called before a grand jury to testify. But the issue was decided narrowly, with the nine-man Court splitting four to four and its decision resting on a singularly narrow opinion of Mr. Justice Lewis Powell for the fifth vote. What may be particularly important is that, in *Branzburg,* the Supreme Court hitched the First Amendment star to news gathering: "Without protection of the right to gather news, the First Amendment rights of the press would be eviscerated." Publishing had long been protected, but *Branzburg* represented the first explicit recognition by the Supreme Court that the right to gather news was protected by the First Amendment.

Subsequent Supreme Court actions denying reporters access to interview prison inmates on their own terms have raised doubts about how firmly First Amendment rights are fastened to news gathering. But, since *Branzburg,* federal courts have protected the right of reporters to protect their confidential sources, a right of signal importance in the context of the presidency. So great is the power of the incumbent president that the bulk of the major revelations about controversial and corrupt presidential and executive branch actions come from sources in the executive or legislative branches who would not dare to speak if their identity were revealed. Similarly, insights into complex foreign and domestic policies of a president are often available to the working press only on a background or nonattributable basis.

Just as the thin white line stands between a compact car and a Mack truck speeding in opposite directions on a highway, so the thin line of the First Amendment stands between the press and the power of the presidency. With few, if any, exceptions the press is no economic match for the presidency, and the fragile nature of its economic viability is not likely to change. It remains for the federal judiciary to provide the protective armor the press needs to continue as a free and powerful counterforce to the exercise of presidential power.

The second critical role of the federal judiciary in putting presidential power in perspective relates to the preservation of individual rights. The years 1965 and 1966 were among the most legislatively productive for the Johnson administration. The "Great 89th Congress," as the president and press hailed it, enacted, as we have seen, scores of bills that gave the federal executive unprecedented access into everyday American life and all manner of private institutions.

At the same moment in our nation's history, the Supreme Court sensed and acted on the need to carve out an especially resilient shell to protect the individual. As Johnson constructed the present-day model for a profoundly interventionist presidential government, the Court simultaneously erected safeguards to help preserve the citizen's treasured liberties from the inevitable encroachments of the powerful state.

Some sense of the importance of the Supreme Court's intervention on behalf of the individual—and its relevance to the protection of individual rights in the face of executive power—can be gleaned from a few of its decisions during the 1966–1967 term, two years before the era of the Warren

Court came to a close, at the peak of Johnson's legislative and executive power:

—In *Berger v. New York*, the Court struck down a New York state statute which allowed eavesdropping upon the oath of the attorney general, or any district attorney or police officer who stated that "There is reasonable ground to believe that evidence of crime may be thus obtained." The Court found that this statute violated the Fourth Amendment's command that a warrant can be issued only upon probable cause, as well as its prohibition against unreasonable search and seizure.

—In *United States v. Wade*, the Court held that the Sixth Amendment guaranteed an accused the right to counsel, not only at his trial, but at every critical confrontation with the prosecution during pretrial proceedings.

—In *In Re Gault*, the Court applied the due process requirements of the Fourteenth Amendment and the Fifth Amendment privilege against self-incrimination to a fifteen-year-old juvenile. The Court held for the first time that juveniles charged as delinquents (and their parents) were entitled to adequate written notice, and the right to be represented by counsel.

—In *United States v. Laub*, the Court held that a citizen could not be deprived of the right to travel abroad without due process of law, and struck down an indictment of fifty-eight U.S. citizens whose passports, although otherwise valid, were not specifically endorsed for travel to Cuba.

—In *Keyishian v. Board of Regents*, the Court held that public employment could not be conditioned upon the surrender of constitutional rights and that mere membership in the Communist party without specific intent to further its unlawful aims was not a constitutionally valid basis for sanctions. The New York State teacher loyalty laws and regulations involved were declared unconstitutional.

Repeatedly, in 1966 and 1967, the federal judiciary acted to protect individual rights in the face of increasingly intrusive government at every level. This role snugly fits the constitutional requirement that the courts face a case or controversy before acting and falls well within the boundaries of their moral power. Americans, left, middle, and right, treasure what remains of their options for individual choice and are likely to support the Supreme Court in this area. There will, of course, be controversy, especially over the individual rights of criminal suspects. But as larger numbers of Americans face the burdens and inhumanities of dealing with the central executive bureaucracy (and other bureaucracies as well), they will more and more come to appreciate the politically priceless value of the federal judiciary in this area. Over time, the Supreme Court may well acquire a broad popular sovereignty if it acts forcefully to protect individual rights in the face of any improper encroachments of incumbent presidential power.

Less clear is the role of the court in the politics of presidential aspirants. For almost two centuries, the federal judiciary considered the drama of presidential politics too unstructured for any attempts at judicial script writing. Then, on March 26, 1962, in *Baker v. Carr* and thereafter in a series of related decisions, the Supreme Court stepped into what Justice Felix Frankfurter had characterized as an out-of-bounds "political thicket." They ruled that political divisions not drawn to give one man's vote equal weight with another's were unconstitutional. It was the kind of negative ruling that required extensive action, reapportionment on a scale that impacted critically, first on state legislatures, then on congressional districts.

In 1972, the federal courts moved to center stage in the quadrennial drama of presidential politics. The Circuit Court for the District of Columbia twice reviewed the formula by which Democrats had allocated delegates among the several states and found it constitutionally sound. Lower Federal courts assumed a leading role in the credentials contests of the Democratic party, interpreting party rules and reviewing the compliance of the politicians with them. Issues relating to seating the George McGovern delegates in California and the Richard Daley delegates in Illinois reached the Supreme Court on the eve of the Democratic Convention.

Largely because of lack of time, the Court declined to review the merits of those cases, but not without revealing the mixed feelings of several justices about the need and judicial propriety of intervention into such profoundly political events.

Lower federal courts have indicated a willingness to move somewhat more forcefully onto the political stage, apparently concerned about the value of an individual's vote in the process by which electorate choices for president are effectively narrowed to two candidates. Judicial lines between the constitutional freedom to organize a political party and the need to protect the precious vote of each citizen are difficult to sketch. But it seems fair to conclude that the federal judiciary is likely to move into this area in a gingerly effort to protect the vote of each individual. In January 1975, the Supreme Court decided that national party delegate selection rules are beyond the reach of state law, but the mix of opinions in that case leaves room for judicial intervention to monitor at least some elements relating to the fairness of party presidential nominating procedures. The concern of legal commentators, like John Kester in the *Virginia Law Review*, about this prospect is reminiscent of the early Jeffersonians: "If the political process itself becomes structured, organized, and restricted by government [the courts], what check on government [the courts] is left?"

There remains, in any analysis of the presidency in judicial perspective, the whirlpool of legal controversies that swirled about the Watergate scandals. As indicated earlier, the Supreme Court blessed the doctrine of executive privilege, but refused to honor it in the face of a prosecutor's subpoena for evidence relevant to a criminal trial. The right to indict a sitting president remains unresolved, but the Court's refusal to hear argument on the grand jury's citation of Richard Nixon as an unindicted coconspirator leaves that action standing. The power of a grand jury, prosecutor, or defendant in a criminal case to subpoena a president also was not clearly resolved, but the deferential language of the Supreme Court in the Nixon executive privilege case and the actions of the special prosecutor and lower courts during

Watergate investigations and trials tend to indicate that no such power would be held to exist.

But these are issues relevant to presidents suspected of criminality, in possession of evidence relevant to criminal proceedings, or involved in activities sufficiently questionable to justify a serious impeachment inquiry. The ramifications of such determinations are likely to have little effect on the institutional forces at play on the power of the presidency. In rare situations, the judicial resolution of these issues can make it easier or more difficult for a president to overstep the bounds of public morality, perhaps even into criminality. Such cases will be rare. The actions of the federal judiciary are likely to be of less significance than those of the Congress, the press, and the American people in inhibiting such conduct in the future.

What the federal judiciary does to strengthen the rights of the press and individual citizens is of much greater significance in positioning the power of the presidency in democratic perspective than any steps the courts are likely to take in head-on confrontation with the presidency itself. The power of the Supreme Court to say "no" to the exercise of executive power against the press or the individual citizen under the Bill of Rights is of much more importance in curbing abuses of presidential power than its ability to define the limits of executive privilege or the powers of a grand jury or congressional committee to investigate the president. The Supreme Court has become the critical battleground for the protection of individual liberty and institutions that give meaning to that liberty in the face of necessarily intrusive governmental power.

A free press is always likely to (and should) stand in a persistently skeptical, often adversary, relationship to government. To the extent that government cannot use the press to achieve its goals, it is inevitable and natural that government will fight back. Can the free press hold its own against the presidentially concentrated power of the federal executive? Not unless it can count on the Supreme Court as a sure and trustworthy defender. Even if the Supreme Court provides relentless support for the press, the resolution of the issue is by no means free from doubt. States' rights and private property rights bowed to the presidency before the pressure of popular government, technology, and national economic and social crises. The 1960s and early 1970s have borne witness to repeated instances of popular wrath targeted at a press perceived to be the maker rather than the messenger of bad news.

If, as Justice Robert Jackson suggested, the cause of "effective" government is of special constitutional importance to the Federal judiciary, the cause of individual freedom will always be in jeopardy. As problems, such as population and environmental control, human and traffic congestion, inflation, unemployment, and the maldistribution of wealth, emerge to threaten the survival of the American civilization, the public pressure for discipline, regimentation, and "effective" presidential government is likely to increase, at the expense of individual and press freedoms. The press has learned a great deal about the abuse of presidential and political power from the Watergate scandals, but the politicians have also learned a great deal about the press.

The critical question for the Supreme Court, as it views the presidency, is not the proper apportionment of power among the various branches, levels, and agencies of government. Nor is it the proper role of presidential government in the economic and social affairs of the United States. Those questions, after two hundred years of history, have finally been resolved.

The federal judiciary must address, in the context of the modern presidency, the ancient dilemmas of personal liberty versus public welfare and of personally treasured individuality versus state-sponsored egalitarianism. Alexis de Tocqueville suggested that those were the critical issues of American democracy. What is the appropriate quantum of private freedom in the face of transcendent social problems which may only be solved by deep and pervasive intrusions of presidential power? Given the multitude and magnitude of the foreseeable problems, there is no certainty that the balance can be maintained between personal liberty as guaranteed by the Bill of Rights and the effective, aggressive, problem-solving presidential government that may be required for survival. It is here, where the power of the presidency and the rights of the people and the press meet, that the federal judiciary faces its greatest opportunity and challenge—to put that power in the perspective of those rights.

IX

---··❦··---

PERSONALITY:
The Paramount Demand
for Loyalty

The presidency is not self-executing. Its power must be exercised by human beings, endowed with free wills and fallible, corruptible human natures like any of us. Yet, as F. Scott Fitzgerald noted of the very rich, presidents are different from you and me. The electoral process through which they pass to achieve office in their own right is both exhausting and invigorating, brutalizing and humanizing. It tends to exaggerate their strengths to the people who vote to elect them and to themselves, and to expose their weaknesses to their opponents and their personal and professional intimates. Surviving the political obstacle course to the White House demands a single-mindedness of purpose that subordinates family, friends, and sometimes personal health and material wealth—all that most Americans value—to the quest for presidential power.

Men who covet presidential power believe they can exercise it more effectively than any of their 220 million fellow Americans. For them, election to office transubstantiates their belief into objective fact. They arrive at the White House exhilarated by the cheers of Inaugural Day supporters, with a somewhat self-induced conviction that the presidential cup could not have been passed to better hands, determined to deploy all the power at their disposal to fulfill their publicly celebrated responsibility to serve the people.

How presidents exercise their power to fulfill that responsibility reflects their personality characteristics. To the extent these characteristics are common to that special breed of American who seeks and acquires presidential power, the identification and understanding of them can serve to inform the national effort to put presidential power in perspective. Psychohistorians tend to focus attention on personality and psychological idiosyncrasies of individual presidents. Such characteristics can, of course, affect a particular presidency. But they are less relevant to the development of systematic and institutional checks and balances on the exercise of presidential power than the identification of personality traits common to most presidents.

Personality, for purposes of this analysis, is essentially the body of inherited and acquired emotional, behavioral, spiritual, and character traits, informed by life experience, that a president brings to the exercise of power. Truly invested personality traits should not be confused with superficial personality differences. The sheer politics of attaining the presidency and the media coverage of presidents tend to exaggerate the publicly received images of personality disparities between successive presidents. The presidential aspirant seeks to project a personality contrast not only with his opponent, but also with the incumbent, whether or not they are members of the same political party. If elected, the new president will recognize that the American people chose him, in part at least, because they wanted a stylistic change from his predecessor. Providing that "change" is usually his easiest campaign promise to fulfill. New presidents, with the enthusiastic collusion of the White House press corps, tend to hyperbolize their differences in style and personality from their predecessors.

Even as they pursue the same policies, most presidents will almost certainly want to project public personalities quite different from their immediate predecessors. The patrician

Roosevelt was succeeded by the country-boy, down-to-earth Truman. Eisenhower was a fatherly president, appearing to move deliberately and slowly, in contrast to the "I'm one of the boys" Truman manner that sometimes projected to the American people a sense of shooting from the hip. The predominate "get the country moving again" ambiance of John Kennedy's brief presidency was as pointedly contrasted with Eisenhower's two-term reign as their disparate athletic symbols, touch football and golf. Kennedy played the impatient son to Dwight Eisenhower's cautious father. Lyndon Johnson was a striking public personality in contrast to Kennedy—earthy Texas versus sophisticated Harvard; shrewd and experienced Southern legislator versus buoyant, inexperienced Lancelot.

Richard Nixon and his image makers strove mightily to provide a superficial personality impression of sharp divergence from Johnson and Kennedy. Where Kennedy was glamorous and Johnson flamboyant, Nixon was molded middle-American and square. In contrast to Johnson's voracious consumption of newspapers, wire service tickers, news magazines, and evening television shows, Nixon's men portrayed a president who had no time for such transient early drafts and polaroid photographs of history. Nixon's lonely contemplation played well against Johnson's gregarious image.

For Gerald Ford, the task of projecting a public personality contrast to Nixon was aided and abetted by a more than willing Washington press corps. He was open, not secret; a common man living in a middle-class Virginia suburb, not an imperial leader with two seaside estates. After Nixon's long separation and eventual divorce from the Congress, Ford sought not the traditional honeymoon but a lasting marriage. His would not be a "Madison Avenue" presidency, his aides backgrounded, but rather one of substance working on the problems of the average American. Although never explicitly stated from the White House, the message was clear: Ford was an honest man, not a corrupt politician; perhaps not brilliant, but certainly not malevolent.

Such public projections are, more often than not, superficial differences, "received impressions" as Republican speechwriter Ray Price put it. These publicly presented personality attributes are more image than reality. They can provide temporary tactical cover, but rarely do they evidence the kind of personality traits that affect the selection or achievement of public policy objectives by an incumbent president.

Nevertheless, the people's perception of the public personality of an aspiring presidential candidate can be decisive in determining whether they give him an opportunity to exercise presidential power. The overwhelming victories of Lyndon Johnson in 1964 and Richard Nixon in 1972 are testaments to the electorate's perception of their and their opponents' public personalities. The people perceived Johnson as a man with the personality to hold the nation and the world together and on course; he had performed brilliantly in the wake of the Kennedy assassination and the economy had begun to sparkle. By contrast, Goldwater was the mad bomber of the nuclear age, erratic and extreme, splitting even his own party apart. In 1972, despite an embryonic uneasiness about Watergate, Nixon was perceived as holding things together, winding down the Vietnam War, bringing an era of relative domestic tranquility after the turbulent final years of Johnson. In contrast, the people sensed a fearful disorientation in George McGovern's publicly revealed personality, reflected in the split of the Democratic party, his radically perceived ideas about drugs, demonstrators, and demogrants, and the Eagleton fiasco.

Over the course of a four- or eight-year incumbency, the American people and the media are remarkably adept at peeling off the publicly projected image of their president to reveal his true personality. Those true personality characteristics can mark not only the way an incumbent president exercises his power, but also the amount of power he has to exercise. They can often be decisive in his achievement of public policy objectives and, within broad ideological commitments, occasionally determine the selection of those objectives he seeks to achieve.

As we shall see, the personality traits common to most

presidents include ambition, the desire to exercise power, egocentricity (sometimes, but not always accompanied by self-confidence), the ability to lead men, the willingness to sacrifice (consciously or unconsciously) personal and family life in the pursuit and exercise of presidential power. Presidential personalities commonly reflect an ability to act with pragmatic (sometimes cold and ruthless) detachment to accomplish what they perceive as worthy national goals, an ample measure of calculation and secretiveness in molding and responding to events, and an awareness that history will someday render a judgment on their presidential trusteeship. Persistence, skepticism informed by a peculiar combination of curiosity and insecurity that inspires meticulous attention to detail, and a burning desire to achieve also mark the presidential personality. The depth and dominance of each of these common personality traits will vary with individual presidents and at different moments during their incumbencies, but the paramount characteristic common to most presidents is their need for loyalty and a determination to satisfy that need so consuming that it occasionally ignites latent sparks of paranoia.

The need and demand for loyalty should be apparent to anyone who reads presidential history and is obvious to those who help a president make it. Most presidents vigilantly confine their confidences to advisors of demonstrated loyalty. There are wide differences of degree, but the bruising realities of national politics and presidential incumbency tend to summon whatever paranoia lurks within the personality of a chief executive. Nixon's paranoia helped drive him, and his top aides, beyond the bounds of constitutional fidelity and moral decency. But Roosevelt, Kennedy, and Johnson, as well as Truman and Eisenhower, were persistently concerned that those serving close to them evidence an overriding sense of "loyalty to the president." Mistakes, even occasional incompetence, could be understood and forgiven, but not disloyalty.

Presidents tend to equate loyalty to integrity. Eisenhower could not believe that Sherman Adams received anything from Bernard Goldfine because he could not accept that a man so loyal would commit an act that indicated a preference for Goldfine (or even himself) over his president. Truman's reaction to the Harry Vaughan scandal reflected a similar attitude. Johnson shattered his father-son relationship with Bill Moyers less because he felt Moyers was promoting himself than because Johnson came to believe it was being done at his expense and, hence, disloyally. When Johnson talked about the split after the event, he would say with evident personal hurt, "That boy lacks integrity." Early in his presidency, Kennedy tried to sweep the executive branch clean of Eisenhower men not only to assure that policy-making positions were manned by loyal Democrats, but because so many Republicans were thought to lack the necessary integrity. Johnson told Nixon in late 1968 that one of his mistakes was not to replace many of the Kennedy loyalists promptly after he assumed office, because he felt their loyalty to the Kennedys compromised their integrity.

The congenial reflection of a president's demand for loyalty is his need to feel politically and personally comfortable with the men around him, particularly those on the White House staff. It is no surprise that John Kennedy placed so many "Irish mafia" on his staff: Kenneth O'Donnell, Larry O'Brien, Richard Donahue, or that his staff was so crowded with Roman Catholics. It was natural for him to reserve his greatest confidences for his brother, Robert, whose loyalty was total and unwavering. Similarly, it is no accident that Lyndon Johnson brought so many Texans to the White House: Jack Valenti, Bill Moyers, Harry McPherson, Walter Jenkins, Marvin Watson, Horace Busby. So, too, the staff of Richard M. Nixon reflected his California instincts and ambitions with men like H. R. (Bob) Haldeman, John Ehrlichman, Robert Finch, and Herbert Klein. Men like this are essential for a president. They are intimately close to him; they have shared many of his experiences; they satisfy his need for personal loyalty.

For the most part (with notable exceptions like Henry Kissinger during the Nixon and Ford administrations) the men on the White House staff are young and have clearly hitched their political and public-service ambitions to the president. They are men whom a president believes will serve him personally, who have not reached that stage of life where they want independence of schedule and who have enough physical energy to work twelve to fifteen hours a day, six or seven days a week.

Most importantly, they have demonstrated their personal loyalty to him by commitments that have involved real sacrifices of other human values: family, personal comfort, independent lives. That loyalty often transcends ideological beliefs. Marvin Watson was Lyndon Johnson's appointments secretary; he was conservative politically, perhaps closer ideologically to John Tower and Barry Goldwater than even the Democratic middle. But he worked as hard as anyone on the Johnson domestic staff to achieve the most liberal legislative goals announced and achieved in this century.

There is an ideological chasm between the strident cold-war foreign policy often expressed by John Kennedy and some of his national goals (like placing an American on the moon by the end of the sixties, whatever the cost) and the foreign policies and domestic priorities enunciated by Robert Kennedy in 1968 and by Edward Kennedy in the 1970s. Yet the same men who served John Kennedy in the early sixties displayed identical, unwavering loyalty to his brother Robert in 1968 and his brother Ted in the seventies. The trust the Kennedy brothers placed in these men was founded in their personal loyalty, not their ideological commitment.

The psychological need of a president for loyalty reflects the reality of his political position. Presidents need men around them who bleed when they are cut. That kind of dedication can be essential to extracting from those men the utmost their talents can produce to deal with seemingly intractable public problems; for example, to seek settlements in the Middle East; effective arms-control agreements; and solutions to the racial, poverty, and economic problems that confront this nation. But if a presidential personality demands a knee-jerk loyalty that suffocates debate and inhibits public policy options from reaching his desk, then it has merely reflected his own insecurity and has badly served his interests and those of the people. Such a personality

penchant intrudes seriously to the detriment of the intelligent formulation of public policy that the people have a right
to expect. The president holds loyalty in its most productive
perspective when he perceives loyalty rendered by aides
who argue with him, press him with new ideas, and help him
to face unpalatable realities.

The complexity of modern government and leadership
requires that a president assemble a variety of skills on his
White House staff. Although the talents and abilities of his
staff members may differ widely—one may be expert in national or international affairs, another an economist, others
proficient writers, systems analysts, or lawyers—they will
commonly incline to identify the public interest with the
interests of the president they serve. Rarely do these specially skilled presidential staffers become intimates of the
president in the way Hopkins was to Roosevelt or Valenti to
Johnson. But, unless the president perceives them as loyal,
they are not likely to get close enough to use their skills
effectively and others will soon replace them.

Every president has (and needs) a few intensely loyal staff
members who will do exactly what he directs. But wise presidents keep such staffers out of the public policy process and
concentrate their efforts in administrative and routine political matters. They make sure all the details of political trips,
meetings, television appearances, speeches, and ceremonies
are exactly as the president wants them. Their self-described
task is the important one of "easing the administrative burdens of the president." They occasionally also perform some
unpleasant and delicate work for a president (firing a cabinet
officer, for example) and can be relied upon to perform such
work precisely as directed. Kenneth O'Donnell filled such a
role for Kennedy; Marvin Watson for Johnson. Nixon's man
Haldeman candidly described his own view of this role, "Every president needs a son of a bitch and I am Nixon's."

But, when to render loyalty to a president requires commission of a crime for him, then this presidential personality
trait has become warped beyond the bounds of national tolerance. The president's demand for loyalty has combined
with his sense of indispensibility or self-preservation (or both)

to endanger our democracy. That kind of loyalty is morally and politically unacceptable in any humane society. But the experience of the American nation in the early 1970s with corrupt loyalty (to the point of perjury and obstruction of justice) should not blind us to the essential and healthy role a president's demand for loyalty plays in the fulfillment of his constitutional responsibilities and the legitimate exercise of his power.

Presidential attitudes toward press leaks are bottomed in their overriding concern about loyalty. Presidents prefer debates over public policy alternatives to be conducted within their official family and not in the public press. One of the most serious breaches of the relationship between a president and a White House aide or cabinet officer can result from the unauthorized (by the president) or premature release of information. Presidents regard unauthorized leaks as acts of disloyalty to them. This is the psychological basis of the rage that every recent president has expressed over leaks of information. Where the information is classified, they are, of course, concerned about the national security. But the true basis of their anger, and the precipitate action it often inspires, is their conviction that the leak evidences an act of disloyalty. Presidents and White House national security advisers at presidential direction have leaked more classified information since 1960 than all the disaffected State Department, Defense Department, and Central Intelligence Agency employees combined. During the Nixon administration, Henry Kissinger provided more classified information to selected reporters than they had ever before received. Yet Nixon, in his paranoid obsession about disloyalty, with Kissinger designating targets, took the most severe steps, including wiretapping his own aides, to "stop the leaks."

Kennedy and Johnson were often enraged about leaks. The Kennedy White House searched for sources of leaks out of the Pentagon in a manner that made patriotism (national security) and loyalty to the president synonymous. Johnson's ire at leaks involving future personnel appointments sometimes reflected his desire to have "all the ducks in a row," particularly where the slightest problem with Senate confirmation could be anticipated. Where Johnson changed appointments because of leaks, he usually suspected that the proposed appointee was the source of the news story. Then his action was motivated not so much by annoyance at the leak as by concern about the loyalty of the proposed appointee. Johnson felt that a man, who could be seduced by the allurements of the press corps even before he was appointed, could not be trusted to choose president over press after appointment to a position that would make him even more desirable prey. (Here, as so often, the exception helps prove the rule. When Johnson concluded that the leak of Walter Washington's appointment as the District of Columbia's first mayor stemmed from Washington's intimate friendship with Washington *Post* metropolitan editor Ben Gilbert, he went forward with the appointment because of the significant advantage he thought that relationship might provide the first Black mayor of the capital city.)

Presidents prefer to fill posts in their administration with appointees who have demonstrated their loyalty. With the hundreds of appointments available to a new president, he will not know most of his appointees, much less be able personally to judge their fidelity to him. Where such judgments cannot be based on personal experience, presidents and their aides have other means of making some tentative judgments about loyalty: the past career of the proposed appointee, the FBI reports of the full field investigation that usually precedes appointment to a major position, conversations with friends and enemies, professional and personal associates. Where such information is insufficient to assure the loyalty of the prospective appointee, presidents can usually seek a demonstration of personal devotion. Will he take a lesser position for a few months until the big opening occurs? In a cruelly demanding sense, the prospective appointee can be left in an ambiguous position for weeks or months under the president's watchful eye. This can be nerve-racking for the individual, witness the months Nicholas Katzenbach served as "acting" attorney general after Robert Kennedy left to run for the U.S. Senate, and the agonizing hiatus between establishment of the Department of Housing and Urban Development and the Johnson nomination of Robert Weaver to be its first secretary.

But the president often considers loyalty of sufficient importance to justify long periods of testing. The post of attorney general is a particularly sensitive one and presidents like to be sure of the man they put in it. Kennedy wanted his brother; Nixon his former law partner and campaign manager, John Mitchell. Katzenbach passed the brutal waiting test during the Johnson administration and became one of the president's wisest and most respected advisers, not simply on legal matters within his jurisdiction as attorney general, but across the spectrum of public policy, including a most influential (if unsung) role, as undersecretary of state, in the Vietnam decisions reflected in Johnson's March 1968 speech withdrawing as a presidential candidate. But dangling a man who yearns for permanent status in an acting position for too long is not without risks. L. Patrick Gray destroyed incriminating Watergate files while he coveted the permanent post of FBI director.

Not every presidential appointment is predicated on the president's psychological and political need for loyalty. The men a president appoints to his cabinet, to chair commissions, and to head the major agencies of the government sometimes reflect his personality and experience, but to a significantly lesser degree than do his White House staff appointments. There are often overriding considerations. Some of the positions, like the president's science adviser or the chairman and members of the Council of Economic Advisers, are highly specialized. Others, such as secretary of defense, are so inordinately demanding managerially and intellectually that most presidents will go far beyond their own circles to seek qualified appointees.

Sometimes men with distinctly different talents are needed at various times in the development of the same department. During 1964 and early 1965, when the bulk of his most controversial and far-reaching health and education proposals was working its way through the Congress, Johnson needed a secretary of health, education and welfare who knew how to lobby, had experienced the rough-and-tumble insecurity of elective life, and understood that congressmen could not be asked to cast votes or take actions that endangered their constituency support. The legislation was of critical importance: medicare and medicaid; the elementary, secondary, and higher education legislation; and a number of important related measures. For this task Anthony Celebrezze, the secretary already appointed by Kennedy, was ideal. He was bright, affable, respected on Capitol Hill as a successful politician, and comfortable in the give and take of tough legislative battles. He was effective in what the president regarded as his major task, to help persuade a majority of the Congress to enact the legislation.

Once this complex legislation was passed, however, Johnson needed someone who could add a special prestige to service in the department and who could attract the kind of brilliant and imaginative talent necessary to operate programs as sophisticated as Johnson and Celebrezze had persuaded the Congress to enact. When Celebrezze became a federal judge, the president chose John Gardner for the second phase. With credentials as an intellectual and his background as president of the Carnegie Foundation, he brought a level of establishment prestige unprecedented for that department. Johnson's estimate of Gardner's ability to attract bright and talented assistants to the Department of Health, Education and Welfare was on the mark. He lured William Gorham, a brilliant systems analyst from Robert McNamara's pool of whiz kids. He made the indefatigably dedicated Wilbur Cohen his undersecretary. Harold H. (Doc) Howe became the commissioner of education. Better doctors and scientists were attracted to the National Institutes of Health and the Food and Drug Administration. Gardner provided the department with leadership and an ambiance that made it the kind of place where bright young lawyers, analysts, educators, scientists, doctors, and social workers wanted to be.

Presidents can also use their power of appointment to help achieve broader political or social goals. To some extent, such appointments may reflect a president's personality penchant for loyalty, but it is not the paramount consideration. Lyndon Johnson believed that it was not simply enough to pass and enforce civil rights laws, that it would be difficult to change the habits and prejudices of several generations, and that it was important to show to the large institutions of American society, like business, labor, and the professions, that there were Black men and women in America who were capable of performing the most important tasks of our society. Johnson considered it especially important to demonstrate to the young Blacks on the streets of Watts, Harlem, and Hough and on the poor farms of Alabama, Mississippi, and Louisiana that, in the United States, there was room for them at the top.

He set out quite deliberately to place Blacks in the highest and most visible posts in the nation. He appointed young blacks like Roger Wilkins and Clifford Alexander to top positions—Wilkins as an assistant attorney general at the Justice Department, Alexander as chairman of the Equal Employment Opportunity Commission.

He named the first Black cabinet officer, Robert Weaver, as secretary of housing and urban development. He carefully picked Weaver and orchestrated the announcement of the appointment with the same shrewdness Branch Rickey displayed when he brought Jackie Robinson to the Brooklyn Dodgers. Preparation for the appointment was as tough on Weaver as it had been on Robinson. Support was carefully lined up on Capitol Hill and in January of 1966, shortly after the 90th Congress convened, the first Black nominated to the cabinet was swiftly confirmed by the Senate.

Johnson first met Thurgood Marshall when they worked together to get a Black student admitted to the University of Texas. He groomed Marshall, as solicitor general, for more than a year before nominating him to the Supreme Court. When Justice Tom Clark resigned on June 12, 1967, it was clear within the White House staff that, if Johnson decided to appoint a Black to the Supreme Court, Marshall would be the one. But there was an alternative to Marshall, for some thought that Johnson should place the first woman on the Supreme Court. One evening shortly before the nomination of Thurgood Marshall was announced, I was sitting in the family bedroom with the president and Mrs. Johnson. He was discussing the question of Supreme Court nominations, as he had undoubtedly done with any number of people. During the discussion, Mrs. Johnson displayed a preference for appointing the first woman to the Supreme Court. Her point was not political; it was a typically straightforward argument. She thought it was important to put a woman on the court; it was time and there were several qualified women. The woman in Johnson's mind was Shirley Hufstedler, a judge sitting on the Federal Court of Appeals in California. However, it became abundantly clear during the discussion that Lyndon Johnson had made up his mind to put the first Black on the court.

That left the Federal Reserve Board, the austere body that controls the federal banking system in the United States. When Canby Balderston's term expired as a member of the Board and the search began for a replacement, the initial reaction of many people in government and banking was that no Black bankers or economists were "technically sophisticated" enough to sit on the Board. Johnson refused to accept that assessment. Eventually he found, in his own bureaucratic back yard, Andrew Brimmer, who was then an assistant secretary of commerce. Brimmer was bright, Harvard educated, and more "technically sophisticated" than many of his predecessor Federal Reserve Board members. Johnson liked his record, and was impressed by the reports he received from Gardner Ackley and the Council of Economic Advisers on Brimmer's ability to handle the job.

On the day before the appointment was to be announced, Johnson became concerned about whether Brimmer would support his policies, most notably whether he shared Johnson's sense of the importance of low interest rates. It was, in some ways, remarkable and amusing. The president called and asked if I were absolutely certain that Andrew Brimmer would support his desire to hold interest rates down, or whether he would be overwhelmed by someone as brilliant and persuasive as William McChesney Martin, then chairman of the Federal Reserve Board who, to Johnson's distinct displeasure, had recently increased the discount rate.

"Has he gotten so involved with big business in the Commerce Department that he's forgotten what it's like to be a Black man?" Johnson asked.

"I think Brimmer favors low interest rates. That's what Gardner Ackley tells me," I replied.

The president shot back, "Thinking is not good enough. I want you to know so. Brimmer doesn't go on the Board until we know."

I called Ackley and others who knew Brimmer well professionally. Brimmer was reluctant to talk to them about what his policies would be once he became a member of the Federal Reserve Board; he considered it inappropriate. I tried, as discreetly as I could, to make it clear to the economists supporting Brimmer that if he considered it inappropriate to discuss his views on these subjects, the president might consider it inappropriate to put him on the Board. Eventually, on a Saturday afternoon, we contacted Brimmer; he had a talk with the president, at which the president concluded, as he later said, "Andy Brimmer hasn't forgotten what its like to be Black, to be a small farmer, to be a candy-store owner, to be a corner druggist, who needs to borrow some money to keep his business going without paying an exorbitant amount of interest to the New York bankers." Brimmer's nomination was promptly sent to the Senate.*

As an individual appointment, Brimmer, like Weaver and Marshall, reflected Johnson's overriding policy objectives more than his personality. The presidential demand for loyalty was in evidence, however: personal loyalty from Weaver, who was to head an executive branch cabinet department, and ideological loyalty from Marshall and Brimmer, who were placed in independent posts. (One of Johnson's special personality characteristics played a role in the sum total of those appointments. A Truman or a Kennedy might have concluded that desegregating the armed forces or placing the first Black in the cabinet was enough to make

*Once on the Federal Reserve Board, Brimmer voted his conscience and his expertise. He became as concerned as others there about the economic pressures prompted by the "guns and butter" budgets and the difficulty of obtaining congressional enactment of the necessary fiscal measures.

the point. Not a Johnson. Only the triple crown—the cabinet, the Supreme Court, and the Federal Reserve Board—would satisfy him.)

Whatever the dominant motivation in a particular appointment, however, presidents will expect loyal service and they will return that loyalty to those who provide it. Indeed, the significance presidents attach to loyalty is demonstrated by the politically costly actions they have taken in expressing loyalty down to those who have served them faithfully and well. An intense display of loyalty down is largely founded in the presidential perception of its importance to inspiring loyalty from others. Yet, while presidents from Washington to Ford have recognized that the bottom line is to protect their own presidency, such displays of loyalty down are not without altruistic motivation. Personal loyalty to close colleagues has often prompted presidents to take inappropriate actions or unnecessary political risks. Presidential history provides many examples, like Harry Truman and Harry Vaughan, Dwight Eisenhower and Sherman Adams.

The actions of Lyndon Johnson during the ferocious 1968 battle to obtain Senate confirmation of Abe Fortas as Supreme Court chief justice well illustrate the complex mixture of self-interest and altrusim that prompts presidential displays of loyalty down at high personal and political cost. A friend, adviser, and lawyer since New Deal days, Fortas had been one of Johnson's key intimates from the time of the president's razor-thin (87 vote) election to the U.S. Senate in 1948. When Johnson had pressed Fortas to go on the Supreme Court in 1965, Fortas sent a poignant hand-written plea to the president asking that he not be appointed. He expressed an obligation to stay with his law firm, and he enjoyed the good life that required a substantial income to maintain. Just a few minutes before Johnson announced the appointment at a July 1965 press conference, he told a reluctant Fortas, "I'm sending 50,000 American boys to Vietnam and I'm sending you to the Supreme Court as an associate justice. You can either watch the announcement on television in my office, or come with me to the East Room."

Three years later, when Earl Warren submitted his resignation, Johnson decided to nominate Fortas to be the new
chief justice and Federal Court of Appeals Judge Homer
Thornberry to replace Fortas. For Johnson, this represented
a Court that would continue in liberal support of his own
public policy viewpoints, particularly on racial issues. But it
also fulfilled one of his frequent claims, that he always gave
more than he promised to those who served him loyally, as
Fortas had, even to the point of becoming an associate justice
when he preferred to stay in private law practice.

The Senate Judiciary committee hearing was stormy. Most
senators knew that Fortas the Supreme Court justice had
remained a close adviser to the president on everything from
the Vietnam War to economic policy and domestic disturbances. Several expressed serious reservations about the propriety of a member of the highest court maintaining such an
intimate public policy and personal relationship with an incumbent president. Initially couched in separation of powers
rhetoric, the issue took hold in the context of cronyism,
fueled by the fact that, like Fortas, Thornberry was a close
personal and political friend of Johnson.

Rumors started to circulate one day that Senate Minority
Whip Robert Griffin had "something that would kill the Fortas confirmation." That afternoon I received a call from Paul
Porter, who with Fortas and Thurmond Arnold had built one
of the finest law firms in the nation. Porter wished to see me
immediately about the Fortas nomination. As soon as he sat
down in my office, it was clear that he was profoundly sad and
disturbed. He handed me a copy of a letter he had written,
with the addressee blocked out, soliciting $5,000 for Fortas
to conduct a seminar at American University during the
prior summer. As soon as I read it, I asked, "Was this sent to
clients of Arnold and Porter?"

"To five of them" Porter replied, "and they all contributed." Tears were welling in the eyes of this singularly
big-hearted and humane man. Fortas was not only his former
law partner; Porter was bound to him in the kind of friendship that is stronger than any blood ties. "Of course," Porter
continued, "Abe disqualified himself from any matters in-

volving our law firm or any of its clients."

Neither of us verbalized what we were thinking: If Griffin had the letter, we would never be able to get the two-thirds Senate vote necessary to block the coming filibuster. In the climate that existed in the Senate over the Fortas nomination —the charges of cronyism, the covert Nixon request that the nominees be held up until after the election, the threads of anti-Semitism, the liberal complexion of Fortas and Thornberry, the lame-duck status of Johnson—we both knew it was over.

Late that evening, I told Johnson about Porter's visit and showed him a copy of the letter. There had been some difficult decision on Vietnam, and he was not pleased with the day as it had gone. "What do you think?" he asked in an exhausted voice.

He knew the answer that I would give. "It's all over, unless we can find a miracle." Johnson paused to think and then said, "We will not withdraw the nomination. I won't do that to Fortas."

"Larry Temple [the White House Counsel who was monitoring the Senate vote count on the Fortas confirmation] thinks we can still get it on the floor," I commented, since the two of us had already talked about the letter.

"I know that and I want to have a full Senate vote on cloture," Johnson said. "Even if we do not get two-thirds, we will get a majority on the floor. With a majority of the Senate for him, Abe will be able to stay on the Court with his head up. We have to do that for him."

Johnson pressed the Senate, which refused to invoke cloture on October 1, 1968. But a majority of those present (45–43) cast their vote to impose cloture, and by implication to support Fortas. Undoubtedly a mixture of presidential motives was involved. But I always felt that the paramount consideration in Johnson's mind was his loyalty to Fortas, a man who, whatever his weaknesses, had served Johnson faithfully and skillfully in many battles through many years. The risks were enormous for Johnson (and Fortas as well) because Fortas had been much more deeply involved in presidential actions and policies than the Senate Judiciary hearings had revealed. He had reviewed every State of the Union message, drafted the bulk of Johnson's politically charged attack on then Governor George Romney during the 1967 Detroit riots, and had even assisted in analyzing the constitutionality of acts passed by the Congress and in assessing the legality of Johnson's imposing wage, price, and credit controls without seeking special statutory authority. Despite these risks, Johnson's loyalty drove him to a bitter confrontation in the Senate, to press senators to vote for a losing and highly controversial cause, and to tear apart his long friendship with Georgia Senator Richard Russell.

Johnson's actions reflected a motivation quite common to the exercise of presidential power, a motivation of loyalty, mixed with guilt, because the president put the loyal aide, friend, or adviser in the difficult situation in the first place. For a president, such a politically risky display of loyalty down has a significant element of self-interest. It is essential that the hundreds of men and women who help him run the executive branch and who support him on Capital Hill realize that he will stand behind them. That is also why a president often stands behind officials who make mistakes, though he would never have taken the action in question and, indeed, might have opposed it.

X

PERSONALITY:
The Other Common Characteristics

Many of the common characteristics that mark the presidential personality are so obvious that they require no explanation. Ambition, the desire to exercise power, leadership ability, and the willingness to sacrifice personal and family life in the pursuit and exercise of presidential power are axiomatic traits of the presidential personality. The sense that history will render judgment on each man's presidency can be either an inspiration or a justification for a particular president; but it will inform all presidential personalities and motivate many presidential actions. There are other characteristics of the presidential personality whose commonality may not be so readily apparent.

An element of pragmatic, sometimes cold and ruthless, detachment is a personality ingredient common to most presidents. Such detachment can be essential to a president who wishes to take maximum advantage of unexpected events or to respond effectively to them. The exercise of presidential power often involves the selection of the lesser of two evils. The choice of high unemployment, with its corollary of human misery, or inflation, with its severe impact on the elderly and others on fixed incomes, is a classic example. The decision to wage war in the interest of national security requires a president to be sufficiently detached to bear the personal agony that derives from his knowledge that individual men and women will die prematurely as an inevitable result of his decision.

Lesser events also reflect a level of detachment. Presidents may sometimes chose the less-qualified candidate for a job, in order to secure the vote of a congressman considered essential to passage of major legislation they believe to be in the public interest. They often are required to take actions in pursuit of public policy that they know will end personal friendships extending back for decades or precipitate immediate and bitter opprobrium. More frequently than most Americans realize, they expose their own lives to danger in leadership appearances that are strongly opposed by the Secret Service.

Lyndon Johnson often displayed this quality of pragmatic detachment in using events to achieve his objectives. The Fair Housing Act was proposed by Johnson in 1966, 1967, and again early in 1968 without much success. The bill had passed the Senate but had been bottled up in the House Judiciary Committee for more than two years. Then, when Martin Luther King was assassinated, Johnson used the tragic event to press the Congress to pass the legislation. Within hours after King's death on April 4, 1968, Johnson began working to revive the moribund bill. He called House leaders of both parties and several other congressmen, urging them to bring the Senate bill to a vote on the floor of the House of Representatives. Johnson divided House members among the White House staff for them to contact in order to muster a majority for enactment. On April 10, 1968, six days after King's death, the House passed the Fair Housing Bill. Johnson signed it into law the following day. With mixed success, Johnson employed similar tactics to move stymied gun-control legislation through the Congress in the wake of the assassination of Robert Kennedy. After the initial shock, there was little time for grief in either situation.

This willingness of a president to use events with pragmatic detachment can also have an impact on the achievement of foreign policy objectives. When India experienced severe famine in 1966, its government requested that the United States provide millions of bushels of wheat to avoid mass starvation. Johnson decided to seize his opportunity.

For some time, he had attempted to move the Indian government to act forcefully in two areas: to require hoarding provinces to share their wheat with provinces in which millions were malnourished and dying of starvation; and, perhaps most important from Johnson's point of view, to proceed with a full-scale national birth control program. Sensitive to the much-violated article of State Department faith that "the United States does not get involved in the internal affairs of a foreign government," Secretary of State Dean Rusk, National Security Affairs adviser Walt Rostow, and others had gingerly attempted to move the Indian government to act in these areas. Subtle suggestion and discreet prodding had characterized their futile efforts. When Johnson said, "No wheat for India until they move on birth control and the hoarding provinces," they were appalled. So were Agriculture Secretary Orville Freeman, Foreign Aid Director William Gaud, and Averell Harriman who brought the Indian ambassador by to see Johnson one sunny afternoon and pressed for the wheat on behalf of the Indians. The visit served mainly to harden Johnson's position and to increase his skepticism about the advice he was getting from the State Department, AID, and the Agriculture Department. The president finally got his message across; his detached and cold persistence forced the Indians to embark urgently on a more effective and widely publicized birth control program and to pressure hoarding provinces to share their harvests.

Franklin Roosevelt's cold and pragmatic detachment in pitting his cabinet officers and his allies on Capitol Hill against one another to achieve his legislative goals is often cited as one of his uniquely sinister characteristics. While Roosevelt was known for his manipulation of top aides, often to their personal embarassment and discomfort, in order to achieve his objectives, most recent presidents have not hesitated to use similar tactics when they deemed it necessary. One of the best examples in the Johnson administration in-

volved Treasury Secretary Henry (Joe) Fowler and House
Banking Committee Chairman Wright Patman. Fowler was
one of Johnson's favorites in the cabinet and Patman had
been the president's friend and political ally for a generation,
beginning during the New Deal. To stem increases in the
prime rate by the major banks in early 1966, Johnson wanted
to turn loose the power of his administration and to deposit
federal funds in banks that held down interest rates (as well
as to remove such funds from banks that increased them).
Although generally inclined to use executive power to hold
down prices and wages, Fowler opposed the particular jawboning and action program Johnson sought to put into effect.
Johnson requested and received an analysis of interest rates
for the period Fowler had been Treasury secretary and discovered that, in percentage terms, those rates had risen
more during Fowler's brief tenure than during that of any
previous secretary in the twentieth century. Johnson immediately called Wright Patman and said, "Wright, there's
something you've just got to know. Interest rates have risen
faster under Joe Fowler than under any secretary in this
century."

Patman was appalled. "Something's got to be done about
that, Mr. President," he said.

"That's why I'm telling you," Johnson continued. "If I were
you, I'd send him a blistering letter and have him up to
testify. You've got to build a fire under him."

"You're absolutely right, Mr. President." By now Patman
was getting angry.

"You know, Wright, unless Fowler starts moving on these
banks, the New York bankers will just keep hiking the interest rates and rolling in the money. Your committee can't
stand for that."

"I'll write him today, Mr. President. We'll call him to testify this week."

By the time Johnson hung up, Patman was sputtering mad.
When Fowler received Patman's scathing letter, he called
the White House. Johnson passed the word that Fowler had
"better tell Patman you'll turn loose some pressure on the
banks or else he'll turn your hearing into a Texas barbeque."
Fowler agreed and Johnson got a jawboning program with

the banks off the ground. Fond as he was of Fowler, Johnson was sufficiently detached to realize that he had to give him a hard shove to get him moving.

Johnson often contrasted his own tough detachment with Hubert Humphrey's "politics of joy" during the 1968 campaign. There were occasions when he thought that Humphrey was losing because he would never go for the Nixon jugular. "You know the difference between Hubert and me," he told me on one of those occasions. "When Walter Reuther walks into the Oval Office and sits there with his hand in his pocket, telling Hubert that unless he puts more money into the Detroit ghettoes they'll burn the city down, Hubert will sit in this rocker listening and smiling, but thinking all the time: how can he get Reuther to take his hand out of pocket so he can shake it. When Reuther comes to me with a threat like that, I'm sitting in this rocker, listening and smiling, but thinking all the time: how can I get him to take his hand out of his pocket so I can cut his balls off!"

A measure of detachment is also essential to most presidents if they are to weather the bitter struggles that precede the most satisfying victories as well as the devastating defeats that occur during any incumbency. Every president assumes office with friends and enemies. Once in office, they are likely to make more enemies than friends. It is imperative for the good of the nation and the functioning of the government that a president have sufficient pragmatic detachment to distinguish when he has made a profoundly personal enemy from when he has simply been in a politically or ideologically professional fight over an issue.

Johnson's reaction to the defeat of the Fortas nomination, for example, was one of sad resignation. He harbored no personal grudge against senators like Everett Dirksen and Richard Russell, whom he believed had committed to vote with him and then backed off. He had no sense, as Richard Nixon did after defeat of the nominations of Clement Haynsworth and Harold Carswell, that a group of intense personal enemies had conspired to deny him in the Senate. Of course, Johnson didn't like losing; no president does. But he realized that, even in the twilight days of his presidency, there was work to do and he would need some of the men who voted against Fortas to help with that work.

Where presidents fail to recognize that an enemy on one issue can be an ally on another, they serve the people badly. The relationship between Johnson and Senate Foreign Relations Committee Chairman William Fulbright is an example of a total break. Johnson and Fulbright were split on two central policies of the administration: the Vietnam War and civil rights for Black Americans. Their personalities clashed more sharply with each nasty jibe the other heard second-hand. On his final night in office, Johnson mused to me, "Perhaps it would have been different with Fulbright if we had only talked to him more, had him over here more, found some things to agree with him on. We should never have let the fight become so personal."

If the Johnson-Fulbright relationship is the how-not-to of presidential personality politics, the Johnson-Wayne Morse relationship is the how-to. Senator Morse was among the earliest and most vociferous of Johnson's opponents on the Vietnam War. Morse was also a critical linchpin in the enactment of the education legislation during the Johnson administration. Both as chairman of the Education Subcommittee of the Senate Committee on Labor and Public Welfare and as a respected proponent of federal aid to education, his support was essential in securing passage of the Elementary and Secondary Education Act, the Higher Education Act, and a number of other bills. And Morse was experienced and expert in labor law and labor politics and a valued Johnson adviser in this area.

As a result—and also because they liked each other personally—Johnson never permitted a break with Morse, even when Morse called for his impeachment for waging an unconstitutional war in Southeast Asia. At lunch one day with Harvard professor Richard Neustadt and me, during the early stages of the 1966 airline strike, Johnson concluded that we would have to stop the strike and set up an emergency labor board. He picked up the phone under the dining room table and asked the operator to get him Wayne Morse. When Morse got on the line, Johnson said, "Wayne, I know why you are always calling for my impeachment and why you want Bobby Kennedy to be president. It's because of all those tough jobs I ask you to do on our education bills and labor problems. Well, I've got another one." By the time the conversation had ended, Morse had agreed to chair the emergency board, which Johnson considered critical to the maintenance of the wage-price guideposts, a significant line of defense against inflation.*

Presidents must have a sufficiently detached perspective to recognize that there is little place in the Oval Office for permanent enemies. The American people were morally and socially revulsed at the compilation of a permanent enemies list by Richard Nixon. But they evidenced little recognition of the extent to which such a personality trait inhibits a president from performing his duties or leading this nation to fulfillment of national objectives. Each president has people he does not like. But he must learn to subordinate such feelings to broader interests. To say Lyndon Johnson was no fan of Robert Kennedy would be the understatement of his administration. But contrast his attitude toward Robert Kennedy with Nixon's covert Chappaquidick operation intended to destroy Edward Kennedy.

Johnson's conversation with me, four days before he announced his decision to withdraw as a presidential candidate in 1968, illustrates the importance of personal detachment in political relations more effectively than any essay. Johnson was sitting at the table behind his desk signing some routine appointments and letters. At first, he asked if I would take over the poverty program since Sargent Shriver was going to Paris as our ambassador. Typically, he asked me to take it on as an additional duty—and seeing the horror on the face of a White House aide who was already working fifteen hours a day, he said, "I will only ask you to do it if I run again." For some reason, it was intuitively clear to me that he had virtually decided not to run again. He must have sensed what I

---

*Neustadt, the innocent luncheon bystander, became a member of that board during the Johnson-Morse phone conversation, the president typically appointing him without asking if he could serve, because Johnson remembered that Neustadt had been secretary to a labor board Morse had chaired during the Truman administration. The strike was eventually settled, but not within the guideposts.

felt, and as best as I am able to reconstruct it, the conversation went like this:

C. I have never really focused on that possibility.

P. Well, focus on it now. Who do you think will get the nomination?

C. Bobby Kennedy. My guess is that he would easily take McCarthy's people away from him.

P. What about Hubert?

C. I don't think he can beat Kennedy.

P. What's wrong with Bobby? He's made some nasty speeches about me, but he's never had to sit here. Anyway, you seem to like his parties.

C. [Nervous smile]

P. Bobby would keep fighting for the Great Society programs. And when he sat in this chair he might have a different view on the war. His major problem would be with appropriations—getting the programs funded. He doesn't know how to deal with those people and a lot of them don't like him. But he'll try.

C. Mr. President, if you run, I think you'll win.

P. Win what? The way it is now we can't get the tax surcharge passed and Ho Chi Minh and Fulbright don't believe anything I say about the war.

Presidents are human beings, not unemotional political machines, and every president has moments of anger that sometimes come into public view. Any number of New Deal historians have recorded the angry flashes of Franklin Roosevelt. Harry Truman's views of columnist Drew Pearson and music critic Paul Hume made headline stories. So did John Kennedy's characterizations of the steel executives and his ban of the New York *Herald Tribune* from the White House. In *No Final Victories*, Larry O'Brien has recorded Kennedy angrily plunging a letter opener into the top of his desk on learning that his $1.25 minimum wage legislation failed to pass the House by one vote, 186–185. Emmett Hughes has given us an unvarnished view of Eisenhower's temper, and any aide to Lyndon Johnson at one time or another felt his wrath or witnessed its expression at the actions and attitudes of others. Johnson was enraged publicly and privately when House members laughed to temporary defeat his rat-control legislation. Richard Nixon shoved his own press secretary in a moment of anger at reporters who were following him. Gerald Ford was reported furious at the press for questioning his motives in granting Nixon a pardon. On another occasion, he called Senator Henry Jackson to angrily complain about one of the senator's aides criticizing the Vladivostok arms limitation agreement with a quip that "the next time Ford should be more careful with foreigners who drink vodka." Such reactions are human, understandable, and healthy for a man whose every action is analyzed in the public print day after day. To a president, virtually every reporter and columnist seems a Monday morning quarterback seven days a week, analyzing each of his failures to solve promptly or brilliantly essentially intractable problems.

A measure of detachment can provide a sense of perspective essential to the control of presidential anger and frustration. The frustration begins shortly after a president moves into the Oval Office. What seemed possible, likely, or even desirable on the campaign stump often appears impossible, unlikely, or undesirable once the candidate becomes the president. His reaction to such perceptions is often a function of his personality. What the president perceives as obviously in the national interest and readily achievable, the Congress or the media may consider antithetical to that interest, too expensive, or not attainable. Sometimes he succeeds over his opposition, but often he fails.

Both his successes and failures are promptly recorded on evening television news shows and the front pages of daily newspapers. Sometimes he reacts properly to them. Sometimes he over- or underreacts, or (to the detriment of us all) misses the point. The president gets hurt. If he can remain sufficiently detached to recognize, as Benjamin Franklin did, that "the things which hurt, instruct," he grows and his personality develops in a healthy way. But bruising political blows that sharpen policy alternatives and the means to achieve them for one president can be simply an embittering experience for another. The presidential personality that can accept such blows with detachment is an enormous asset for the nation. Such an attitude can also help a president realize that he is never as good as the editorial writers and columnists say he is when they praise him, or as bad as they say he is when they attack him.

Like Truman, Eisenhower, and Kennedy, Johnson certainly could get angry at his opposition. In January of 1966, he directed an aide to blast the steel companies in the midst of a major price rollback fight during the Vietnam War. The aide's characterization of them as "war profiteers" made headlines, but it was mild compared to Johnson's earlier reaction when the steel executives raised their prices late on the afternoon of New Year's Eve. Nor did he appreciate the roasting the Catholic bishops gave him about his views on birth control. But in both these cases, he made sure that neither he nor his staff ever cut the cord permanently because, as he put it, "We need to hold this thing together. We need those steel companies to train and employ Blacks," and "we may reach the point where the only people that will support the poverty program will be the Catholic bishops."

The best antidote for presidential rage is a presidential sense of humor. Both Roosevelts had good senses of humor and John Kennedy was blessed with a spectacular one. Johnson may have lacked Kennedy's ability to laugh at himself, but a robust life in elective politics had provided him with a magnificent sense of humor. His humor was more needle-pointed than Kennedy's, particularly about the press. When the White House press corps caught him proclaiming, before countless millions of South Koreans in Seoul, that his grandfather fought at the Alamo, he cracked, "If Hugh Sidey ever had a crowd like that, he'd claim he was a great-grandson of George Washington." And, late one evening during the Washington riots that followed the Martin Luther King assassination in 1968, I told him of a report that Stokley Carmichael was organizing a group at 14th and U Streets to march on Georgetown and burn it down. "Georgetown," he said with a mischevious twinkle, "I've waited thirty-five years for this day."

Persistence is an essential personality ingredient for a strong president and most presidents amply exhibit this char-

acteristic en route to the Oval Office. Gerald Ford, who became president by appointment to the vice-presidency and
succession without election, was not required to evidence
this trait before assuming office. His publicly relaxed manner
was politically refreshing after the Byzantine years of Nixon's
Watergate, but he will need to develop the quality of persistence his predecessors have repeatedly displayed if he is to
make significant progress on the difficult public policy problems that he faces. Franklin Roosevelt's persistence eventually led him to the means to change the attitude of the Supreme Court on his domestic social and economic regulatory
programs and to provide (lend-lease) aid to Great Britain
before this nation entered World War II. Kennedy persisted
on the religious issue during his presidential campaign, and
he put the pieces together after the Bay of Pigs, including the
pharmaceutical company ransom of the Cuban invasion bri-
gade.

From the moment of assumption of the presidency, persistence is required to shape the executive branch into a
responsive instrument of presidential policies. Richard Neustadt's book on *Presidential Power* has documented how few
presidential orders are self-executing and how intransigent
the executive bureaucracy can be in resisting new directions.
The appointment of ideologically sympathetic and personally loyal cabinet officers and agency heads is only a small first
step in that direction. Changing the emphasis of domestic
grant-in-aid programs demands repeated presidential intervention, particularly when these programs have constituencies created and nourished by legislative mandate. The Hill-
Burton hospital program has for years encouraged the
construction of medical facilities in rural areas. Efforts to
move the focus of hospital construction to urban ghettos and
suburban population concentrations required the repeated
intervention of Johnson and the White House staff during the
1960s. Truman ordered the Armed Forces desegregated, but
the officer corps was essentially white, until both Kennedy
and Johnson, over an eight-year period, with the persever-
ance of Defense Secretary McNamara, virtually ordered that
Black officers be promoted and that ghetto components, like

mess attendants, be broken up. Even then, special reporting systems had to be established to provide a recurrent check on the recalcitrant bureaucracy.

Politics may be the art of compromise. But presidential politics with the Congress is the art of compromise practiced by a president with a personality trait of tenacious persistence. Lyndon Johnson empirically and intuitively sensed that the most significant tool he could put in the hands of Black Americans was the voting lever. Once they were behind the curtain of the voting booth, politicians would have to reckon with them as a major force. Without that democratic outlet for release of their political views, Johnson feared for the viability of our society.

The Voting Rights Act of 1965 was his first major civil rights proposal as president (the 1964 act was originally introduced during the Kennedy administration). He devoted a staggering amount of his time, energy, and political capital to breaking the Senate filibuster and passing the act in August of 1965. He spent hours negotiating with Senate Republican Leader Everett Dirksen, he called financial and labor supporters of other senators, he tried private persuasion with senators like Richard Russell, and publicly cajoled border-state and conservative senators. When White House head counts indicated the critical cloture motion was likely to fail, he gathered key staff members around the cabinet table and assessed the legislative situation senator by senator, in search of the necessary votes. Hubert Humphrey, then the Senate whip, later told me that, during the 1964 Civil Rights Act Senate battle, Johnson even had one senator's mistress contacted to have her persuade her lover to vote to break a filibuster.

Johnson deliberately signed the Voting Rights Act at the Rotunda in the Capitol, on live prime-time television, to dramatize its importance. He monitored its implementation with the meticulous care of an obstetrician during a difficult labor and delivery. He prodded the Justice Department to make sure monitors were present at each voting place in the affected Southern states. He overtly and covertly encouraged civil rights organizations to get their people out to vote and to run for sheriff, city councilman, county commissioner.

He followed the statistics on increased Black voter registration as closely as he watched his own polls. He knew that Black mayorality candidates or Black candidates for county commissioners, local judges, sheriffs, and tax assessors across the nation would benefit from the Voting Rights Act of 1965. After any election, he recited the latest figures on the number of elected Blacks across the nation to persuade more Blacks to run for office and register and vote. He insisted on appointing a Black mayor for Washington, D.C., because he wanted to encourage Blacks to run for mayor in the big Northern cities. He pressed young Black leaders, like Walter Fauntroy, to subordinate the ministry to a life in politics.

Johnson rightly recognized the social and economic implications of the ballot for any minority in our nation. The Irish, the Italians, and sometimes the Jews entered the American mainstream in cities like New York and Chicago, Boston and Philadelphia, by way of politics. Denied access to the professions, to the financial community, and often to the best colleges in our nation, these immigrant groups were able to make their way in America by taking hold of the political reins. So Johnson saw the Blacks, as needing political power in their hands, not only because of the responsibility that the possession of such power brings to those who hold it, but also to make it clear that they would have to be dealt with as men with the power of local, state, and national governments behind them. And Johnson saw the overriding need for presidential persistance to achieve these goals.

Johnson persisted to the point of nagging through the enactment and implementation of the voting rights legislation. After he left office, in retrospective looks at his presidency, he noted its wide impact across the South and characterized it as the most important piece of domestic legislation passed during his years in the White House. At the LBJ Library Civil Rights Symposium, in the last major speech before his death, Johnson decried the fact that not enough Blacks were voting and prodded those present to devote their energies to registering Blacks and urging them to vote.

Unrelenting skepticism is another common presidential personality trait essential to the conduct of an effective presidency. Like the need for loyalty, skepticism twisted into paranoia can be dangerous. For skeptecism to serve most effectively as a presidential personality trait, it should be accompanied by a shrewd (almost psychiatrically expert) understanding of human nature. A president must be skeptical enough to pay meticulous attention to detail, to discount advice for bureaucratic loyalties and for the (sometimes unconscious) personal, intellectual, and ideological prejudices of his aides and advisors. The line between skeptical caution and cynicism in dealing with public and private leaders, as well as subordinates, is politically and psychologically fine, and most presidents would prefer to err on the side of cynicism. History is replete with examples of political and personal treachery and incompetence and those who move to the Oval Office from a public or political life have accumulated abundant direct experience in the foibles of human nature. Without sufficient political experience to know how justifiable is a healthy measure of suspicion about the accuracy of facts and the purity of motives, a president will find himself in deep trouble early in his incumbency.

On the White House staff, some of us had a quip about Lyndon Johnson's skepticism: "The only person Johnson trusts is Lady Bird; and then only 90 percent of the time." The wisecrack overstated the point, but the skeptical quality of Johnson's personality contributed to his presidency. As much as any other personality trait, it inspired his phenomenal attention to detail: Was the legislation ready to go to the Congress the day the presidential message was to be sent? Did all the budget figures check out? Would the program achieve its goals? Have the House and Senate committee chairmen agreed to hold hearings? When? Did you remember to call Arthur Krim (his wife is interested in mental health, you know)? And the vice-president (Hubert has a special interest in mental retardation)? Have you figured out what the headline of the story will be? And on and on. While not all presidents shared as deep-seated a skepticism as did Johnson, every aide of Roosevelt, Truman, Eisenhower, Kennedy, and Nixon with whom I have discussed this trait has confirmed its existence in the personality of the man he served at the White House.

The empirical realities of politics sharpen presidential skepticism about the motivations of advisors. Johnson, for example, would discount what Labor Secretary Willard Wirtz recommended as to manpower policy or a noninflationary wage settlement because "he has to live with George Meany when it's over," or what Commerce Secretary John Connor said about the economic ramifications of a price increase because "his entire life has been spent in business and he wants to retain the approval of his friends." Similar qualmish scrutiny characterized his reactions to farm programs suggested by Agriculture Secretary Orville Freeman or conservation projects recommended by Interior Secretary Stewart Udall. At the same time, however, he knew that cabinet officers such as these could severely damage their ability to serve him well unless they maintained their positions of confidence with their constituent interest groups.

All of the facts are rarely, if ever, available to a president at the time he must make most decisions. Those that are often turn out to be half-facts or incorrect as they are subjected to careful analysis. That is why presidents are so suspicious about the "facts" that are initially presented to them on any major issue, particularly fast-breaking events. Like newspaper editors with young reporters and lawyers in their initial interviews with clients, presidential skepticism is based on the repeated difficulties they have experienced in obtaining an account of events as they occurred, not simply as they were perceived.

A president with a healthy measure of skepticism in his personality make-up will be more demanding in the preparation of government policy and legislative programs and in their operation. Johnson was constantly concerned about the possibility of corruption in the poverty program. He recognized that funds were being disbursed rapidly and through a wide variety of groups. By design, the funds were placed in the hands of many who were not accustomed to the kind of responsibility that attends public accountability. He fully appreciated that, in the ghettos and the rural poverty areas, effective ways of getting results did not necessarily comport with the way federal regulations were written by Washington bureaucrats. He valued greatly Office of Economic Opportunity Director Sargent Shriver's talents and considered his contagious enthusiasm essential to the momentum of the poverty program. But Johnson was skeptical that a man of Shriver's nature would be as concerned with the detailed monitoring essential to keep the ammunition of corruption out of the arsenal of the program's enemies. As a result, he eventually appointed, as Shriver's deputy, Bertrand Harding who had measurably strengthened the internal auditing procedures of the Internal Revenue Service. In Johnson's eyes, Harding's central mission was to institute controls on the poverty program that would afford maximum protection from the danger of graft and corruption.

Johnson's concern was less that his administration could be stained (although that was of profound moment) than that the poverty program could be destroyed by the finding of a single case of serious corruption or misuse of government funds. He followed with great care every investigation of alleged misuse of funds in the poverty program. From where did this deep skepticism emanate? It came not only from his life in politics but also from his own experience as a National Youth Corps administrator during the New Deal. He believed that some of the Roosevelt programs, like the National Youth Administration, foundered because inadequate accounting and auditing procedures exposed them to attack by anti-New-Deal politicians who, with great success, camouflaged their opposition under cover of corruption charges.

The absence of a deeply rooted streak of skepticism can be costly for a president. Dwight Eisenhower simply could not believe that Sherman Adams was involved with Bernard Goldfine until it became a national scandal that tarnished his presidency. Both Eisenhower and John Kennedy were insufficiently skeptical and, hence, inadequately prepared for what they faced in their summit meetings with Nikita Khrushchev. Johnson, who was skeptical to the point of triple checking every assertion about a proposed new domestic program or the predicted head count for a House or Senate floor vote, displayed a remarkable willingness to rely on Pentagon and State Department assurances about the Vietnam

War during 1966 and much of 1967. Skeptical during those
months in late 1964 and the first half of 1965 when he was
trying to formulate a Vietnam policy, he seemed almost to
abandon that attitude for the two-year period that followed
his July 1965 decision to send large U.S. troop contingents to
Southeast Asia. As with the Eisenhower and Kennedy decisions to go forward with the Bay of Pigs planning and invasion, our nation paid dearly for this costly lapse of skepticism.

Whatever the publicly received personality image, most
presidential personalities are shrewdly calculating and secretive. This is particularly reflected in the way in which they
prefer to conduct the process of formulating national policies
and the timing of public announcements of major decisions.

Calculating personalities can serve presidents well in the
foreign policy area. John Kennedy and the Democrats
reviled John Foster Dulles for his "brinkmanship" in dealing
with the Russians. But calculated brinkmanship was an essential ingredient of Kennedy's foreign policy, just as it had been
for Eisenhower and would be for Johnson, Nixon, and Ford.
Indeed, the Cuban missile crisis is probably the most successful act of calculated brinkmanship in foreign policy during
the modern presidency. And the call up of the reserves during the Berlin crisis in 1961 achieved its calculated objectives
at home and abroad.

Foreign nations expect a president to be calculating and
they often measure his intentions by what his administration
spokesmen say. Kennedy recognized the importance of this.
One of Kennedy's most politically explosive confrontations
with the Congress was over his right to censor all public
statements by military officers, with particular scrutiny of
those concerning the Russians and Chinese and their relations with each other. During Senate Armed Services Committee hearings on this subject in September 1961, Kennedy
personally invoked executive privilege to protect the identity of those individuals in the Pentagon who had censored
particular speeches. It was the only formal invocation of executive privilege during his presidency. Johnson repeatedly
ordered that world leaders not be criticized personally, no

matter what they said about the United States, because he wished to control precisely our dialogue and his relations with them.

Calculation as a facet of personality plays a role in the lesser elements of American politics as well. As the analysis in Chapter V demonstrates, Kennedy and Johnson were as calculating with the media as Eisenhower and Ford. All recent presidents have displayed an awareness that a particular reporter is likely to serve the presidential interest by injecting a particular tone into a story, that it sometimes is most helpful to play one White House staff member off against another, one cabinet officer against another, one senator against another, a governor against a mayor. These are the calculations which can sometimes be essential to the achievement of policy objectives.

Calculation often walks hand in hand with a secretive element in the personalities of most presidents. Most presidents come naturally to secrecy—for their success has given them an acute sense of the importance of the timing public announcements to the achievement of public policy objectives. Secretiveness can sometimes push presidents over into dissembling, however, at least temporarily. Eisenhower tried to avoid the truth about the U-2 incident; Kennedy had a "cold" at the time of the Cuban missile crisis and misled the press about CIA pilots; Johnson played Vietnam too closely for his eventual political comfort. The press pushed Eisenhower and Kennedy to level with the American people about the secret reconnaissance over Russia and the U.S. involvement in the Bay of Pigs invasion. The Pentagon Papers constitute a case study of secret orders and involvement of both the Kennedy and Johnson administrations in connection with Vietnam.

Presidents get accustomed to keeping secrets in foreign affairs and national security matters, but there is another reason why they hold matters tightly. The longer they can keep secrets, the longer they can keep their options open. The premature (from the presidential viewpoint) revelation of decisions or alternatives under consideration often forecloses courses of action that might otherwise be available to a president, especially when the revelation catches a president by surprise. Presidents are not always wrong about this and it is difficult to balance, even in retrospect, the value of openness at early stages of public policy formulation against the risks and benefits of premature release of information.

In early 1966, after months of work, Lyndon Johnson had committed to the Model Cities program, an especially complex legislative package designed to rebuild the most dilapidated ghetto sections of major cities. By a carrot (money) and stick (only if you get organized) approach, the federal government would join with the cities on a systematic basis to rebuild ghettos, coordinating health-care facilities, job training (for work that would be needed in the revitalized area), sewer systems, fire and police protection, housing and transportation projects. The proposal was so intricate that I recommended the selective briefing of urban affairs experts for the wire services and major newspapers about ten days before we sent the message to Congress so that they could begin writing stories to assure better public understanding of the program. The alternative of a short White House press conference, subsequent to informing key senators and representatives and simultaneous with release of the presidential message to the Congress, seemed certain to lead to confusion.

Johnson disagreed. The Congress had to be the first to know, he argued. "Senators and congressmen don't like to find out about legislation heading for their committees in the newspaper." Moreover, he added, early release would give opposition forces a chance to organize. When we released the message, the stories, even in the most sophisticated newspapers, such as the New York *Times* and the Washington *Post*, were confused and misleading. When Johnson mentioned this to me on the following morning (and suggested that my press briefing was at fault), I reminded him of my earlier recommendation. Johnson snapped back, "I'd rather have the *Times* and the *Post* confused than not pass the program." After one of the toughest legislative fights of the Johnson administration, the Congress passed the legislation. Johnson commented to me that evening that, if the press had been writing about the Model Cities program for weeks before we sent it to the Congress, the program would never have been enacted. Whatever the merits of his strategy (and I still had doubts about it), I thought to myself that evening, this president was convinced it worked on this legislation.

Calculation also leads to cautious, sometimes misleading consultation by which a president tests the validity of conflicting arguments from his advisers or the reaction of special interests which a proposed policy move might affect. Johnson was constantly consulting men and women with divergent views on major economic issues, not only to get their opinion but also to calculate the political realism of suggestions from his aides at the Council of Economic Advisers, the Treasury, the Commerce and Labor Departments, and the Bureau of the Budget. Particularly when measuring the value of divergent recommendations, he would present the labor arguments to a Henry Ford and the business arguments to a George Meany. Press leaks from White House visitors unable to distinguish between Johnson's closely held true leanings and the views he tested on what he anticipated to be an adversary mind occasionally resulted in confused stories about the direction of economic policy. But such consultation was invaluable to the president. Not only did it inform the substance of the proposals, it added a knowledge of the posture affected interests would take that could be critical to the achievement of selected policies.

Egocentricity is a personality characteristic common to all presidents and to some degree essential for the conduct of the office. A president must have some sense that he is "the center of the center," to borrow the marvelously descriptive phrase Stewart Alsop attached to the White House. He must believe that he can lead the nation better than anyone else. A president of sincerely expressed public humility, like Harry Truman or Gerald Ford, may begin simply by recognizing that "history" has placed on his shoulders the constitutional responsibility and authority to lead the American people, particularly during an incumbency to which they were not elected. But, as Truman's self-justifying memoirs disclose, he shortly will conclude not only that his decisions were the right ones, he will be convinced that no one could have done better under the circumstances.

In a common expression of presidential egoism, the elected president will identify himself as the representative of all the people. After his 1948 defeat of New York Governor Thomas E. Dewey, Truman repeatedly noted that he was the only government official with a national constituency. Roosevelt once overruled his administrative assistant James Rowe with the admonition, "No, James, I do not have to do it your way and I will tell you the reason why. . . . the people of the United States elected me president, not you." Johnson was more curt. "There's only one name on that ballot," he often said, "and it's not Califano or McPherson. No one elected you boys to sit in this office." Ford, like Truman and Johnson during their completion of the Roosevelt and Kennedy terms, has been deeply conscious that he has not been elected by the people. Not only did he take pointed note of that fact in his first prepared remarks upon being sworn in, within days thereafter he announced that he intended to seek a national mandate from the people in 1976.

Ego helps cushion the relentless reality expressed so well on Harry Truman's desk plaque, "The buck stops here." It is a psychological source of self-confidence and it can motivate presidents to noble actions. In early 1966, Johnson became deeply concerned about the impact on his defense secretary of so many stories characterizing Vietnam as "McNamara's war." "They'll destroy that man," he told me. "This isn't his war. If it belongs to anybody, it's my war. Let's stop him from talking so much about it and I'll start defending our position." John Kennedy promptly made the judgment that he alone would assume "full responsibility" for the Bay of Pigs debacle. Gerald Ford took the extraordinary step of testifying before a House subcommittee to dramatize his personal responsibility for the controversial Nixon pardon.

A well-developed ego is essential to the ability of a president not only to accept the reality of the difficult tasks that confront him, but also to learn from his successes and his failures. In this sense, Erik Erikson's description, in his book

Insight and Responsibility, of ego as "the guardian of meaningful experience" applies with special force to presidents.
Erikson's conclusion that a strong ego is the "psychological
precondition for . . . the will to choose what is necessary"
points up the importance of ego to the occasional individually ruthless but collectively essential decisions a president
must make.

Egocentricity plays a most serious role in the president's
perception of his duty to protect the power of the office
entrusted to him. Conscious of his role as commander in
chief, John Kennedy had a major confrontation with the then
singularly powerful chairman of the House Armed Services
Committee, Carl Vinson, over a congressional attempt to
force the expenditure of funds for a new bomber he felt the
Air Force did not need. The issue was less over the particular
weapons system than it was over Kennedy's establishing his
presidential authority to decide whether to spend funds appropriated by the Congress. Kennedy considered victory essential to preserve the commander-in-chief powers of the
presidency, and he risked a major confrontation with the
Congress to make his point. Harry Truman's dismissal of
General Douglas MacArthur involved the same considerations.

Johnson vetoed a number of bills where he thought the
Congress encroached on the function of the executive
branch. Usually the Congress had legislated a requirement
for congressional committee clearance of what he considered "purely executive" actions, such as military base clo-
sures, before they could be taken. In attempts to roll back
any number of price increases—steel, copper, aluminum,
gasoline, molybdenum—Johnson would always say at the
start, "Let's be sure we can win. The worst thing for the
American presidency would be for one of these steel mag-
nates like Roger Blough to beat the president of the United
States." Once we moved to roll back any price with overt
presidential support, Johnson intimately directed the battle
to make certain the president won. (Years later Roger Blough
told me that if there had not been a steel industry over the
past twenty years, the presidents in office would have in-

vented one to assure some major victories over big business.)

Ego also heightens the awareness in presidents of their need to win. Johnson was as deeply committed to home rule for the District of Columbia as any man that ever occupied the Oval Office. But the unprecedented energies and time he devoted to obtaining a discharge petition to force the home rule legislation to the House floor in 1965 were punctuated by his repeated exclamations, "If they beat us on this, they'll know they can win and we'll have trouble passing any more of our legislation." Compromise marks the political vocabulary of every president, but more often than not it is a code word for victory. The mere possibility of an overwhelmingly Democratic House as a result of the 1974 elections, with the congressional independence from a Republican president that it implied, drove Gerald Ford to the political stump to warn the American people of the dangers of a "legislative dictatorship."

The ego element of presidential personalities does more than self-impose a duty to protect the office they hold and inspire their will to win. It maintains their acute self-consciousness of the supremacy of the office they hold. Presidents do not regard the legislative and judicial branches as equal; separate sometimes, but never equal. Roosevelt regarded the Supreme Court as a body to be shaped in the judicial image and likeness of the New Deal. Kennedy and Johnson considered the federal courtrooms as areas in which to pursue their civil rights policies. Eisenhower regarded the challenge of Orval Faubus as much a defiance of presidential supremacy over the states as disobedience of a court order. When presidents must seek Taft-Hartley injunctions to block strikes that could injure the national security, they consider the courts as rubber stamps for their judgments and shop for judges who will provide the judicial blessing they need. They recognize that each time another branch permits or approves one of their acts, it becomes both *de facto,* and *de jure,* legal.

Of all the common presidential personality traits, egocentricity harbors the sharpest double-edged sword. The environmental trappings of presidential power can be engrossing to the point of egocentric corruption. The planes, cars, and servants, the ability to talk to anyone anywhere in the world by picking up a telephone, the engulfing imagery of power, the parades and the adulatory march "Hail to the Chief!" accompany a president wherever he goes. It is no wonder that presidents begin to feel that all manner of publicly provided convenience is theirs. Johnson once walked up to the wrong helicopter in a line of planes and the Marine sergeant stated, "Your helicopter is the next one, Mr. President." Johnson quipped, "They're all mine, son." Kennedy spoke of and treated the Army Special Forces "green berets" as though they were a private army. In his book *Conversations with Kennedy*, Ben Bradlee writes of Kennedy sailing on his presidential yacht, sometimes becoming annoyed if he were not recognized and saluted by other boats. Nixon came to regard the General Services Administration as a personal decorator for his Key Biscayne and San Clemente retreats.

There are amusing, but revealing, examples of the self-centered possessiveness attendant on any presidency, particularly where a presidential program backfires on the president himself. In 1968, Johnson adopted the concept of building a "new town in town," a program designed to reconstruct completely a portion of a center city into a self-sufficient community. The perfect location seemed to be thirty-five acres of government-owned land in Washington, D.C. that housed only an abandoned vocational training school. With no one living on the property, there appeared to be none of the difficult human relocation problems and aroused neighborhood groups that plague urban redevelopments. Since the government owned the land, the delays and expense of lengthy condemnation proceedings could also be avoided. With some fanfare, the White House announced that the first "new town in town" would be constructed in Washington, D.C., at the abandoned thirty-five acre site. Within days, neighborhood groups of people who lived near the site began to complain. They wanted one or another kind of a community built, or none at all. Some of these groups were financed with federal funds from the Office of Economic Opportunity. As their efforts to thwart the administration program showed some signs of success, Johnson discovered they were financed with OEO money. "Call Shriver," he said during a phone conversation with me one day, "and tell him that these people are using *my* money to fight *me*. How can he justify that?"

On another occasion, the Washington *Post* carried a story that President Kennedy had saved his White House counsel Lee White from making a serious mistake. I called White, a friend and talented public servant, to commiserate with him. "That story doesn't bother me," he said chuckling, "The day I'll begin to worry is when the Washington *Post* writes that Lee White saved that incompetent President Kennedy from making a serious blunder."

The egocentricity that inspires self-centered possessiveness and informs the presidential will to win also serves to make most presidents cautious about picking their issues in order to preserve their political capital and enhance the influence of presidential leadership. Failure to respond to this instinct can be debilitating to the power a president has to exercise. It may be that elected presidents better appreciate how precious and fragile this sort of presidential power is. Gerald Ford, for example, squandered his presidential capital, not only with the pardon of Richard Nixon, but with his naïvely enthusiastic assurance to the American people in August 1974 that the nation should have a national health insurance program by the end of the year, as well as with a number of other unattainable commitments and unsustainable vetoes. The people might soon forget such promises and even place much of the blame on Capitol Hill, but the president diminishes in the eyes of the Congress each time he fails to deliver on a legislative promise or sustain a veto.

Egocentricity carries with it dangers for any president. But in balanced and secure measure, it can be a psychological reservoir of major significance. Egocentricity can be essential in maintaining the self-confidence required to endure the frustrations of infusing the executive and congressional bureaucracies and the self-centered interests of the American people with a sense of national purpose and in accepting with reasonable equilibrium the often unjustified and sometimes cruel criticism of presidential performance.

XI

PERSONALITY:
The Distinctive Characteristics

The personality characteristics common to most presidents are the most important to identify in terms of making national decisions about vesting power in the office or placing restraints on its exercise. But personality traits distinctive to an individual president may also be relevant to such decisions. In the sense that such traits reflect a president's personal experiences and background, they can be related not simply to the means by which he pursues his policy objectives, but sometimes to the objectives he selects.

As George Reedy has noted, a president, to a large degree, can determine how he spends his day. He can make room for frequent golf as did Eisenhower, or occasional sailing and touch football as did Kennedy. Like Truman he can relax in evening poker games, or like Ford he can swim most days. Or he can make room only for work, in the manner of Lyndon Johnson. The almost total preoccupation of Richard Nixon with Watergate during his second term indicates that the executive bureaucracy has a self-generating momentum that can propel the government, however erratically, for an extended period with a minimum of presidential attention.

But a bureaucratically engaged president will focus much of the energy of the national government. The areas to which such a president directs his attention are ones in which new policies and programs are likely to be developed and changes in direction are likely to occur. The distinctive personality characteristics of a particular president, informed by his prior experience, contribute significantly to the targets he selects for special concern.

Dwight Eisenhower had been a military man for virtually all his adult life. He was not as concerned with domestic social programs as his election rival Adlai Stevenson might have been. Eisenhower's public and personal ambitions and desires reflected his broad international military experience, as well as his years as a Columbia University president immersed in the foreign policy establishment dominated by the Council on Foreign Relations. Unlike Stevenson, Eisenhower was not motivated by a desire to seek contemporary academic or liberal media approval. Nor was he particularly concerned about his historical standing on the domestic front. He came to the White House with a guarantee of historical approbation as a result of his success as Supreme Allied Commander in Europe during World War II. His desire to maintain and enhance his global stature led him to end the war in Korea, to move with dramatic caution in Lebanon, and quickly extricate our troops from its shores. But it also led him to the abortive Big Four Paris summit with Khrushchev, Macmillan, and DeGaulle in May 1960.

So predominate was his focus on international policy that domestic problems festered dangerously during his eight years in office. Having observed American business as a high-ranking officer during World War II, Eisenhower had come deeply to admire the way it brilliantly served the war effort in developing the weapons, productive capacity, and logistics essential to win the war. Personally comfortable with American businessmen, he believed that business had done so well in the wartime forties and during the Korean conflict that it could be relied upon to perform its tasks at home. Eisenhower's posture toward the disadvantaged and the poor was to give the private sector as much freedom as possible, almost dogmatically invoking what Lyndon Johnson derided in his book, *The Vantage Point,* as the Republican trickle-down theory of economics. In contrast, Johnson saw the limits of social conscience in the drive for private profit and believed that the federal government should intervene wherever it could effect directly or indirectly the redistribution of wealth or power.

In economic matters, it was not surprising that Eisenhower adopted a hands-off attitude, occasionally speaking of "shared [but independent] responsibility." Unlike Kennedy and Johnson, he had no stomach for "fine tuning" the economy and attempting to manipulate wage, price, and capital investment decisions in the private sector. Both Eisenhower and Johnson recognized that business was the economic generator that powered so much of the nation. But Eisenhower would have been appalled at some of Johnson's attempts to use business as an instrument, not only of presidentially directed economic policy, but of social planning as well. Johnson's interventionist instincts exceeded even Walter Heller's theoretical concepts of the extent to which government could manipulate the economy and would have excited the Fabian Socialists of post-World-War-II Britain.

Despite his parting shot at the "military industrial complex," for the most part Eisenhower perceived large corporations as great American institutions and shared a common sense of purpose with American business as it was. Johnson saw American business as one more tool for the achievement of social and economic objectives and perceived corporate giants as centers of economic power managed by men whose strengths and weaknesses provided the levers to put that aggregate wealth to work for his public policy objectives. During the near steel strike in late August and early September 1965, Eisenhower visited Johnson in the White House. Johnson called me in to brief the former president on the situation. Eisenhower talked in broad institutional terms of colossal forces, powerful steel companies versus the monolithic steelworkers union. Eisenhower trusted big business but not big labor. Johnson was skeptical of both; his perception was not institutional. Johnson's concern was with how to convince I. W. Abel to settle within the 3.2 percent wage guideline when Abel had recently won his election as steelworker union president on a platform espousing a much larger wage increase.

Although Eisenhower had a distinctly noninterventionist
bias, he held to that tenet of the Protestant ethic which
commanded compliance with the letter of the law and adherence to a gentlemanly code of reverential courtesy to the
office of the president. This attitude, as much as his military
sense of the rule of law and order, led him unhesitatingly to
support the Supreme Court's school desegregation decision
against the recalcitrant and demagogic Arkansas governor,
Orval Faubus. Faubus not only refused to play by the rules;
he did so in rude defiance and vulgar disrespect for the presidency itself. Eisenhower saw that the law was strictly obeyed
and the presidency kept on its benevolent but distant pedestal. But he had no desire to push it to new frontiers. For both
Johnson and Kennedy, however, the courts provided yet another instrument to be used for the active pursuit of racial
integration.

Kennedy's buoyant, youthful, swinging ascension to power
in the White House undoubtedly confirmed his belief in his
most optimistic campaign rhetoric. He exuded an optimism
so contagious that he swept the American people to major
investments in a trip to the moon, a supersonic transport, an
antiguerrilla capability to fight limited wars. The first two
and one-half years of his short-lived presidency were the last
will and testament to the world-is-our-oyster view of American capability. In that sense, his personality had a sweeping
impact on his policies.

Kennedy's father had made it very big, very fast, financially and politically. From a sophisticated start, Joseph
Kennedy, Sr., skipped over the lace-curtain-Irish generation
and moved his sons directly into the Northeast establishment
of Harvard. For President John Kennedy, this provided an
intimate family experience to support the proposition that,
in America, any success was achievable once the decision to
move was made. So he set about "getting the country moving
again" with a combination of inspiration, glamour, charm,
blarney, rhetoric, and unabashedly patriotic good intentions.
His policies were an allegro rendition of the old Democratic
party marching song, "Happy Days Are Here Again." His
extraordinarily attractive personality was more inspirational

with the people, however, than it was effective with the Congress.

The successful projection of that personality haunted the Lyndon Johnson White House. It was not enough for Johnson to be the most successful president in our nation's history in terms of enacted congressional domestic programs. So intensely did he covet the retrospectively perceived total popular acceptance of Kennedy, that like so many of us, he forgot that, in the fall of 1963 just before his assassination, John Kennedy was under attack on many fronts, for his failure to pass his legislative program, the lagging economy with five million unemployed, improper news management, and even the loss of rapport with the intellectuals.

The Johnson perception of John Kennedy—whom he greatly respected—was one of the shadows that lurked behind several of his policies. Lyndon Johnson's pursuit of the Vietnam conflict to what so many contemporary historians regard as an extension of national ego far beyond the interests of national security, is sometimes credited to the personality of a gun-toting Texan who refused to be the first American president to lose a war. This is caricature analysis at its worst. What Johnson did in Vietnam was undoubtedly the product of the best judgment, experience, and wisdom he could bring to bear on the problem, as David Halberstam's sardonic phrase, "the best and the brightest," suggests. That experience, as many who worked for, admired, or criticized him have noted, was gained during a cold-war adulthood. He entered politics shortly before World War II and became a significant national force after it ended, when suspicions between the Iron Curtain countries and the Western World were at their peak.

While LBJ's "frontier" personality may have had some impact in this area, my own judgment is that it was less significant than another impetus that was central to many of his programs and objectives. Johnson was both blessed and plagued by a self-imposed obligation to fulfill his perceptions of the Kennedy tradition and often to do what he thought John Kennedy would have done. This drive which fueled several of his presidential policies, applied as much to the

Vietnam War as to civil rights programs.

At the same time, Lyndon Johnson was a shrewd and complicated man. His motivations were mixed for the presidential litany he often intoned in support of his Vietnam policy: that he was carrying on the Southeast Asian policy of John Kennedy and his predecessors, Eisenhower and Truman, and that John Kennedy had solemnly recounted his private meeting at the moment of the 1961 transfer of presidential power when Eisenhower ominously warned him of the Communist threat to our national security in Southeast Asia. Particularly in late 1967 and 1968, this invocation of other presidents was largely motivated by Johnson's desire to garner support from those elements of society which opposed the war most effectively and most vocally at that time. But as the Pentagon Papers grimly demonstrate, this invocation was founded in solid historical facts.

It is no accident that presidents as disparate in personality as Eisenhower, Kennedy, Johnson, and Nixon all perceived the Vietnam War as a matter involving our national security. Each acted on that perception until, in the case of Richard Nixon, it had to give way to the reality that the people of this nation would no longer commit their human and material resources to maintain a government suspected of rampant corruption and perceived to be of such tenuous relevance to our national interests. Prior experience and personality traits affected each president's conduct of his Vietnam policy and his explanation of it to the American people, but the manner in which each president pursued the war differed more because of the situation each faced.

Eisenhower was more reluctant to commit American ground forces and less confident of our ability to police the world than either Kennedy or Johnson; but Eisenhower was not faced with the need for a major troop commitment. Only a handful of military assistance program advisors (some six hundred) were stationed there when he left office and their role was narrowly circumscribed to noncombatant zones and functions. Kennedy increased the number of U.S. forces there to some twenty-five thousand, including Special Forces antiguerrilla units to beat the North and South Vietnamese

Communists at their own game, and he changed their mission by moving them into combat zones with authority to fire when fired upon. As the Pentagon Papers put it, he changed a "gamble" into a "broad commitment." Johnson then sent massive numbers of conventional ground forces to South Vietnam, but he explicitly rejected recommendations for the Cambodian invasion and saturation bombing of North Vietnam subsequently ordered by Nixon. One need not accept the determinist view of history to conclude that, aside from tactical decisions (which, of course, can be tragically translated into human lives), each of those presidents is likely to have acted similarly to protect a perceived national security interest had their times in office been exchanged. To posit that Fulbright, McGovern, or Goldwater would have acted differently is to beg the question. They were never elected president by the American people.

It is, however, worth distinguishing between exchanging tenures in the Oval Office and extending them. Had Presidents Eisenhower, Kennedy, and Johnson been in office for more extended periods, somewhat different Vietnam policies might well have evolved, for time and experience in the presidential crucible have an effect on the incumbent. Despite his penchant for regional security pacts like SEATO (Southeast Asia Treaty Organization), Eisenhower's eight years in office politically confirmed his military concern about becoming bogged down in a land war on the turbulent Southeast Asian peninsula. Kennedy started anew in 1961, with empirically uninhibited optimism about the American capability to shape events in Vietnam and around the world. But, by June of 1963, in his American University speech, Kennedy publicly began to defrost his chilling Inaugural Address rhetoric. His January 1961 call to arms gave way to an incipient recognition that achievable and desirable peace was "not a Pax Americana enforced on the world by American weapons of war." In a September 1963 interview with Walter Cronkite, Kennedy recognized that the war in Vietnam was "their war. . . . the people of [South] Vietnam, against the Communists."

Johnson, in turn, confronted Vietnam without the military

misgivings of Eisenhower or the White House experience of either Eisenhower or Kennedy. But by early 1968, he, too, had come to sense the futility of continued escalation in Vietnam and had begun in earnest the Vietnamization program that Nixon embraced with such public fanfare. The point is not simply that Johnson would have ended the war more rapidly than Nixon, or that Eisenhower would have been more reluctant than Kennedy to increase the number and nature of our forces there and alter their mission. Rather, it seems fair to speculate that had any of these presidents had more extended tenures (as distinguished from exchanged terms), their decisions would have been different.

The manner in which the four presidents solicited public support for the war reflected not only the different situations they faced but also, and perhaps more decisively, their distinctive personality traits. Eisenhower had little need to muster support for U. S. involvement in Southeast Asia. Kennedy held a hawkish televised press conference with maps of Laos and Vietnam during the first spring of his presidency, and carried American popular support through the eloquent cold-war rhetoric that began with his Inaugural Address and hallmarked so much of his presidency. Nixon wrapped the war in the flag that he pinned to his lapel in an attempt to appropriate it as a symbol of loyalty to his administration. His appeal was essentially to the right of the American political spectrum, with some vicious innuendo directed at the liberal press and with conspiracy charges aimed at dissenters and antiwar demonstrators.

Johnson's personal experience also influenced the manner in which he sought to maintain the support of American citizens for the war. He had been profoundly touched by the McCarthy era. Many of the men and women who were destroyed by the neofascist movement that McCarthy seeded and nourished in the arbor of anti-Communism had been Johnson's friends and political allies. He was particularly offended by the defamation of Helen Gahagan Douglas, of whom he spoke highly.

During the 1964 presidential campaign, Johnson enthusiastically accepted Goldwater's invitation to paint the Republican candidate as a mad bomber on a global scale. His focus then was on the middle and the left and, as Philip Geyelin points out in his book, *Lyndon B. Johnson and the World,* he spoke perceptively of the "illusion that the United States can demand resolution of all the world's problems and mash a button and get the job done." While recognizing that our nation had "accepted the responsibilities of world leadership," Johnson pointedly noted that "we are not the sole captain of the ship." In this respect, he shared the sentiments Kennedy expressed shortly before his assassination when he said, "We can't expect these countries to do everything the way we want them to do it. . . . We can't make everyone in our image, and there are a good many people who don't want to go in our image." But faced with the need to make decisions delayed during 1964 and early 1965, Johnson fell back on his experience during the late 1940s and 1950s. In the aftermath of the presidential campaign against Goldwater until the fall of 1967, Johnson's concern about what would happen in America as a result of the Vietnam War was predominantly with the right. He feared that there was a latent strain deep in the American people that supported a bomb-them-into-the-stone-age posture against the North Vietnamese. During those years, he often expressed his concern about the danger of the right forcing some precipitate action that would incite the Chinese Communists to intervene overtly if the war were not pursued with measured, escalating force.

Johnson misjudged the eventual power of the left in American society, particularly its influence on the formulation of American public opinion. Despite repeated urgings by several members of his staff and many of his friends outside the government, he refused to cloak the Vietnam War in the American flag. On rare occasions, he would release flashes of frustrated anger, privately or publicly attacking dissenters to the war as "nervous nellies" or "bomb throwers." He wanted "draft dodgers" and draft-card burners prosecuted. But for too long, Johnson kept looking over his right shoulder as the people moved up on the left. What he did not realize at that time, and what Richard Nixon was eventually forced to accept, was that, for the American nation, the war in Southeast Asia was simply too far away and directed by a government perceived as too corrupt to justify the loss of thousands of young American lives.

Presidents since Roosevelt have pursued essentially similar foreign policy objectives on the major issues that face this nation abroad. Where change has come in the easing of cold-war tensions or foreign economic or aid policy, it has often been dramatically expressed. But it has invariably evolved through broad, bipartisan consensus. Like foreign affairs, domestic policy is also conducted within a broad national consensus. The national, as well as international, policies of most administrations are founded in a more substantial and nonpartisan ideological consensus than the rhetorical idiosyncrasies and disparate styles and means of most presidents tend to reveal.

The major political parties of this nation are not ideologically based. Each provides safe harbor for a wide ideological spectrum. Their success at the national level has depended on their ability to stay within the moderate mainstreams of American life, with most Republicans mildly more conservative and most Democrats mildly more liberal. The ideological boundaries within which their goals are set have been similar for all politically ambitious aspirants and historically ambitious incumbents since the days of Franklin Roosevelt.

With the exception of Barry Goldwater (and that exception may be more rhetorical than real), no aspiring or incumbent American president since the forties has suggested attempting to repeal the New Deal. Each has journeyed down the road to welfare-state capitalism at a different rate of speed, but there have been few detours and no U-turns. Social Security is still on the books, as are the laws establishing the alphabet regulatory agencies which have become an accepted, if shopworn, part of the American system.

Nevertheless, distinctive personality characteristics and prior experience can significantly affect the public problems a president targets for special concern, and the men and women from whom he seeks advice as well. The composition of the Johnson task forces is illustrative. Throughout most of the Johnson presidency, a large number of task forces were at work to devise solutions to a variety of domestic and international public policy problems. Johnson personally approved the memberships of each task force, which was usually composed of experts outside the government—academicians, economists, scientists, doctors, businessmen, labor leaders, lawyers. When I would submit a list of names, he would often call suggesting additional members. Pointedly he would say to others, "Joe thinks the Great Divide is everything between the Berkshires and the Rockies and that no one with any brains lives there." He insisted that individuals from the Northwest and the Southwest and the Central and Southern states be placed on task forces. When the White House domestic staff visited universities, seeking new ideas, Johnson insisted that those trips not be limited to Yale, Harvard, MIT, and UCLA. At his prodding, we also went to such universities as Texas, North Carolina, Chicago, and Tulane. Partly this was because Johnson sensed the importance of having a broad base of intellectual ideas. But it also reflected his sense of betrayal by the Eastern and Western liberal establishments and his own personality clashes with them. As he often remarked, "I'm passing all their legislation and they're still cutting me up." Whatever the reason, the result was substantively significant. In the mid 1960s, the Midwest and South were much more conscious of environmental issues and more concerned about protecting wilderness areas and clean air and water than the Eastern intellectuals, who were more deeply involved with the problems of urban ghettos and the war in Vietnam. Task force members from those Midwestern and Southern areas helped focus Johnson's concern about clean air and water and the problems of solid waste pollution.

Johnson's personality was rooted in a tough, lower- and middle-class upbringing in the rugged Hill Country of Texas. It was nurtured first by teaching Mexican-American children and then by his service as a National Youth administrator. As a young congressman, he "put in his whole stack of chips" to support the New Deal. These experiences contributed

mightily to his sense of national obligation toward the poor
and the Blacks. Kennedy witnessed poverty in Appalachia
during his campaign against Hubert Humphrey in West Virginia and was deeply touched by it. Lyndon Johnson learned
about poverty when he lived in its midst with poor Mexican-
Americans in Texas. He knew the indignities of segregation
and discrimination in the South from personal experience,
not as many of his advisers learned of it, from reading Gordon
Allport's book on *The Nature of Prejudice.* Often Johnson
talked about the travels of his cook, Zepher and her husband,
driving a Johnson car from Washington to Texas across the
South, with few, if any, places at which they could stay because they were Black. His experiences go a long way toward
explaining his concern about tearing the nation apart over
failure to resolve the race issue. His personality consumed
the issue and directed his energies at eliminating racial discrimination. He used every tool at his disposal to achieve that
goal.

Individual personality traits can also have an impact on the
way in which the president decides and is able to lead the
nation. Eisenhower projected a secure leadership, always
keeping the distance of a benevolent father from the people
he often treated as members of a family in need of wise
guidance and patient discipline. Gerald Ford has led with
humility, as one of the boys. His lectures on the economy
have often displayed the ambiance of a college football coach
trying to inspire a losing team at half time. His "WIN" but-
tons, to enlist support to fight inflation, were greeted with
snickers in the sophisticated salons of the East, but he hoped
they would provide a rallying symbol for the middle American, the greatest potential source of his political support.
John Kennedy had a publicly seductive style which he
shrewdly used to lead the people initially toward the emotional acceptance and ultimately toward the avid support of
a particular goal or issue. Within weeks after his election, we
accepted the possibility of a nuclear attack on the United
States; within months we were enthusiastically building
bomb shelters and stocking water and canned food in our
basements. Once we appreciated the technological reality

that we could put a man on the moon, he led us to make the enormous financial commitments necessary to achieve the goal. He knew the value of high visibility in political leadership—whether it was fifty-mile marches to improve the physical fitness of American youth or green berets for our counterguerrilla forces. He went directly to the people because that was where he was best, and he tended to shy away from the congressional corridors because there he was least comfortable.

Johnson's attempts to obtain support from a large segment of the American public, as distinguished from the power elite, were much less effective after his landslide victory in 1964. On the other hand, Johnson was, indeed, both student and master of the Congress, comfortable with the complex of Washington forces emanating both within and outside the Capitol. He knew well the Rube Goldberg nature of Washington power and often, when he pressed the button, only he truly appreciated the labyrinth of forces he had set in motion to achieve his goal.

Kennedy and Johnson tended to fight for their common goals in areas most familiar to them. Like all other presidents, they tried to play to their own strengths and away from their own weaknesses, both with mixed results. The same instinct that led Johnson to obtain a Gulf of Tonkin Resolution for Vietnam misled him to place too much reliance on it. The same sense of public relations that led Kennedy to help organize the August 1963 civil rights march misled him to overestimate the ability of even such a magnificently orchestrated peaceful demonstration to obtain congressional action without persistent legislative follow-through.

The personal idiosyncracies of each president affect his conduct in office in any number of less visible ways. Johnson was inordinately sensitive to his characterization in the press as a "wheeler-dealer." As a result, he issued unprecedentedly strict conflict-of-interest directives and repeatedly prohibited his staff from involvement in any antitrust or regulatory commission cases. Johnson's determination to shake the wheeler-dealer image made him extraordinarily reluctant to grant any pardons. By contrast, Nixon perceived the pardon power as one more presidential tool to achieve political objectives.

The personality differences between Eisenhower, Kennedy, Johnson, Nixon, and Ford are pointed up sharply in their different styles of conducting the business of the Oval Office. Eisenhower's staff system was military; his appearance fatherly. Kennedy's staff system was less structured; his appearance exhuberant and energetic. Johnson's staff system was frenetic, seeking a cure for every ill; his appearance one of indefatigable perpetual motion, in constant conversation and consultation. Nixon's staff system was elaborately structured; his personal style one of lonely contemplation and suspicion, speaking to an unprecedentedly small number of aides. Ford's staff system is middle-America, a group of the boys trying to work things out; his personal style neighborly, sincere. There is a good measure of truth in son-in-law David Eisenhower's remark about the tone of the Watergate White House staff, "Maybe it was the personality of Richard Nixon that inspired it."

What does the analysis in these three chapters tell us about personality and the presidency? The examples, largely but not entirely, are from my own experience, particularly with Lyndon Johnson. I have selected them much as a novelist uses key characters, to illustrate general propositions with specific incidents and hopefully to illuminate the impact of personality on the exercise of the presidential power. They are similar to incidents described in the literature and lore of other presidencies. On the whole, they are designed to illuminate not the personality traits peculiar to Lyndon Johnson, but those that should be familiar to any aides who have served in the White House and to students of presidential history.

From the foregoing analysis, the importance of personality to the selection of presidential objectives and the manner in which he seeks to achieve them—indeed, whether he achieves them—should be apparent. Personality is often decisive to the style in which presidential power is exercised. How a president perceives the problems he faces is profoundly affected by his personality.

To some extent, a president is a prisoner of historical forces that will demand his attention whatever his preference in policy objectives. Where the president is faced with an event or crisis that requires an immediate response, personality can notably affect history. Every president is a victim as well as a molder of events. The consistently dovish rhetoric of Democratic presidential campaigners since Woodrow Wilson did not change the historical fact that war touched the presidency of most successful candidates. Wilson no more wanted World War I than Roosevelt wanted World War II: Truman the Korean conflict; Kennedy the Russian probe of his strength and will during the Berlin and Cuban missile crises or the early conflict in Vietnam; Johnson the full-blown Vietnam War. Each president has unexpected successes and makes unintended mistakes, particularly in foreign and economic policy and in responding to immediate crises. As the time within which a president must react to a crisis is telescoped, the time for considered reflection before action becomes reduced. Each reduction of calculated input creates room for an increase in personality input. It is in such circumstances—race riots in major cities, hourly hot-line exchanges with the Russian premier over a Middle East crisis, the half-hour to decide whether this is the moment to force the anti-civil-rights bill filibuster to a cloture vote—that personality may well be decisive in establishing (or failing to establish) major national policies.

Distinctive personality characteristics can affect the manner in which presidential power is marshaled and deployed; and that, in turn, can influence whether a policy objective is achieved. But what brings a president to political and social beliefs that give birth to ideological commitments is a combination of his conviction as to what is right, his aspirations for his place in history, and his sense of where the country should go, tempered by his perception of where the American people are willing to take it. This is true whether the president comes from Kansas via West Point, the Hill Country of Texas via the Senate, Irish-American Boston via Harvard, California via Wall Street law practice, or Grand Rapids, Michigan, via the House minority leadership.

Whatever a man's path to the White House, he will arrive

with certain characteristics common to most presidential personalities. The demand for loyalty is the paramount characteristic of every presidential personality. Ideally it will be accompanied by a sufficiently mature sense of security to permit loyal dissent and disagreement. Similarly, the egocentricity that leads men to conclude they can be a better president than anyone else should be tempered by the kind of curiosity and flexibility that instructs changes of view and informs perspective.

Persistence, occasionally to the point of stubborness, is essential to the achievement of most controversial presidential objectives. Unyielding, "I'm-from-Missouri-you've-got-to-show me" skepticism is critical to the intelligent analysis and selection of policy options. So is the sense of security that comes from a well-balanced ego that makes a president personally comfortable in testing policy alternatives on a variety of aides, government officials, outside experts, special-interest representatives, casual office visitors, and opponents. The difficulty in having the relevant facts before a presidential decision is made and the need to take most presidential decisions without all the relevant facts make these particularly desirable personality traits.

All these qualities are likely to be accompanied in most presidential personalities by full measures of shrewd calculation, secretiveness, and pragmatic detachment. The mix will, of course, vary individually, and the dominance of one or another of these traits is likely to differ at various times, as personal pressures and untimely events confront the presidential personality. But most presidents are imbued with these personality traits in greater or lesser degree.

Identification of common personality traits is of critical importance to the formulation of recommendations designed to enhance, curb, or guide the exercise of presidential power. It is difficult, perhaps impossible, to devise rules to deal with personality traits peculiar to individual presidents, except at the outer limits of weakness or criminality. But proposals that fail to take common personality traits into account are founded in political quicksand.

The more power the people give a president, the more

they expect from him. But when all is said and done, written, and rewritten about presidential personality and public policy, at the core must be a recognition by all Americans that, like their own, presidential human nature is fallible, subject to the seductive temptation of personal indispensability, and just as likely as any other to rationalize the misuse of power for goals personally perceived as worthy.

Human nature is complicated and the motivations of most presidents are difficult to identify with any precision, even by the president himself. Many of us on the Johnson staff often used to think that if we could identify the ninety-nine reasons why Johnson took a particular action, we had probably overlooked the decisive one. That is certainly true of many presidents, if not of most leaders, throughout our nation's and the world's history.

Those who seek to structure institutions and devise systematic changes to put presidential power in a perspective conducive for the development of our democratic system must appreciate the relevance of common personality traits to the exercise of presidential power. They must understand how specially difficult it can be for a president to personally admit (much less correct) mistakes, as distinguished from accepting public responsibility, and to resist the temptation to accept or acquire more power to pursue what he perceives to be overriding national objectives. We need to know a great deal more about the impact of personality on the presidency and the impact of presidential power on the personalities of the men who hold the office. Few men ever achieve positions or are placed in situations where they realize they may be capable of doing anything; even fewer have at their disposal the power to act on that realization—and presidents are at the top of this select group.

The forces that play upon an incumbent president undoubtedly have an impact on his personality and they will affect his perception of the office he holds. Most presidents learn from their experience in the Oval Office. How fast they learn is more a function of their intelligence than their personality; what they learn may well be more a function of their personality than their intelligence.

XII

———✦———

PRESIDENTIAL
POWER IN
CONTEMPORARY
PERSPECTIVE

Like Dorian Gray at death, by the time he resigned in August 1974 Richard Nixon was severely scarred with pockmarks of a corruption that will dominate historical autopsies of his administration for decades to come. While the pardon granted by Gerald Ford might have eased some of the immediate personal pain, the historical lacerations are permanent for the former president. The lasting impact of the sordid events our nation remembers as Watergate on the office of the presidency and the real powers which it harbors is less certain.

The extent to which these events will have any such impact depends on the institutional forces and public and private interests that have the potential to temper the exercise of presidential power. Without changes in the fundamental counterpoint forces and interests in American society, it is unlikely that the tendency of the presidency and the executive branch to strengthen their political, economic, and social muscle will be significantly allayed, even in the aftermath of Watergate. No successor president, elected by the people or appointed by his predecessor, as Gerald Ford was, is likely to relinquish the powers he acquires when he assumes the office. Whatever the objective perception of the ubiquitous intensity of presidential power, the incumbent president will never consider it sufficient to achieve his (the nation's) objectives. For him, each power vacuum is an inviting opportunity that, if filled, may help achieve some desired national goal.

In the wake of Watergate and the abuse of federal police and intelligence powers, several restrictions are likely to be placed on the president's ability to designate those who have access to individual tax returns; the wiretapping issues will be redebated in the Congress and the law may be changed; executive branch intelligence and investigative activities, particularly the Federal Bureau of Investigation and the Central Intelligence Agency, will be more closely scrutinized by the Congress and subjected to additional controls. These legislative safeguards are important to protect civil liberties and citizen privacy. But other likely changes may be more superficial than real: Both the ostensible size of the White House staff and the conspicuous opulence that attended the Nixon presidency will probably be reduced. The attitude and style of the men who sit in the Oval Office during the last quarter of the twentieth century may be most noticeably affected, but the reality of the power they assume will not be essentially trimmed. Gerald Ford's early incumbency has already demonstrated that.

Watergate and all that word came to symbolize in the early 1970s embody at once the most pervasive personal and political corruption in the history of the American presidency. It is important to separate the two. Psychohistorians, political scientists, and law professors will spend decades disecting the intentions and motivations of Mr. Nixon and the legal nicities of his situation. But there are sufficient uncontested facts on the public record to conclude that the depth of personal corruption was unprecedented in the history of the American presidency and that the federal criminal code already contained the statutes necessary to prosecute those involved. There are (and were during the Nixon years) laws on the books that deal with tax evasion and fraud, the conversion of government property, corrupt campaign financing practices, the use of political campaign contributions for personal purposes (especially without the proper personal income tax treatment of those contributions), bribery, extortion, the sale of government offices (like ambassadorships), perjury, and obstruction of justice. The issue is less whether new laws are needed than whether these laws can (and will) be enforced against a president and his aides in a timely fashion.

Beyond that, the personal corruption of Watergate raises questions of morality. While a moral people can inspire fair laws and administer them with justice and mercy, there are no statutes that can create a moral people. No Congress in history has been wise enough to enact legislation to eliminate every possible avenue of temptation and every weakness of human nature. There surely will be future presidents and aides who will use their office or certain of its perquisites to enhance their personal financial situation in the post-Nixon years, just as the Grant and Harding administrations were infected by corruption in the pre-Nixon years. The vast publicity that attended the revelations of corruption in the early 1970s makes it likely that future presidents will be distinctly more sensitive than Richard Nixon to the use of public funds and public office for their personal financial gain. Some statutory tinkering is indicated here, but it is difficult to conceive of significant additional legal ,or institutional safeguards against the personal corruption that permeated the presidency in the early 1970s. In reviewing the ocean of proposals to inhibit presidential power that have flowed from the Watergate experience, we must remember, as former White House counsel Harry McPherson has written, "Most . . . would not have prevented the cover-up. Those that would have succeeded in limiting Mr. Nixon's ability to abuse power would also have impeded a better man in the proper use of it." The benefits of inhibition must be weighed against its risks.

To the extent Watergate reflects the personal corruption and weakness of a man and his colleagues and the moral fragility of human nature, there is little point in seeking profound political, social, or theological insights that will lead to legislative and institutional changes to prevent its recurrence in the future. Every phase of recorded history abounds with acts of personal corruption and immorality. In political, as well as personal terms, the Watergate scandals have ample precedent in the development of the Judeo-Christian ethic that, at least rhetorically, dominates American society. There are saints in this world and the recorded history of mankind. But the prophets of the Old Testament and the parables of Christ teach that most men will succumb to the allure of corrupting temptation whenever the benefits seem sufficiently great and the risks of suffering adverse consequences sufficiently slight. In these terms, presidents are like children at the cookie jar of power. They will keep going back for more so long as they can reach it without getting caught or without being slapped on the wrist.

At this point, the personal and political corruption of the events encompassed by Watergate overlap. It is here that we must focus our national attention. How long ago were the seeds of Watergate abuses planted? Was the office of the presidency visited with such power that its grotesque exercise to achieve presidentially perceived worthy goals was simply a matter of time? Were the institutions and forces of countervailing power so self-centered and debilitated that the president would perceive them as too inner-directed for the timely recognition of an overreaching exercise of power, and too weak to do anything if they did recognize it? The political corruption that Watergate accentuates provides a contemporary perspective essential to understanding the dangers of the failure to counterpoint presidential power more effectively in the last quarter of the twentieth century.

The attacks directed at the executive branch, the Congress, the courts, the press, the opposition political party, the private-sector institutions (like American business), those perceived as political enemies or ideological deviants from administration policy (like Larry O'Brien or Daniel Ellsberg), should be examined with a full appreciation that the president and his top White House staff believed their own actions to be in the national interest. As President Nixon noted in his late evening diary dictation of March 21, 1974, "they [White House aides and others] were all . . . involved for the very best of motives." The conviction of so many Watergate actors, vested with vicarious but nonetheless effective presidential power, that the ends they perceived as legitimate justified their bizarre means points up the importance of invigorating the constitutionally conceived counterpoints to presidential power.

Control of the executive branch is the first goal of every American president. With several million civilian and military employees, achievement of this goal is no task for a president reluctant to exercise his power. A substantial measure of such control is essential if the contemporary president is to have any hope of fulfilling his campaign promises and moving toward the accomplishment of those objectives he sets for the nation during his administration. A wise president, however strong, seeks talent as well as loyalty, integrity as well as industry, men and women in top policy-making positions who will be partners as well as patrons. So it should begin, and probably does, with any new administration.

But loyalty can soon become far more important than ability, personal allegiance more essential than integrity. The government bureaucracy may find itself infiltrated by a cadre of people whose loyalty to the president is transcendent. The same tight control of the executive branch which is essential for efficient program operation also facilitates the use of those programs to help mount the re-election campaign. Where existing organs of executive power do not support the president's concepts of what is in his and the national interest, their top officials may be removed (as, in fact, they were in the Nixon administration) or new organizations established. When FBI Director J. Edgar Hoover balked at the Nixon-approved plan to ferret out the source of leaks to protect the national security, a separate police organization manned by ideological fanatics was established in the White House.

The dysfunctional organization of the executive departments and the congressional rejection of the several reorganization proposals of recent presidents, discussed in Chapter II, has encouraged presidents to establish *ad hoc* organizations and to deploy their personal staffs as a superjurisdictional corps of executive vice-presidents. Notable recent examples involve economic policy, energy, domestic affairs, and national security; but there are any number of other areas in which less publicized White House aides and *ad hoc* arrangements provide a point of functional responsibility for the president. Such arrangements necessarily reduce the stature of traditional cabinet and agency heads. They place in *de facto* control men whose responsibility and loyalty run to the sole source of their authority, the president. The departments and offices, established by the Congress, with nominal and often explicit legal responsibility, are ignored or by-passed by the president because of their functional irrationality. In the early 1970s, the executive bureaucracy was an organizational clay pigeon for the unhealthy increase in presidential power at the expense of the stature of the cabinet and agency officials.

As was the case with the federal executive bureaucracy in the late 1960s and early 1970s, the Congress was so out of political shape that the presidency, on the whole, was an easy institutional winner. Even though the Congress was in the control of the opposition party, the use of presidential power further eroded its stature during that period. Most presidents joust with the Congress during their terms in office and some, like Harry Truman, have even run for election against the Congress. But few have mounted a systematic effort to debilitate a fellow branch of the central government.

Normally, a successful presidential legislative program depends on achieving a majority vote in each house of the Congress. However, Richard Nixon was a president more interested in holding back any new social or economic intervention by the federal government and eliminating programs (or reducing appropriation levels) established by earlier Congresses than in passing new legislation. Like Eisenhower whose forty-four vetoes stymied the decidedly

Democratic 86th Congress, Nixon needed the votes of only one-third-plus-one of the members of either the House of Representatives or the Senate to sustain a presidential veto and block affirmative congressional action. The formidable nature of the veto power came into sharp focus when numerous health, education, and other social programs were eliminated or curtailed by the development of a minority of the Congress in support of the president. The shrewd use of the threat of a veto also had a significant impact on the level of a number of major funding bills and the tone of legislative measures authorizing domestic programs.

Where the veto was not likely to be successful or where the investment of presidential capital in sustaining a veto was not considered worth the effort, the president impounded appropriations to deny or limit funds to programs (like the Community Action Agencies of the Office of Economic Opportunity) he wished to discontinue or redirect. It was the courts, often at the request of potential recipients of appropriated funds, that eventually moved to curb this practice, at least in the most egregious cases. But they, too, became prey for the presidential hunter of the late 1960s and early 1970s.

Political ideology and social philosophy have long been accepted as legitimate considerations in making judicial appointments (although lifetime tenure has provided political appointees with a sense of independence that has surprised many presidents). Roosevelt nominated judges who he believed would uphold his view that the Constitution justified the intervention of the federal government deep into the American economy. Johnson nominated scores of men and women to federal circuit and district judgeships, in large part because he believed they shared his philosophy about equal rights and racial discrimination. President Nixon campaigned in 1968 on assurances that he would bend the courts away from the liberal Warren era with judicial nominees and an attorney general who held less permissive, more conservative "law and order," property-oriented philosophies.

The end and means of Richard Nixon were superficially legitimate and within the traditional exercise of presidential power to fill judicial vacancies and make top appointments in the Justice Department. What characterized the unprecedented and disturbing intrusions of presidential power during the late 1960s and early 1970s was the contemptuous arrogance with which Nixon pursued his goals. With the nomination of Harrold Carswell to sit on the Supreme Court, he glibly dismissed the nation's need for excellence with back-of-the-hand mediocrity. By accepted standards of judicial temperament and legal talent (independent of political philosophy), Carswell was unworthy of appointment. His sense of justice and integrity was such that he dissembled about his racist activities before the Senate Judiciary Committee during his confirmation hearings. Eventually, Nixon appointed William Rehnquist and Lewis Powell to the Supreme Court; both men shared his conservative judicial philosophy and both were eminently qualified to sit on the highest court in terms of legal intellect and personal integrity. But before he did that, he tried deliberately to demean the institutional prestige of the Court with the third-rate nomination of Carswell.

President Nixon's treatment of federal district judges also reflected a sense of institutional contempt for another branch of the government. Richard W. McLaren was whisked into a judicial vacancy in Chicago in the early stages of the ITT investigation, either because he opposed the administration treatment of the ITT, or knew too much about it, or both. Neither the president nor his chief domestic aide, John Ehrlichman, evidenced any sense of impropriety in contacting Judge Matthew Byrne, during the course of the Daniel Ellsberg trial, to tempt him with the possibility of the FBI directorship. Similarly, as the edited transcripts of the presidential tapes released in May 1974 revealed, the president and his aides had no qualms about the intrusion of partisan objectives in their relationship with Charles Richey, the federal district judge who handled the civil suit of the Democrats against the Committee to Re-elect the President resulting from the break-in to Democratic National Committee headquarters in June 1972. So self-confident was the conviction of the president in the ubiquitous reach of his power that there appear to have been no second thoughts about its exercise deep into the reaches of the federal judiciary.

In the 1960s and early 1970s three Supreme Court justices set at least some precedents for this attitude. Chief Justice Warren Burger supported Richard Nixon's handling of the Vietnam War, delivering him a note in support of the Cambodian invasion that several Congressmen and many Americans considered an unconstitutional exercise of presidential power, and he made no secret of his support for the president on controversial domestic matters. When asked about his cozy relationship with Lyndon Johnson after he went on the bench, Abe Fortas asked, How can you turn a president down when he has such difficult problems and seeks your advice? In August 1964, then Supreme Court Justice Arthur Goldberg wrote President Johnson with partisan political advice suggesting five steps he should take "similar to those which the Labor party in Britain has taken, to minimize serious strikes during this [presidential] campaign," including private talks "with Meany, Reuther, other labor leaders and politically friendly industrialists." No wonder Elizabeth Drew concluded her analysis of the federal judiciary in the October 1972 *Atlantic Monthly* with the question, "whatever happened to checks and balances?" Novelist Herman Melville was more pointed when he warned almost one hundred years ago: "If there are any three things opposed to the genius of the American Constitution, they are these: irresponsibility in a judge, unlimited discretionary authority in an executive, and the union of an irresponsible judge and an unlimited executive in one person."

The clashes of the press with American presidents are a chronic fact of political life. Woodrow Wilson believed that the press never supported him adequately on the League of Nations. Franklin Roosevelt considered the press a mouthpiece for the Republican opposition and the voice of the "economic royalists." John Kennedy banned a newspaper from the White House because he did not like the stories it had written and repeatedly expressed his distress at newsmagazine stories to his friend, then *Newsweek* Bureau Chief

Benjamin Bradlee. There were few White House correspondents who were not called by Lyndon Johnson or one of his aides to complain about one story or another. But none of those presidents, even in their most charged moments of anger, ever used their power to systematically undermine public confidence in the integrity and credibility of the free press in America or to drain its economic strength.

Early in the Nixon administration, Vice-President Spiro Agnew attacked the major Eastern newspapers and media, particularly those most critical of the administration, like the Washington *Post*, the New York *Times*, and the news departments of the three major television networks, ABC, CBS, and NBC. In the Pentagon Papers case, the Justice Department attempted to impose the first prior restraint on free speech in the two hundred-year history of our nation. That same department then pursued New York *Times* correspondent Earl Caldwell, in an attempt to deny reporters the right to protect the confidential sources of information essential to most investigative stories, a move that the *Yale Law Journal* characterized in 1971 as a "divergence from previous Justice Department policy."

The most vicious attack on the press was mounted in response to the Watergate stories of the Washington *Post*. The effort was both verbal and economic, with official after official in the White House and the administration leveling salvos at a series of stories that later turned out to be correct. (Perhaps, as a result, during much of the Watergate revelations, the American people on the whole believed those speaking from the narrow perch of executive power, not those working on our daily newspapers.) Economic attacks included attempts by friends of the Nixon administration to have revoked the FCC licenses of two local television stations owned by the *Post*, in Miami and Jacksonville, Florida. TV stations customarily provide a return on investment at a much higher rate than newspapers, and are important to the economic viability of any communications enterprise. The potential of federal intervention through the Federal Communications Commission is a constant threat to the networks and broadcast licensees.

The Watergate revelations also illustrate the power of an unscrupulous president to divide and conquer the opposition political party. The events are well known: They include the bugging and attempted burglary of Democratic National Committee headquarters; the forged Muskie letter using the opprobrious "Canuck"; the forged false accusations of sexual misconduct against Senators Hubert Humphrey and Henry Jackson; the Internal Revenue Service harassment of Democratic National Committee Chairman Lawrence O'Brien. Any number of snafus and strange occurrences plagued the Democratic primaries and the presidential campaign of George McGovern, some of which were likely the work of the president's staff and campaign aides. What should concern the nation is not only that men played such dirty tricks in the 1968 campaigns. More profoundly disturbing was the vulnerability of the opposition party, not simply because of its own ideological fragmentation, but because of its distinct financial and media disadvantages in the face of an incumbent president. These disadvantages account in no small part for the fact that so many of these corrupt practices did not surface before the American people until months after the 1972 presidential election.

The most frightening lessons of the early 1970s lie in the demonstration of the power of the president to reach out across American institutions, public and private, to protect and sometimes rationalize the most insidious abuses of presidential power. Three ingredients were essential to make these abuses possible: the distortion of political values, secrecy, and money.

The awe in which most Americans hold the presidency produces an environment in which ends can justify means, the distinction between the man and the office can become blurred, and the difference between public and private morality and public and personal responsibility can become confused. National political administrations, like lesser institutions and families, do not like their dirty linen washed in public, but few institutions have traditions of "national security" and "executive privilege" to keep their activities secret. Because of the penetration of federal executive power into virtually every facet of American life and its potentially decisive powers over most aggregate economic interests, the money for the political campaign of an incumbent president—in 1972 some $60 million—has been delivered with surprising ease when he has been favored for re-election. In greater or lesser degree, there were precedents in all these areas—people and their confused values, secrecy, and money—to set something of a stage for the grotesque distortion of democracy on which the Nixon administration embarked.

The predominant confusion that has plagued the people's perception of the presidency, particularly since the time of John Kennedy and the television presidency, has involved their difficulty in distinguishing between the office and the man. The founding fathers were sensitive to this distinction. Elitist political theory was the rationale of family-blood monarchy and dictatorship that led many of them to renounce their European citizenship and sail the perilous seas in search of a new nation. Because of their bitter experience with and concern about that kind of government, they drafted a Constitution very much based on a system of law that takes into full account the fallible, human nature of the few who from time to time have been entrusted with governing the many. The Constitution was deliberately designed to protect the body politic from the bad man in the good office and to distribute power in healthy conflict for the good of the people. By providing clear lines of succession; by setting forth the procedures for the impeachment of a felonious federal judge, cabinet official, vice-president, or president; and by limiting terms of office for elected officials, the founding fathers recognized that human history was plagued by death, corruption, and excessive concentrations of power. They drafted a Constitution designed as much to protect the office from the man as it is to give the man who holds the office the authority he needs to serve the people.

It is much easier to recognize the distinction between the office and the man when a federal judge is involved, for there are so many federal judges; or when a congressman or senator is involved, for there are 435 congressmen and 100 senators. Indeed, in a brief submitted during the criminal case of Spiro Agnew, the Justice Department drew a distinction between the "indispensable" president whom it claimed could not be indicted while in office and the "dispensable" vicepresident whom it claimed was subject to the criminal justice process during incumbency.

There will always be aides around a president—particularly as he seeks to satisfy his understandable demand for loyalty—who will merge the office and the man and act on the sincerely held conviction that the good of the office can never be separated from the good of the man who occupies it at any given moment of time. One need only reflect on the attitude of some of Franklin Roosevelt's closest aides when Harry Truman took office, or the bitterness that developed between those aides of John Kennedy who left shortly after his assassination and those who remained to serve Lyndon Johnson, to realize that a merger of office and man is psychologically natural and humanly understandable. That same transitional staff bitterness plagued the early months of the Ford administration.

Recognition of the difference between the office and the man is difficult enough; acting on that recognition takes a level of dispassionate examination rarely found in the partisans who worked with the man during his campaign for the presidency and who are the first to drink with him from the Holy Grail of presidential power. Even late arrivals to a president's administration fall prey to this misconception. The failure of General Alexander Haig, the chief of staff drafted by Nixon when Haldeman and Ehrlichman resigned, to make this distinction led him to believe that he had to defend Nixon to protect the presidency. With apparent, if misguided, sincerity, James St. Clair claimed he was representing the office of the presidency when he was trying to save Nixon the man from impeachment and criminal prosecution.

In Washington, there is generally a tendency to view the office of the presidency very much through the glasses of the man who occupies it, because the politicians and bureaucrats there are well aware of how differently the office is sculptured by the hands of a conservatively passive Eisenhower than by the hands of a liberally aggressive Johnson. In a much less sophisticated way, the average American identifies the office and the man as one; for, in psychological perception and publicly received image, the presidential shield takes on the shape of the man who holds it.

The mass of the American people are likely to continue to identify office and man psychologically, programmatically, and politically. They recognize that the man must retain his legitimacy to hold the office by election at least every four years. But it seems quite clear that the American people prefer to merge the office and the man until they themselves have an opportunity to go to the polls and separate the two. Their reluctance to urge impeachment for so long in the face of the most profound and pervasive political corruption in the history of the presidency bears persuasive witness to this observation. Other factors contributed to that reluctance in 1974: their distrust of the politicians voting on impeachment and the margin by which they had rejected the Democratic candidate who ran against Nixon in 1972. But, essentially the people believed that they had merged the office and the man by their votes. In a sense, the men around President Nixon affirmed by their actions the psychological identification shared by the overwhelming majority of their fellow citizens.

The merger of the office and the man in the minds of those who serve a particular president becomes more dangerous because of the confusion in American political life between public and private morality. John Courtney Murray, the great American Jesuit philosopher, decried the failure of the modern world to distinguish between the moral standards that govern individual morality and those that govern national morality. The American citizen, as an individual, is steeped in private morality. He learns it from his parents, his schools, and his church. There are some absolutes, but private morality is essentially that which is right or wrong for an individual, as an individual, to do or not to do at any given time under any given set of circumstances.

Public morality is little taught in our schools, rarely preached in our churches, and within the personal experi-

ence of only 1 or 2 percent of our population. For one man
to kill another may be murder; acting as agent for a nation
at war, killing may be justifiable and publicly moral. For one
man to steal from another for personal gain is privately immoral and perhaps publicly punishable as a crime; for one
nation to steal the secrets of another nation is legitimate
within current standards of public international morality.

This distinction between private and public morality is of
major importance for any man who aspires to presidential
leadership. Often a president's pursuit of public objectives
will accord with standards of both public and private morality. But consider, for example, whether or not resignation is
an appropriate course of action for a president. If the paramount consideration in his mind is personal morality, the
decision may be quite different than if the paramount consideration is public morality. Negligence, bad judgment in making appointments, lack of specific knowledge, refusal to face
tough facts—the presence of any or even all of these factors
would still permit a conclusion that a man did not commit a
personal wrong sufficient to require his resignation from
office. But the presence of these same factors might very well
justify resignation because of the offense they give to any
reasonable standards of public morality, since no acid more
rapidly erodes the respect of the people essential for effective political leadership in a democracy than public immorality.

The Watergate scandals offered repeated instances of the
disturbing failure of many individuals to evidence any sense
of public morality. John Ehrlichman casually dismissed the
burglary of Daniel Ellsberg's psychiatrist's office with a
"don't-do-it-again" admonition to the burglars on his own
White House staff, apparently confusing his public obligation
with his rationalized sense of private innocence because he
did not personally enter the psychiatrist's office to steal the
patient reports. Patrick Gray equivocated in statements to
the press, campaigned while acting FBI director for the
Republican presidential candidate, and destroyed "politically dynamite" documents without any sense that he was
giving offense to public morality; but his Catholic upbringing

and schooling would not permit him to lie under oath because that involved personal morality and perhaps serious individual sin. Nixon presidential aides Haldeman and Ehrlichman, in their letters of resignation, paid lip service to public morality, but protested their private morality as though that were the ultimate standard by which their exercise of the public trust should be judged.

Where a distinction between public and private morality has been rhetorically recognized, too often it has been used to justify some extraordinary action that would otherwise be immoral or criminal. The special obligations attendant to public morality have rarely been recognized in the contemporary exercise of presidential power. Public office has been perceived as a magic looking glass that vests those it reflects with the-end-justifies-the-means right to take actions that would otherwise constitute unquestioned immorality. Too rarely has public office been seen as imposing separate and higher standards of morality on those who hold it. For a John Mitchell, almost any action may be justifiable to maintain incumbent presidential power, if the alternative available on the other side is bad enough. For a White House aide like John Ehrlichman, it may not be possible to draw any lines to limit presidentially authorized activities.

Perhaps the most common distortion of the distinction between public and private morality is reflected in the firm conviction of most presidents that under special circumstances they have a right to lie, that standards of public morality justify levels of evasion and outright dissembling that are beyond the bounds of private morality. Arthur Sylvester, the first assistant secretary of defense for public affairs under President Kennedy, was the only government official in recent times to state publicly, with the ironic candor that characterized his public service, that the government had a right to lie to preserve the national security. His comment was made in defense of the way Kennedy handled the Cuban missile crisis and was based on the commonly held belief of high government officials that there are some things the people should not be told in order to protect them. The rationale

for this often self-serving tenet is that the people have vested
this authority in their leaders and that dissembling to prevent the revelation of certain information is well within the
bounds of public morality; indeed, that it may be required to
fulfill public responsibilities.

For a president, there are three ways to keep secrets: the
use of the national security classification system, the scheme
of deniability which has been domesticated from CIA use,
and evasion or, if necessary, outright lying. While Nixon
broke new frontiers of abusing presidential power in the use
of these techniques, the basic principles had been established
as acceptable long before he took office. Most presidents are,
as James MacGregor Burns characterized Franklin Roosevelt, both lion and fox, and their foxiness is often displayed
in their misleading and evasive discussion of public policies.
FDR was certainly less than candid when he said shortly
before World War II that our boys would never fight on
foreign soil. John Kennedy's placid public description of his
hair-raising Vienna summit with Khrushchev was hardly
forthcoming. Dwight Eisenhower's initial disavowal of CIA
intelligence flights over the Soviet Union was outright misleading. Both Kennedy and Johnson played their chess game
in Vietnam too close for eventual national comfort in the
early stages of the war.

All those presidents undoubtedly believed that the secrecy
they treasured was so essential to the national security that
it justified occasionally misleading the American people. For
the most part, the American people accepted their judgment. While the precedents are not directly in point, it
should have come as no surprise that someday a president
would intone the political chant of "national security" to hide
from the American people any number of embarrassing if
not criminal actions. Of course, Nixon went beyond the self-
imposed limits of his predecessors when he invoked the
chant of national security to drive the demons of criminal
responsibility from the West Wing of the White House. But
the key point is that the limits were self-imposed by prior
presidents and there was some precedent for Nixon to exercise the accepted presidential prerogative of determining

what to keep secret and to what lengths it was appropriate to go to maintain secrecy.

The pressures of incumbency and the seemingly insoluble problems presidents face tempt most of them to reach for and use all the powers at their disposal. To the extent they can use some of those powers secretly, they are not likely to have the political and moral grace to resist the temptation to use them improperly. During his showdown with the steel industry, John Kennedy dispatched Washington attorneys to Pittsburgh, discreetly to threaten top corporate executives with meticulous and relentless Internal Revenue Service audits of their personal income taxes if the price increase was not rolled back. He approved the use of all manner of dirty tricks in an attempt to topple the Castro regime. Lyndon Johnson is reported to have used the FBI to wiretap potential adversaries during the 1964 Democratic National Convention and on other occasions. The true role of the CIA in the domestic affairs of our nation during the 1960s and early 1970s may never be fully disclosed. But it seems clear that it served the partisan political purposes of Richard Nixon and it is likely, with or without explicit presidential direction, that its activities during the Nixon administration were not without some precedent during the Kennedy-Johnson years.

The presidential handmaiden of secrecy is deniability— the ability of an individual ordering an act performed to deny with publicly received credibility that he had anything to do with that act. It is common for White House aides and cabinet officers to take actions specifically directed by the president in a manner which permits the president either to deny that he had anything to do with those actions or even publicly to reprimand the aide or cabinet officer for taking them. When John Kennedy ordered the Pentagon to establish a procedure permitting press interviews only in the presence of a public affairs officer, the order was issued by Assistant Secretary Sylvester (who refused to let a presidentially loyal Robert McNamara sign it). The press reaction was (as Sylvester had predicted) vocal, antagonistic, and persistent. When reporters' pleas for revocation of the order fell on deaf ears in the Pentagon, they went to the White House where they were told that it was a matter for the Pentagon to handle and that the president would not overrule the secretary of defense. Pentagon knowledge that Kennedy had ordered any new procedure was unusual during the McNamara regime. McNamara's policy had been never to reveal whether he or the president was ordering an action, a procedure he customarily followed and some other cabinet officers occasionally adopted to protect the president from public involvement in potential controversy or public responsibility for a mistake.

During a spurt of food price increases in 1966, Lyndon Johnson told me to direct Agriculture Secretary Orville Freeman to hold a press conference deploring rising food prices. Johnson thought such a statement by the secretary of agriculture would be unusual enough to attract wide attention. Coming from the secretary of agriculture, Johnson also thought it would make clear that he meant to jawbone farmers to hold down produce and meat prices. He was explosively correct on both counts. When farm interests came to the White House to demand Freeman's scalp, Johnson, of course, refused to give it. But he was not beyond deploring such a politically indiscreet statement by his secretary of agriculture, although he pointedly told one group, "Food prices must sure be out of sight if Orville Freeman is complaining publicly about them!"

Ideas are commonly floated at presidential direction to test them on the American people, in a way that permits the president total deniability. The presidential reasoning is that such trial balloons can open a public dialogue without prematurely foreclosing presidential options. Opposing politicians are often attacked by administration aides in the same way and for similar reasons. When *Newsweek* reported John Kennedy's annoyance at the liberals for messing up policy formulation, he asked the bureau chief to put the words in the mouth of White House aide Kenny O'Donnell to protect his own position. All of this has long been regarded as well within the bounds of contemporary American political morality.

Richard Nixon carried the established political precedents

of his predecessors in preserving deniability to unprecedented lengths. White House aide Douglas Hallett has reported that most White House political memos were "ad-
dressed to Haldeman to preserve the president's deniability
in case of any leaks; in turn, many presidential memos were
either signed by Haldeman or unsigned altogether." Nixon
added elements of CIA dirty tricks deniability and used them
to confuse and conceal individual criminal responsibility.
The sheer size of the Nixon White House and Re-election
Committee staffs provided unprecedented opportunities to
assure deniability. The difficulty for a president in controlling
such a large number of White House and campaign aides was
matched only by the difficulty of the special prosecutor, the
Senate Watergate Committee, the House Judiciary Committee, and criminal juries in assessing individual responsibility
for specific Watergate acts.

The rhetoric on the accountability and size of the White
House staff has been shrill, but unless it is accepted by future
presidents, that rhetoric is unlikely to have much practical
effect. There is little the Congress can do to limit the number
of people actually working for the White House. The bureaucratic reality gives the president wide flexibility to employ
men on the payrolls of government departments and agencies. He can also consult and deploy any number of willing
private citizens to act as surrogates or emissaries in conducting the public business. Johnson, for example, sent Abe Fortas to the Caribbean during the 1965 Dominican Republic
crisis; Ford sent a Washington attorney to San Clemente to
arrange the Nixon pardon.

Where deniability fails to maintain secrecy, the upside-
down-cake public morality that has guided the contemporary exercise of presidential power must turn to dissembling.
In our society, it is a criminal offense for a private citizen to
lie to the government. It is no offense for a president or a
public official to lie to the people (unless they do so under
oath). The record of the early 1970s abounds with instances
of White House aides and cabinet officials who lied to the
press and their colleagues repeatedly.

Perjury is a common enough offense, particularly in the

white-collar crime area. Most businessmen and union officials involved in fraud or embezzlement cases have more problems because of what they say about what they did, than because of what they did. Lying is a common weakness of human nature. Even St. Peter, the rock of the Christian churches, lied three times in denying his affiliation with Christ shortly before the crucifixation. But St. Peter realized that he was wrong, just as most private citizens realize it is wrong to lie, and criminally so if the lie is under oath. What marked some of the president's men of the early 1970s was their conviction for so long that there was nothing wrong with their dissembling. They believed they were cloaked with public, presidential robes, morally sufficient to justify dissembling and perjury and taking a series of other actions that would be criminal for those less regally dressed in the mufti of private life. That so many ambitious young (and old) men held this belief is a stinging commentary on the seductive allure of power. There is more than a little truth in Nixon aide and Jesuit Father John McLaughlin's comment that "the exercise of power is an experience as intense as sex."

The confusion between public and private morality and responsibility and the ability to maintain secrecy have seriously corrupted the exercise of presidential power. But the third ingredient, private money, has probably done more to corrupt contemporary political morality than any other single factor. Private money is a uniquely productive fertilizer for the seeds of political corruption.

Campaign financing has long been the Augean stable of American presidential politics. Most experienced politicians have recognized, although they too rarely publicly admit it, that the relationship between private wealth and public office has been detrimental to the healthy development of our democracy. The vitality of a democratic society depends on the exposure of its citizens to a variety of points of view and personalities. The greatest inhibition on that exposure in the last two decades has been the prohibitive cost of running for political office, particularly the presidency. Certainly, without public financing, since the 1960 campaign between

John Kennedy and Richard Nixon, it has not been possible to say to every American that his child could grow up to be president (or even a congressman or a senator), if he were the best man with the best ideas; rather, he could grow up to hold high political office in America only if he had (or could raise) sufficient funds to mount the campaign.

Watergate dramatized for the American people the special money-raising ability of an incumbent administration assured of re-election and willing to use the tools of government as expressed or implied inducements. During the 1972 campaign, the acquisition of political funds through the exercise of presidential power was without precedent. But the termite of financial corruption had long been gnawing at the foundations of government. Many years before Watergate, private wealth had become the most debilitating and corrupting force in presidential and national politics. There had long existed ample warnings to alert the American people to the dangers of private wealth to public politics:

—After spending $250,000 in an embryonic campaign for the Democratic presidential nomination in 1971, Senator Fred Harris quit because he was $40,000 in debt and his financial angels were unable or unwilling to put up any more money.

—Senator Edmund Muskie, another contender in the 1972 presidential sweepstakes, sharply reduced his staff in late 1971 because he began to run out of funds. When faced with a choice between reducing the substantive side of his staff or his political experts, he cut the former, in part, because delegate votes in hand helped keep the money rolling in.

—Herb Alexander, probably the foremost authority on campaign financing in the nation, has estimated that, by the late 1960s, it cost at least $.5 million for a party nominee simply to operate his campaign headquarters at the convention.

—In 1968, the Nixon forces spent $3.5 million dollars solely for the purpose of raising money.

—The reported costs of financing presidential campaigns rose from $6.2 million dollars in 1940 to $44.2 million dollars in 1968, an increase of more than 700 percent. The true expenditures in the 1972 presidential campaigns probably exceeded $100 million.

—*Time* magazine estimated that the 1972 political campaigns cost $400 million for all candidates that ran, with the express caveat that its estimate was likely on the low side.

Political power and money have been mutually reinforcing props in the amorality play of contemporary presidential politics. In the 1972 election, Richard Nixon and his men raised at least $60 million for his re-election campaign. His opponent had some $20 to $25 million. Even had George McGovern been a more broadly appealing candidate, he was not likely to have been a significantly more effective opponent when he was outspent more than two to one in the era of modern communications. Moreover, the $60 million available to Nixon is deceptive, because it does not include the special financial advantages of an incumbent president: the free transportation, access to evening television news broadcasts and daily front-page newspaper coverage, the superb federally financed communications system, the government-paid campaign aides on the White House staff and in the federal departments.

Other powers of the president were also put at the disposal of the fund-raising re-election effort in the 1972 campaign. The clouded ITT and milk price-support increase matters have received wide publicity. The Senate Watergate Committee staff concluded that the White House "responsiveness program" was designed by presidential aides to support political fund raising through the use of federal grants of millions of dollars, the shaping of legal and regulatory actions, and government employment. The Senate committee staff report concluded that the actions appeared to violate federal criminal and civil statutes and "may rise to the level of a conspiracy to interfere with the lawful functioning of government."

Federal criminal statutes prohibit the improper use of government power for campaign fund-raising efforts. It is a felony to solicit or accept anything of value as a political contribution in consideration of any promise of influence in obtaining a federal job. Bribery, extortion, receiving political contributions on federal property or from government contractors or corporations, even promises of "any . . . other benefit," or any "special consideration . . . for any political activity" are federal crimes, conviction of which may result in imprisonment and fine. These statutes attempt to draw a line between the cynical side of Rooseveltian politics (tax and tax, elect and elect) and the raw use of government power for partisan political and fund-raising purposes.

Administrations since the days of Franklin Roosevelt, and probably before, to the extent federal grants and jobs were available, have had the option to place grants in the hands of partisans and those who could be of political assistance. The line between helping Blacks because one believes Blacks need some extra help in Harlem or Watts or Hough and helping Blacks because one thinks they will vote for the administration in power can often be a fine one. So long as the assistance needed exceeds the resources available, judgments will have to be made among competing supplicants. But many of the activities of the early 1970s seemed clearly to cross over the boundary of questionable judgment and Jacksonian spoils politics into the territory of criminal activity.

Over the course of every recent presidency, there has been some relationship between financial political support and certain ambassadorships. Some such posts (England and France are examples) require a substantial level of personal wealth because government pay and allowances are grossly inadequate to cover the expenses of an effective ambassador. Lesser ambassadorial posts, such as those in the Caribbean, have often been considered political rewards for long party service or financial support. But in the early 1970s this nation was called to bear witness to the cash-on-the-line, no-credit-cards-accepted sale of ambassadorial positions to the highest bidder. So blatant did the cash market in ambassadorial posts become that the Senate Foreign Relations Committee now routinely demands complete revelation of political contributions by all nominees. Perhaps the most publicized example in the early 1970s was Mrs. Ruth Farkas, who was named ambassador to Luxemburg after pledging some $300,000 to President Nixon's campaign, $200,000 of which was not even paid until after the re-election of the president, at a time when his campaign coffers groaned under a substantial surplus. Few Americans know about the even more dramatic example of Cornelius Whitney. He was promised the ambassadorship to Spain in return for a $250,000 contribution; when the appointment did not come through, the contribution was returned.

Investments of private wealth to help obtain or maintain political power are sometimes wholesomely motivated. But the larger those investments become, the more suspicions they justify about motivation and the more serious their erosion of the constitutional principle that each man is entitled to only one vote. Why do individuals of enormous wealth contribute substantial amounts of money to the presidential candidates of both major parties when they are running against each other? Perhaps for the politically altruistic purpose of supporting the two-party system, but more likely to hedge their bets, to assure access no matter who gets elected.

Federal regulations declare the appearance of a conflict of interest as abhorrent as its existence, because of the questions it raises in the minds of the people about the integrity of the executive branch officials involved. What of the appearance of campaign contributions to a president (or senator, or congressman) who must act on matters that directly affect the source of livelihood and status of the contributors?

There has been reason for concern about the corrosive influence of money on American politics for some time. States like Maryland and New Jersey have been marked by corruption, particularly among builders, architects, and state and county executives. Political pay-offs for city contracts and favors have been as common in some Amrican cities as in the most corrupt dictatorships. Congressmen and senators have been convicted of accepting bribes or using campaign funds for personal purposes. Most Washington commentators have long known that banking interests are healthy contributors to members of the House and Senate banking committees, that the oil interests help their elected friends on the tax-writing committees of the Congress, and that maritime labor and business take care of their friends on the House and Senate labor and commerce committees.

At the presidential level, the relationship between big money and politics has been cozy for years: the Nixon fund of 1952; the gifts to Eisenhower; Goldfine and Adams; the $1,000 per member presidents' clubs of the Kennedy and Johnson administrations; the frenetic scramble of presidential hopefuls, both Democratic and Republican, to small private dinners in New York and California to raise funds; and the stream of untraceable cash that moves into most major presidential campaigns.

Most scandals are isolated and press reports usually focus on the specific facts, the case to be fixed, the contract to be won, the grant to be obtained, the pardon to be issued. But the greater danger of presidential corruption lies not so much in an individual ITT scandal, as in the desire of major contributors to affect broad public policies, domestic or foreign. Reporters and writers, like Morton Mintz of the Washington *Post* and James Polk of the Washington *Evening Star News*, perceived the broader reach of special-interest money years ago and often wrote about it. But few Americans appreciate that the focus of business, labor, or other money has been less the specific case than the presidential power to set broad policy, particularly through his rule-making and appointment authorities. Institutional money contributors have long recognized that, if the men in office were "sympathetic" and the regulations "realistic," there would be less need to deal with knotty specific cases. As the government grab bag of grants grew, educators for president A, scientists for president B, doctors for president C, and businessmen for president D, felt compelled to organize to raise money for candidates "sympathetic" to their interests and "realistic" about their problems.

In recognition of this danger, campaign financing and corrupt practices laws have customarily been designed to restrain the use of aggregates of wealth, usually corporate or labor. But personal wealth can render the "one-man-one-vote" rhetoric just as hollow. In 1968, for example, Stuart Mott, the well-known liberal grandson of the General Motors scion, attempted to purchase his own foreign policy for 200 million Americans. Mott, whose dovish Vietnam War attitude prompted personal contributions for the presidential candidacies of Nelson Rockefeller and Eugene McCarthy, mounted a buy-a-dove campaign on Hubert Humphrey after the 1968 Democratic Convention. In trying to set up a meeting with Humphrey which never took place, *Fortune* magazine reported that "Mott wrote Humphrey a letter in which he made it clear that the presidential candidate would have to modify his views on Vietnam before he could expect any financial support from this group."

Personal wealth was also the source of the largest reported prenomination contribution in American history, made in 1968 by Mrs. John D. Rockefeller, Jr., on behalf of her stepson Nelson's bid for the Republican nomination. From June to September 1968, Mrs. Rockefeller made eight gifts to the Rockefeller for President (New York) Committee in amounts totaling $1,482,625—more than three times the amount that most American citizens make in their lifetimes. Since the federal gift tax applies to contributions of more than $3,000, Mrs. Rockefeller was presumably subject to taxation of as much as $900,000 on the money she gave. The revelations of gifts and forgiven loans during his vice-presidential confirmation hearings provided a glimpse of the heady use of funds for political purposes by Nelson Rockefeller himself.

In 1974, the Congress finally took action to eliminate private wealth as a decisive factor in presidential politics. For the general presidential campaign, it authorized full public financing; and it provided up to $4.5 million in public funds to match the private contributions raised by presidential primary contenders. Campaign expenditure ceilings were placed on the general presidential election ($20 million per candidate) and the primaries (a total of $10 million per candidate). While the specific legislation may be subject to constitutional challenge, the 1974 act signals a congressional determination to move to a system of public financing, at least at the presidential level. (The Congress, largely at the behest of the House of Representatives, declined to authorize public financing of congressional campaigns. So many House members run for re-election without effective opposition that they did not want legislation that would guarantee an opponent adequate funds to contest their seats.)

The public financing of all political campaigns, while constitutionally complex in view of the First Amendment, is long overdue. The issues of our society have become so complex, and will become even more so in the last quarter of the twentieth century, that candidates who seek responsibility to decide them should not have to spend their time raising money to conduct political campaigns and to carry on a dialogue with the electorate. Money should be removed as a factor in the decision whether to run for office, how to campaign for office, whether to remain in public life after an unsuccessful candidacy. Once elected, leaders should not have to be concerned about patronizing someone who is or was "good for a big contribution."

In an institutional sense, the legislative reform of the campaign financing system may be the most important positive development for the presidency to result from the revelations of the early 1970s. But the influence of individual and aggregate private wealth not only affects the exercise of presidential power directly. It also renders inordinately difficult, for the wrong reasons, the achievement of presidential legislative objectives. The persistent inability of the national government to deal effectively with inflation and other economic problems is in large measure a function of the unhealthy influence of private funds in congressional political campaigns. As early as 1966, Johnson recognized the economic need for a tax increase to take some money out of the economy. He was stymied by the political reality vividly reported at a late 1965 meeting with the bipartisan leadership of the Congress. Then House Minority Leader Gerald Ford told him, "I think you would get about 15 votes in the House for a tax increase." Then House Majority Leader Carl Albert trumped Ford, "You wouldn't even get that many!"

President Ford faced the same problems when he assumed office in August 1974. The series of economic summit meetings served as forums for special-interest groups to espouse their self-interest. Several of those groups—particularly segments of business like the potent oil industry and the big labor unions—speak through the amplifier of financial resources that can be committed to political campaigns.

Beyond campaign financing reform, the legislative and institutional ramifications of Watergate on the presidency are difficult to predict. Any number of specific and relatively narrow proposals to enact new laws or amend old ones have been and will be made for years to come. Some are discussed in the final chapter of this book. But their impact on the presidency is not likely to be substantial. They are in the nature of political plastic surgery. This is so not because intelligent men of intimate experience with the presidency and political leadership are failing to search for the changes the Watergate experience demonstrates to be warranted. It is so because the American presidency does not need radical surgery; the other institutions in our society do. It is so because Watergate represents problems more of personal immorality than of institutional deficiency in the Oval Office.

The press is widely given credit for unveiling the Watergate corruption for all to see. But Washington reporters and editors would be the first to agree that it was not the press, but two reporters and four editors with the unwavering support of the head of a well-heeled and highly motivated communications empire, who broke and kept alive the Watergate story. Eventually (but not promptly) the New York *Times* joined the Washington *Post* and then other major news organizations moved in. But, with the exception of the Providence *Journal* breaking the story of presidential income tax evasion, major Watergate stories have come from a handful of well-staffed news organizations, with the substantial financial resources needed to mount a major investigative effort into presidential corruption. Whether the militant skepticism of the press toward the presidency persists and grows will provide a fair measure of how well it has learned its Watergate lessons.

The courts responded somewhat erratically to Watergate. The sentences of various convicted Watergate criminals provide convincing, if unfortunate, testimony to the difference a judge makes. In the federal district courts of Washington, the result can be decisively different if a Watergate case comes before a John Sirica or a George Hart. The criminal justice system at the preindictment level often rewards those who have committed more serious offenses, if they can lead the prosecutors higher up the ladder of political responsibility. The young campaign aide who knows only that he committed perjury and the person who suborned his perjury is likely to be incarcerated. The attorney general who lied under oath to further his own Senate confirmation can walk out of court a free man because he can lead to other big (or perhaps even bigger) fish for the prosecutor's net. Contempt is a charge the courts can level at the incumbent president, but he has ample opportunity and power to discredit that charge in the public press. When John Kennedy remarked that "life is unfair" he was talking about the military draft. He might have been talking about the erratic manifestations of the application of prosecutorial and judicial power in the Watergate cases.

The relationship to the presidency of the private-sector institutional forces has been affected by the Watergate events, largely because of the vigor of the special prosecutor's office and the actions of the federal judiciary. Those corporations and business executives who were prosecuted and convicted for violating corrupt practices provisions of the federal criminal code are not likely to repeat their actions in the near future. Nor are other companies and individuals. Here, in the arena of money and politics, the deterrent effect of the Watergate revelations and prosecutions has probably been substantial. Indeed, the drying up of big contributors may do more to encourage public financing of future congressional campaigns than any abiding sense of moral outrage.

The short-term congressional response to Watergate was the unanimous vote of the House Judiciary Committee to impeach Richard Nixon. Slow moving, the House committee under the extraordinary leadership of its chairman, Peter

Rodino, gave the American nation a textbook example of the integrity of the congressional committee system in one of its finest hours. It was an important action for the exercise of presidential power. Had the committee members failed to act and force Nixon's resignation in face of certain impeachment, they (more than the institution of the presidency) would have set a new outer limit on the activities in which future presidents could engage. Every White House aide can testify that each president takes the precedents of his predecessors in the exercise of power and moves the next step. Most Americans may have trouble even conjuring what the next step might be, but there is one person who would have figured it out if Richard Nixon had remained in office until the end of his elected term—a future president of the United States.

The long-range congressional response to Watergate is less certain because it depends on the complex political and institutional factors discussed in earlier chapters. But the Congress—as well as the American people—must understand that there is no real repentence on Nixon's part and none is likely for a reason central to understanding Watergate: President Nixon and his aides believed they were doing the right thing for the nation. For all of them this was true at the time they acted; for most it is true to this day. Egil Krough believed the secret police "plumbers unit" to be a legitimate exercise of presidential and governmental power while it was operating. Jeb Magruder considered perjury and obstruction of justice acceptable means in pursuit of Nixon's re-election at the time he lied before the grand jury, federal prosecutors, and Judge John Sirica. The testimony of John Mitchell, H. R. Haldeman, and John Ehrlichman before the Senate Watergate Committee and during their criminal trial repeatedly evidences their continuing personal belief that they were legitimately using government power. Nixon himself, after telling Haldeman on Aril 25, 1973, that John Dean was "supposed to lie like hell" before the grand jury, was able to ask with incredulity on the next day, "Oh, my God, what have we done to be impeached?" The reason Nixon did not publicly admit guilt in his statement accepting Ford's pardon is simply that he does not believe he has done anything wrong except make a few "mistakes in judgment."

Whatever the sincerity of the postconviction and presentencing statements of the Nixon men, the cogent point is that, like all other men in positions of power, they are more likely to enlarge the means they use to achieve what they perceive to be worthy objectives than to abandon the objectives. They are certain to believe that, for the president, actions that would otherwise be illegal or immoral become permissable in pursuit of his national policy objectives. If the Congress and the American people have not learned this lesson from the national nightmare of corruption and abuse of presidential power during the early 1970s, then they may not deserve the protections afforded them by the Constitution. Whether they merit those protections, they are not likely to preserve them.

The sheer drama of the Watergate events—erased tapes, break-ins and burglaries, passing of money among ex-CIA agents, perjury, selling federal jobs for political money—has turned the spotlight on the presidency in a kind of obsessively fascinating who-done-it atmosphere that can be instructive for the American nation. To the extent the sensational disclosures make the people more skeptical about the uses of power and to the extent they examine the office of the president and its relationship to our freedom and the other institutions in our society, then Watergate may come to represent, to some degree, an ironically constructive, if sordid, event in American history. If the lurid criminality of the Nixon administration opens for intelligent and wide discussion the kind of radical surgery needed to protect our freedom against unhealthy and unbalanced concentrations of power, then some purpose may be served by the lives and institutions shattered by Watergate. But if the split-second attention span of the American people passes over Watergate as an exciting, if disgusting, political circus, and moves ahistorically to the next crisis, then this nation may pay an irrevocably exorbitant price.

One need not exaggerate the importance of Watergate or fail to recognize that the individuals involved were weak and corrupt. But that does not relieve the society from its responsibility to decide whether it must place greater restraints on the power available to the president and structurally reshape the system of counterforces that play upon the exercise of that power. Watergate poses some savagely tough questions about our democracy and its institutions. Why the people placed their trust in this man, why these men concluded that the means they used to perpetuate themselves in power were legitimate, why they believed that the American people would accept those actions, why the Congress, most of the press, and the opposition party were so supine for so long, why private interests were so readily corruptible—these and other questions must be examined with brutal candor.

To refuse to pose such questions is to say that we cannot seek the truth, much less face it; that we cannot pointedly ask and candidly answer how we got to Watergate and whether the road is still open for a future journey. It may be to admit despairingly that we are no longer strong enough to live under the most ingenious Constitution ever devised by man. To evade persistent and cold examination of these tragic events is the stuff of a weak and tired people who are so exhausted by democracy that they prefer to end their days in politically hedonistic amorality. It reflects the weary resignation of a tired generation that seeks to avoid any more traumas of its own, even if that quest involves the betrayal of its trust to succeeding generations. It fails to recognize that the events of the early 1970s did not occur in a historical, political, or social vacuum, that a stage of presidential power had been set and that institutional and human tolerance for these events was frighteningly high for a democratic system designed to protect individual freedom by balancing and fragmenting power.

At the very least, Watergate has provided decisive, if tragic, contemporary validation of James Madison's admonition to the Virginia Constitutional Convention in 1829. "The essence of Government is power; and power, lodged as it must be in human hands, will ever be liable to abuse." Madison was not willing to rely on the goodness of man to channel the exercise of such power to the public interest:

man is known to be a selfish, as well as a social being. . . . We all know that conscience is not a sufficient safeguard; and besides, that conscience itself may be deluded; may be misled, by an unconscious bias, into acts which an enlightened conscience would forbid.

As to the permanent interest of individuals in the aggregate interests of the community, and in the proverbial maxim, that honesty is the best policy, present temptation is often found to be an overmatch for those considerations. These favorable attributes of the human character are all valuable, as auxiliaries; but they will not serve as a substitute for the coercive provision belonging to Government and Law.

XIII

---◆◆◆---

THE FUTURE
PRESIDENCY

This is no time to gather, like political Lilliputians, to tie the presidential Gulliver in miles of string. Any national evaluation of the White House and the men who sit there should recognize the real need for a strong presidency. The objectives should be both to appreciate the importance of presidential power and the need to put it in healthy democratic perspective by rendering its exercise accountable, responsive, and credible and by advancing the nominally countervailing institutions of society into position to call the exercise of such power to account.

The potency of presidential power must be measured against the other forces in our society: the executive branch, the Congress, the states and cities, the federal judiciary, the press, private institutions, and partisan political organizations. In any such reckoning we must understand the double-edged nature of all power: that powers vested in the presidency for benign purposes can be used by a particular president for malevolent ends. As this analysis has indicated, the persistent trend of the last several decades has been for countervailing power centers to become dependent on and subservient to the presidency. They have become weaker or grown in power less appreciably than the presidential office and the executive branch it can deploy.

Putting presidential power in perspective also requires realistic acceptance of the fact that presidents have common, as well as special, personality characteristics and that they and their men are human beings with all the weaknesses and fallibilities that attend human nature. In proposing new directions for the presidency and the counterpoint forces in society, we must identify those areas which can be affected by legislative changes and those elements of the human condition and morality where the laws of men cannot change the nature of man. An increased measure of accountability for broken promises and ill-advised actions and of responsiveness to the broad public interest require that we not subject those who exercise presidential and White House staff power to virtually irresistible temptations to abuse that power. Recommendations for change must also reflect the need to restore credibility to the highest office in the land. As justice rendered is justice perceived, so power exercised in the public interest is power seen to be used in that interest.

While the most urgently needed changes involve the non-presidential power centers in our society, there are significant modifications in the presidency itself that are likely to render the exercise of presidential power decidedly more accountable, responsive, and credible. To the extent those modifications strengthen the presidency, they can be safely made only if countervailing forces to the exercise of presidential power are simultaneously restructured

Clinton Rossiter's description of *The American Presidency* as "one of the truly successful government institutions ever created" is being seriously questioned by many thoughtful political scientists and commentators, largely as a result of presidential involvement in the Vietnam War and Watergate and the misuse of government police and intelligence agencies. Nevertheless, the presidency is the oldest surviving democratic office in the modern world. Most monarchies have passed into history books. Those which remain, like England's, are markedly different from their original conception. A variety of dictatorships—communist, fascist, nationalist, but rarely, if ever, of sustained benevolence—have been recorded in the pages of history. But the American presidency has charted and sailed a steady course of accumulating prestige and power over the two hundred years of its existence. Today, as Rossiter has written, the presidency is

> ... a whole greater than and different from the sum of its parts, an office whose power and prestige is something more than the arithmetical total of all its functions. The President is not one kind of official during one part of the day, another kind during another part—administrator in the morning, legislator at lunch, king in the afternoon, commander before dinner, and a politician at odd moments that come his weary way. He is all these things all the time, and anyone of his functions feeds upon and into all the others. He is a more exulted chief of state because he is also voice of the people, a more forceful chief diplomat because he commands the armed forces personally, a more effective chief legislator because the political system forces him to be chief of party, a more artful manager of prosperity because he is chief executive.

These roles must be examined against the conglomerated powers at the disposal of a president performing them. Increments of presidential power have too often been unperceived until too late. The potency of the president has increased as the sheer power, economic and military, of the United States has increased. It grows with each addition to the burgeoning federal budget. Discretion so broad has been vested in the presidency that it has been difficult (sometimes impossible) to construct standards against which its exercise can be called to account.

Even less appreciated at the time of their vesting is the cumulative impact of each piecemeal accretion of power by the presidency. Immediate need for forceful action to end the Depression led the Congress to vest broad economic regulatory powers in the executive branch during the Roosevelt administration. Urgent social needs led to the congressional authorizations for the executive branch to operate hundreds of new domestic programs during the Johnson administration. The financial plight of the states and cities and the economic and energy crises of the late 1960s and early 1970s led to granting the president limited revenue-sharing allocation discretion and wide price, wage, and energy regulatory powers during the Nixon administration. Notably absent at the time these powers were lodged in the presidency was any systematic attempt to measure them against then existing presidential powers. What is needed is a Presidential Powers Impact Statement Act to require the Congress and the executive branch to analyze the impact of each significant new legislative program or administrative action on the powers of the presidency.

To understand how a Presidential Powers Impact Statement Act would work, let us assume that the president proposed to the Congress a constitutional program for the compulsory nursery-school education of children from three to six years of age, in legislative recognition of the importance of formal education for children at that young age. In addition to justifying the program itself, the president's message and supporting documents would have to contain an analysis of the extent to which that program would impact on existing presidential powers. The presidential proposal would be required to include a discussion of related federal legislation such as the Elementary and Secondary Education Act, and programs such as day-care centers and health care for children, as well as welfare laws and regulations. Such a statement would also set forth the then existing roles of the states, cities, local communities, and the private sector, and describe the way in which the then existing distribution of power would be altered if the proposed presidential program were enacted. The Presidential Powers Impact Statement accompanying this compulsory nursery-school legislation would include a discussion of the alternative means by which the same objectives could be achieved, including an analysis of capabilities, costs and benefits of assigning all or part of the task to states, cities, and/or private educational institutions. The Congress and the public would have available an analysis of the extent to which the compulsory nursery school program affected the power of the president and his branch over children.

The objective of a Presidential Powers Impact Statement would be to place before the Congress and the public some real sense of the extent to which a significant proposal would affect presidential power, so that an informed judgment on that issue could be an integral part of the public policy formulation process. This proposed act would not require any specific actions to increase or decrease presidential power. Its purpose is to require the Congress and the public to confront what they are doing to the most important public office in our nation and how that will affect the balance among institutional counterforces at the time they decide to act.

The subtleties of power relationships are difficult to subject to objective analysis. Yet it is essential that we try. The Congress considers our physical environment so precious that it has imposed the requirement that an environmental impact statement be prepared prior to taking any significant federal administrative or legislative action that might affect the environment. It is a telling commentary on the value we place on our political environment if we fail to undertake a similar kind of analysis with respect to new powers to be vested in the president and the executive branch over which he presides. The first step up the spiral staircase of intelligent precaution against the dangers of a too powerful presidency is an assessment of the extent to which new actions, legislative and administrative, will affect the power of that office.

Effectively enforced presidential accountability and responsiveness, as well as enhanced presidential credibility, require public measures of performance against promise. The Congress, with its legislative oversight function, is the body constitutionally responsible for measuring presidential performance on a continuing basis. Privately, most congressmen and senators recognize that the Congress has not performed this function well. Some have tried repeatedly to bring this to the public attention.

The deficiencies lie almost entirely within the power of the Congress to correct. The Constitution of the United States requires the president to report each year to the Congress on the "State of the Union." By tradition, largely political, the president normally goes before the Congress in January and informs its members and the American people (a) what a wonderful year it has been (or why others are responsible for the problems of the past year) and (b) what programs he thinks are needed to make future years even more wonderful (or how to solve those problems). Over the past twenty years, State of the Union messages have been optimistic sermons from a radio and television pulpit which the president has naturally used to enhance his power as the chief executive and his stature as the leader of the nation. Directed more at the American people than the Congress, these messages provide the president with a special opportunity to characterize the issues not necessarily as he views them over the past and coming year, but as he wants the American people to view them over that span of time. Like any lawyer, he knows that characterizing the issues can be the key to winning the case.

The Congress should enact permanent legislation which would require that certain specific reports accompany the presidential assessment of the State of the Union to which it is constitutionally entitled. These reports would be similar to the congressionally mandated Economic Report of the President which describes the manner in which the economy (e.g., prices wages, unemployment, capital investment, balance of payments) has changed during the prior year as compared to earlier years and which projects the outlook for the future. These reports should cover such matters as social programs, ranging, for instance, from the United States's standing in terms of infant mortality, to population shifts in the nation, housing starts, environmental quality, and so forth; and foreign relationships, including significant new treaties, executive agreements, and trade and aid pacts.

Near the end of each session, the Congress should review the events of the prior year and, by resolution or legislation, identify any special areas on which it desires presidential reports early in the next session. The lists could be endless; but the point is quite simple: If the president were required to report specifically, both orally and in writing, in a more detailed message each year on his stewardship of the country during the prior year, then the State of the Union message might become a more meaningful political event. It will still represent his statement of the issues; but at least the Congress can have a hand in establishing those issues.

The president should also be required to present to the Congress an annual National Posture Statement, with reports that provide a specific measure of his branch's performance against legislative programs enacted by the Congress and promises the president has made about those programs. To level such a requirement on the president would force him to measure his statements more carefully as well as provide an added incentive to perform up to promise, an ingredient essential to the restoration of credibility to the American presidency. The lack of tools and standards by which to measure the glowing hot metal of promise against the cold forged steel of performance has been an invitation to presidents to join with the other forces of American society, including, too often, the Congress and the media, to reduce the American public policy dialogue to rhetorical tinsel.

Under this proposal the president would be required to develop and project the five-year costs* of all domestic program decisions, and their expected relationship to the threats they are designed to meet, such as those arising from collapsing cities, malnutrition, pollution, congestion, and inflation. The executive corollary to the Congressional Budget Office is to require the president to submit to the Congress, as part of his budget, a domestic National Posture Statement that carefully assesses domestic priorities and needs, projects the costs of the programs designed to meet these needs for a five-year period, and measures competing claims of various domestic programs for tax dollars.

The National Posture Statement should do more than present alternative ways of abating pollution or rebuilding cities; it should set forth the basis for selecting one alternative over another. This statement should provide analyses and recommendations on the choices that should be made, considering the longer run as well as the present, among competing

---

*Five years seems to be about as far in the future that most reliable estimates can be made.

programs: air pollution versus child health versus rebuilding cities versus job training. Included in any such analyses and five-year projections should be the costs—financial and social —of failure to pursue a particular program or meet a particular need. The president should also be required to prepare a posture statement on military and foreign policy objectives and the costs of achieving them (similar to the detailed posture statements submitted by Robert McNamara when he was secretary of defense).

In preparing five-year projections and analyses, the president would be required to assemble the kind of information on which to make long-range judgments about his own recommendations to the Congress. The Congress would have before it the kind of information essential for intelligent and informed decision making among the extraordinarily difficult choices that lie ahead. Most importantly, the American people, particularly through the interest groups that represent segments of them, would be able to make better judgments about the resources necessary to protect their national security at home as well as the commitments necessary to protect their national security abroad.

The president is the leader of the American establishment, especially the American political establishment, and if that establishment is to regain the confidence of the American citizenry, its rhetorical commitment must more neatly track reality than it now does. The day-to-day battle of political campaigns and presidential messages to the Congress for inches of newspaper lines or seconds on an evening television show has grotesquely distorted our political dialogue. Too many campaigning presidential aspirants deliberately distort the realities of which they are more aware than the voters they are trying to persuade, and who they should be trying to educate. Presidents, even incumbents in their second and final term, are essentially campaigning to write the first draft of the histories of their years in office.

The American people have become so jaded with political promises that most hold politicians in less esteem than frontier settlers held snake-oil salesmen. Over the past generation, the drum beat of exaggerated promise has been far more debilitating to the politically cohesive fabric of American society than even the grossest dissembling of Richard Nixon, and Ron Zeigler, during their historically brief occupancy of the Oval Office.

The rhetorical commitment of the American political establishment—executive and legislative—is, indeed, magnificent. Unfortunately, it is not the language of American reality. A few examples of presidential and congressional commitments in the laws passed by the Congress, particularly during the Johnson administration, will provide a sense of the importance of requiring an annual reconciliation of the public books of promise and performance.

—*The Housing Commitment.* The Housing Act of 1949 declared that the "general welfare and security of the nation require the elimination of substandard and other inadequate housing through the clearance of slums and blighted areas, and the realization . . . of a decent home and suitable living environment for every American family." In the 1968 Housing and Urban Development Act, the Congress realized that, for twenty years, the promise had not been kept, noted the failure as "a matter of grave national concern," and rededicated itself to "the elimination of all substandard housing in a decade."

Yet, in the mid-1970s, more than twenty-five million Americans still live in housing unfit for human habitation.

—*The Cities Commitment.* The 1966 Model Cities legislation declared as congressional policy that "improving the quality of urban life is the most crucial domestic problem facing the United States" and stated as its purpose the provision of "financial and technical assistance to enable cities of all sizes . . . to plan, develop, and carry out locally-prepared . . . programs . . . to rebuild and revitalize large slum and blighted areas."

Yet, some ten years and two presidential administrations later, we continue to stand by as a nation, while the physical plant of most of our cities further decays and obsolesces, and the postwar suburbs of the forties proceed through the first stages of severe deterioration.

—*The Antipoverty Commitment.* The Economic Opportunity Act of 1964 declared "the policy of the United States to eliminate the paradox of poverty in the midst of plenty in this nation by opening to everyone the opportunity for education and training, the opportunity to work and the opportunity to live in decency and dignity."

Yet, more than a decade later, some thirty million Americans are still locked in poverty—and the number seems to be going up, rather than down.

—*The Crime Control Commitment.* The Omnibus Crime Control and Safe Streets Act of 1968 recognized the urgency of the national crime problem as a matter that threatens "the peace, the security and general welfare of its citizens," and made it "the declared policy of the Congress to assist state and local governments in strengthening and improving law enforcement at every level by national assistance."

Yet, year after year since 1968, crime has continued its persistent rise. The Safe Streets Act has been funded at 50 percent or less of its programmed level, and the American public has been presented with a series of preposterous assurances that there is a cheap and easy way to eliminate street crime.

The rhetorical commitments of the president proposing this legislation and the Congress enacting it were magnificent—but they have the timbre of hollow echoes against the reality of performance. They provide good reason for Americans to believe that our national security is at stake as we face our domestic problems. They also provide ample justification for Americans to conclude that the president and the Congress do not mean what they say. The president and the Congress have repeatedly refused to act in accordance with their own rhetorical and legislative commitments.

It is no wonder that the American citizen is so profoundly troubled. Largely as a result of the gap between political rhetoric and national reality, the average American voter everyday accumulates evidence that nothing in the government works the way it should. Fear more than hope has become the fragile link that holds together Americans concerned about the future of the nation. Hope is born of vision and reality and, for most of the past two hundred years, our political leaders have somehow been able to provide the vision seeded in reality essential to inspire our people to attain their goals. This is not so today.

In part, this is no longer true because it is increasingly difficult for the American citizen to measure the performance of his political leaders in any systematic or objective terms against the promise—until it is too late. Instead, the test has become the gut reaction of the American who, in 1974, waited on gasoline lines, although he did not believe there was a gas shortage; who demonstrated against war, only to have it continue for years; who saved his money in the 1960s only to find that the inflation of the 1970s outstripped the value of his savings; who accepted price and wage controls without knowing how ineptly they were administered, until shortages began to show up at the supermarket. The visceral nature of such measurements does not lessen their political significance; indeed, it often enhances it. But the cogent impact of a series of such reactions tends to contribute to the emotional despair that plagues our society rather than to a rational assessment that can lead to more thoughtful policies in the future.

If the president were required to provide a series of public reports directed at specific aspects of American life, the gap between rhetoric and reality would begin to close, not only because of the attention that would be given to fulfilling political and legislative promises. Those promises themselves would not be so cavalierly made if presidents knew they would have to report with precision and detail on their performance each year in office. It may be difficult to extend the split-second attention span of the American people, but recurring specific reports would reduce the ability of presidents to rely on it to relieve them of political responsibility for failing to fulfill exaggerated promises. There is no reason to wait for history's judgment on their success or failure to

fulfill their promises, when we have the econometric and technological tools to make many such judgments contemporaneously.

Another debasement of the political dialogue characterizes presidential campaigns, speeches, and messages to the Congress. Rarely are presidents required to provide any indication to the American people as to the cost of keeping the promises they make. Here two actions seem clearly warranted:

—First, every presidential message to the Congress proposing a new federal program should indicate the cost of that program, spread out as best as can be estimated for a five-year period, with supporting data submitted to the Congress and the press, as to the bases for those five-year projections.

—Second, presidential candidates should commit to each other and to the American public to provide best estimates of the costs of fulfilling their campaign promises when they make them. Such commitments can be monitored by the Fair Campaigning Practices Committee and by the press corps through relentless exposure of every failure of presidential candidates to disclose such costs. Newspaper stories reporting on promises of presidential candidates should indicate, alongside the promise to rebuild the cities, that the candidate either estimates that the cost of the program will be so many billions of dollars or that the candidate refuses to provide any estimate of the cost of this program.

This is particularly important for the last quarter of the twentieth century, during which our nation must be willing to commit additional scores of billions of dollars to the public sector if it is to cope effectively with domestic problems and to make some trenchantly difficult choices about the allocation of such resources. In the near term, those choices will be especially difficult in the context of a static gross national product, or one growing at no more than 2 percent annually. In contrast to the horn of economic plenty that characterized the mid-1960s where there was more for everyone, the commitment of more resources to the public sector and the disadvantaged in the late 1970s will involve absolute redistributions of wealth.

During the late 1960s and early 1970s, the proportion of our nation's trillion dollar plus gross national product devoted to the public sector has hovered around 30 percent. During that same period, France and Germany devoted about 38 percent of their gross national product to the public sector; England, about 39 percent; Norway, about 43 percent. In Sweden, almost 50 percent of the gross national product is collected in taxes and devoted to the public sector. If we had followed the French and German example, we would have had in excess of $80 billion more for our public needs.

Failure of our presidents and presidential candidates to remind our people that public services require public funds has been costly during the past several years. With some exceptions in time of severe economic crisis, it appears unlikely that presidential candidates will be anymore forthcoming on this overriding issue in the future, absent persistent public pressure from the press and the Congress. John Gardner has said that history will not treat well a society that refuses to tax itself for its public needs. One might add that history will not treat well political leaders in the future who continue to ignore this issue, bury it in irrelevant discussions of revenue sharing, or limit their proposals to inadequate revenue-producing plans to close tax loopholes or reduce defense spending.

It is no longer adequate for presidential candidates to tell reporters (usually off the record or on deep background) that they cannot survive politically if they suggest raising taxes and committing more of our resources to the public sector of our economy. The severest test of political leadership today may be whether a president can convince the American people to do just that over the long haul. The time has come to impose upon the presidential candidate and incumbent president the obligation to report the true costs of achieving the promises they hold out for our future.

The pursuit and conduct of a sound economic policy presents a similarly severe test for presidential leadership. The

London *Economist* has pointed out that no democratic government has survived a sustained 20 percent inflation rate. History also provides some dire precedents as a result of the reluctance of free peoples to make the sacrifices necessary to stem rampant inflation. Italy, France, and England are recent examples of the overriding impact of self-interest. Business wants to maintain its profits; labor its jobs and high wages. No one wants to pay more taxes. Special-interest groups, from government employees and home builders to lawyers and doctors, seek to protect (or enhance) their own economic condition. Strong presidential leadership is essential to deal with persistent problems like inflation and recession that require sacrifices for the collective welfare by most special interests.

Such leadership can be effectively forthcoming only in an environment where the president is credible not only as a man who speaks the truth, but as one who is, indeed, interested in the national welfare. In the kind of political and economic atmosphere that this nation faces in the last quarter of the twentieth century, the cynical shell games that have too often scarred presidential leadership in the past must give way to a candor that restrains extravagant promise in the face of expectable performance, that distinguishes the temporary relief of instant cures and contemporary approbation from the bitter medicine of the distasteful, but necessary, long-term therapy that can lead to historical vindication.

The need for perceived as well as rendered credibility and integrity underlines the importance of curtailing the role of private wealth in national politics. The analysis of campaign financing in Chapter XII and the experience of this nation with local, state, and national corruption, dramatized beyond fiction by Watergate, should make clear that private wealth has no place in the politics of a democratic society where each citizen's vote should count as one and only one. Public financing of election campaigns is essential to eliminate the disturbingly decisive edge of money in politics, particularly presidential politics. The Congress has begun at the presidential level, but eventually lesser levels—congressional, state, and local elections included—should be a part of a public financing system, with the strictest regulation and severe penalties for violations. By freeing senators and congressmen (as well as governors and mayors) from the need to patronize political contributors, public financing can also help assure that the people receive the benefit of a vigorous loyal opposition to an incumbent president.

Another element critical to the survival of an effective loyal opposition is access to the broadcast media, particularly television, the most effective, and expensive, means of communications in our society. The advantage that attends presidential incumbency must be balanced by requiring television networks to provide leaders of the loyal opposition equal access to respond to televised presidential appearances, whether speeches, press conferences, or personality appearances. Whether the fairness doctrine survives or shrinks in the face of the First Amendment in other areas of public dialogue, special provision must be made to balance the lopsided access of the president to the most powerful means of communication in our society.

The Congress must tend to some of the practical personal financial burdens it imposes on its own members. There should be significantly higher pay for congressmen, as well as sharply increased expense allowances. The pay problem is a relatively simple one to resolve as a practical matter, although it is perceived to be dangerously difficult politically. Congressmen and senators must maintain two homes: one in the state or district from which they are elected, the other in Washington, D.C., where they work most of the year. They need adequate funds to travel to and from their home states. Their salaries should be increased to $100,000 per year, a far more reasonable level than the present $42,500, and they should be reimbursed for the cost of as many trips to their home districts and states as they take. Coupled with public funding of political campaigns, such financial support should sharply reduce the potential for the subtle corruption that infects so many votes on legislation affecting special interests. Of perhaps greater importance, House and Senate members would have more time to consider issues and deal on equal footing with the president's branch, and talent, not money, would be the most relevant factor for men and women deciding whether to seek and hold seats in Congress.

Personal financial matters are of critical importance in maintaining the credibility and integrity of the presidency. The time has come for any man who declares himself a candidate for the office of the president of the United States (his running mate and House and Senate candidates as well) to make available his tax returns and the details of his present and recent financial worth. This must be done prior to the time he runs for office and, if elected, repeated annually, certified independently perhaps by the General Accounting Office. It is essential for the American people to know—it is no longer sufficient simply to hope or believe—that their president is, as only Eisenhower could have said it, "clean as a hound's tooth." Post-Watergate America requires action of this kind by any man who aspires to the presidency.

The sense of Americans that their presidency has become too regal to be responsive must be allayed. It must be made clear that a president cannot unjustly enrich his personal economic situation while in office. Anyone who has worked closely with presidents knows the brutal toll of the job on human energy and on psychological and spiritual resources. It is counterproductive and cruel to deny a president the comforts of personal retreat, whether to Hyannisport, a Texas ranch, or a San Clemente coastal estate. However, a careful accounting should be kept of all government expenditures to make any such retreat safe and its communications adequate for a president. When he leaves office, equipment unnecessary for his continued protection should be removed. To the extent such removal is impractical, the General Accounting Office should be authorized to determine the value of added government facilities and make certain that the proceeds of any sale accrue to the United States, not to the individual president. Should the property be donated to some public or charitable use, the value of government-added facilities should not be available to the former president for tax deduction. These kinds of restrictions may be symbolic, but symbols often assume major importance to the integrity of a secular or religious institution. These have such importance to the office of the president.

After Franklin Roosevelt broke with tradition to be elected for four successive terms, the Constitution was amended to restrict the president to two elected terms, each limited to the four years originally established in the Constitution. Today, the federal government is geometrically more complex and pervasively interventionist than it was in the time of Roosevelt. Partially in response to this condition there have, over the years, been expressions of sentiment to extend the presidential term to six years. Most who favor that proposal urge the establishment of a one-term limit. In 1971, Senate Majority Leader Mike Mansfield of Montana and then Republican Senate dean George Aiken of Vermont introduced Senate Resolution 77 to achieve that objective. In his book, former President Lyndon Johnson urged a constitutional amendment to establish a single six-year term. Several of Johnson's closest aides and advisors, have expressed support for his recommendation.

Like presidential power itself, the six-year term for the president cannot be considered in political isolation. Extending the president's tenure may make eminent political and practical sense, but only if action is taken to increase the tenure of House members from two to four years and the Twenty-fifth Amendment is modified or repealed. Many of the same considerations that support the concept of a six-year term for the president also support an increase in the term of House members. Establishing the six-year term for the president without a simultaneous extension of the term for House members would further tilt the balance of power to the White House. My recommendation is:

—That the president be given a six-year term, with re-election possible for one additional term of four or six years.

—That the two-year term for members of the House of Representatives be extended to four years, with no inhibitions on their right to run for the Senate (or for any other office) during their four-year term.

—That the Senate term remain a six-year term.

—That House and Senate members continue to be eligible for re-election indefinitely.

—That the Twenty-fifth Amendment be repealed and provision be made to conduct a special election for president and vice-president to fill the unexpired term of a vacant presidency whenever two or more years remain in the unexpired term of the vacating president. Pending the outcome of that election or where less than two years of the unexpired term remains, the elected vice-president would succeed to the presidency.

The increased perplexity and apparent intractibility of problems facing any American president need not be described in detail here. The United States of the 1970s is as different from the United States of the 1930s as that nation was distinct from the original thirteen colonies. The international entanglements and responsibilities of the United States are uniquely intricate and significant. As earlier indicated, from 1930 to 1970, government expenditures on the domestic side alone rose from $2.7 billion to $120 billion, an increase of more than 4,400 percent; federal grant-in-aid programs rose from 24 to 500, an increase of almost 2,100 percent. The central executive today touches every American everyday of his life. This involvement, likely to increase, is necessitated by the national nature of many problems, the efficiencies of scale which can sometimes alleviate the need for more taxes, modern technology, and communications. The process of analyzing options for dealing with problems has become more sophisticated, that of selection more time-consuming, and that of implementation infinitely more difficult. In this connection, the budgetary and legislative processes of the federal system underline the need for a six-year presidential term.

A new president assuming office in January 1977, will have his first opportunity to develop completely his own annual budget for a fiscal year beginning on October 1, 1978, and ending on September 30, 1979. Even then, he must submit by May 15, 1977, four short months after he assumes office, any recommendations for new budget authority for the fiscal year beginning October 1, 1978. He would, of course, have some impact on the budget for the fiscal year beginning October 1, 1977 (the year he assumes office) and ending September 30, 1978. With rare exception, however, his impact on that budget is likely to be marginal, because he will be cutting and pasting a budget fully developed by his predecessor during the summer and fall of his election year and submitted to the Congress before the new president assumes office on January 20, 1977. His predecessor's budget will reflect commitments made and programs instituted during his prior years of incumbency. The first year of government operation under a budget totally prepared by a new president's administration will begin during the last three months of its second year in office and the first nine months of its third (and next to last) year.

In *The Imperial Presidency* Arthur Schlesinger, who opposes a single six-year term, dismisses this as a "budgetary argument" and argues that the budget system can be revised. Revised? The issues are why it is the way it is and how it could be revised in the context of our federal system. The Congress, in constitutional control of the federal purse, has something to say about the budgetary system of the government. Its latest revision moved the beginning of the fiscal year from July 1 back to October 1, because the underlying legislative issues that the cold, dull tables in the federal budget reflect (and often obscure) are increasingly difficult to analyze separately, much less relate as a coherent whole. The budget constitutes the financial characterization of many major national issues: defense spending, federal support of housing, foreign aid, poverty, education, health care. It quantifies the relationship of the federal government to the economic state of the nation. A central reason the Congress, in 1974, moved the federal fiscal year back three months was its recurrent inability intelligently to analyze the president's budget in time to act on appropriations bills prior to July 1. Executive departments were operating on continuing resolutions, with no true sense of what their budget would be for a given fiscal year until several months of that year had passed.

Because the issues inherent in budget decisions are at the core of controversial national policies, the budgetary process inevitably is a major hurdle in any new president's race against the four-year clock. As we recognize that the budget increasingly reflects expenditures which in large measure were set in motion years before a new president assumes office, the limitations of a four-year term become more apparent. Most budgetary expenditures are locked in place for years: long-term defense contracts; social security and welfare formula payments; civil works programs involving billions of dollars and years of work on our waterways; and long-term highway, courthouse, and post office construction for which commitments are often made and contracts signed years before a new president assumes office. The president who desires significantly to reorder national priorities by shifting the expenditure of federal resources faces an almost insurmountable time problem in the confines of a four-year term.

All of this must be considered in the context of the entire federal system. True, as some who oppose the six-year term point out, the speed with which a widening variety of new problems confront a president has been sharply accelerated. But the necessary array of financial resources and bureaucratic energies at the national, state, and local level to deal with such problems cannot be effectively marshaled in a four-year term. Indeed, the four-year term tends to institutionalize, to our national detriment, the split-second attention span of the American people. New candidates, running on new issues, divert the pursuit of specific policy objectives before there has been any real test of the viability of recently adopted presidential programs aimed at those objectives.

Assume that a president campaigns on several new proposals, including a promise to build twenty-five new cities in open spaces in our nation to ease the fearful congestion in the Northeast from Boston to Washington and on the California coast. The better part of his first year in office would be consumed in developing in detail an effective program, with a workable financial formula. Such a program would have to identify the scores of statutes to be repealed or amended, provide appropriate legislative authority and standards for the acquisition and development of the land, incentives for people to move there, a viable framework for the states, and some projection of the federal funds that would be required in future years. All this would have to be designed in the context of a politically realistic chance of congressional enactment. The new president assuming office in January 1977 would probably not be prepared to send his new cities legislation to the Congress until early 1978. If he were particularly fortunate, the Congress would pass the authorizing legislation by the end of 1978. He could then request and obtain a supplemental appropriation in late 1978 or (more likely) some time in the spring of 1979, to begin the detailed planning and work with the states to put the program into operation.

At this point the states interested in developing one of the new cities within their borders would be convinced that the national government was serious. It had put some resources where its rhetoric had been. Those states would then put in motion their own legislative machinery to provide whatever matching funds and administrative apparatus were required to develop one of the new cities. The process of passing legislation and appropriations through the state legislatures and the building of the special federal and state bureaucracies to administer the new cities program would consume at least another year, bringing us well into 1980. Thus, the new president would be at the end of his first four-year term before his new cities program ever had the necessary legislative and administrative infrastructure to start the kind of detailed planning that must precede sound operation of any complex new undertaking.

If the president were defeated in his bid for re-election (or decided not to run for office again), another president elected in November 1980 might well have his own ideas about the solution to urban congestion on the East and West Coasts. That newly elected president might decide to abandon the new cities program and start a special urban rehabilitation program in East and West Coast metropolitan centers. Meanwhile, urban congestion in the Northeast and the West would continue unabated, for a lack of federal programs, federal funds, or clear-cut national objectives pursued for a sufficiently sustained period to achieve any real purpose. A president would have served his entire four-year term, newspapers would have trumpeted his proposal for new cities, and, yet, where it counts, with the people, nothing would have happened. For many Americans, it would become another frustrating piece of evidence in the case against the viability of our existing system, another illustration why that system does not work.

This example may seem nightmarishly exaggerated to those uninitiated in contemporary federal and state bureaucratic infrastructure. To the contrary, it is almost exactly what happened to the Model Cities program that Lyndon Johnson proposed in the 1960s. It took a year for the executive branch, with the assistance of outside experts, to develop the Model Cities legislation. The legislation was completed by the end of 1965 and was submitted to the Congress early in 1966. Largely because the 89th Congress was so liberal, the program was enacted in late 1966 (but not without a Herculean presidential effort and an enormous legislative battle). Supplemental appropriations of $10 million were obtained in early 1967. The states and cities then began to prepare to respond to the new federal law. Not until the end of 1968 was the administrative and legislative infrastructure for the Model Cities program in place at the national, state, and local level. In January 1969, when Richard Nixon assumed office, he reviewed the imminently operational Model Cities program and concluded that revenue sharing would be a more effective way to help the cities. Nixon then set out to dismantle the Model Cities program, which has been floundering ever since. The losers? The American citizens in the cities suffering the social and human indecency of urban blight. Had the presidential term been six years, this nation at least would have had some sense of the viability of the Model Cities concept. Instead, we have perpetuated an intellectual, social, and bureaucratic dialogue over the value of such a program, all in the context of new revenue sharing programs which themselves may not be adequately funded and tested before yet another president with yet another program assumes office.

In the complicated federal and technological infrastructure of the last quarter of the twentieth century, the four-year term perpetuates a revolving-door presidency, allowing too little time to establish the staying power of domestic programs to meet urgently escalating needs of significant numbers of our people. The revolving-door presidency is a major contributor to the increasing frustration of all institutions of society dealing with and dependent upon the president's branch. The relentless ticking of the four-year clock contributes significantly to the gap between promise and performance in American society. The six-year presidential term can be expected to encourage more responsible presidential proposals and contemporary accountability, as well as ease the pressure on the White House to employ exaggerated rhetoric and instant programmatic cures. The six-year term is a logical outgrowth of our experience with domestic programs during the 1960s and early 1970s and a practical recognition of the complex realities of the budgetary, legislative, and federal systems.

The president should not be limited to one six-year term. Presidents are by no means infallible and they must understand that they will be judged not simply by God and history, but also by the people who live while they are in office. The most frequently profered argument to limit a president to one term is that the president will be free from partisan politics. Thus, the argument concludes, he will answer only to the national interest. Roosevelt aide Thomas Corcoran answered this argument with a typically wry comment before the Senate Judiciary Committee: "It is impossible to take politics out of politics." Indeed, if limiting the president to a single term were to have a depoliticizing impact on the Oval Office, it would be likely to reduce even further the responsiveness of the modern presidency to the people. That price, in a time of deep concern about presidential accountability and responsiveness, is much too steep. The winds of politics should constantly swirl against the panes of glass around the Oval Office. There is no place for political storm windows in a presidential democracy. As former cabinet officer and Democratic National Chairman Larry O'Brien wrote in *No Final Victories*, "Let the people decide. If the people want a particular man as President two or three or four times, why should their wishes be frustrated? If you believe in democracy, you have to place your ultimate trust in the good judgment of the American people."

There is some concern that an extended term would permit the pursuit of futile policies by a president self-confined to his own prior positions. The Vietnam War is cited as a classic example to illustrate this concern. But the Vietnamization program was begun during the Johnson administration; Johnson had become sufficiently skeptical of military advice on the war to deny the Pentagon request for additional troop commitments in March 1968. By then he had sufficiently witnessed and experienced the sting of popular opprobrium to temper his earlier Vietnam policies. Had Johnson remained in office, it seems probable that our commitments in Southeast Asia would have been reduced more rapidly than they were under Richard Nixon. Certainly, it would not have taken any longer to terminate our involvement there. Indeed, as the discussion of Vietnam policy in Chapter XI indicates, had either Eisenhower or Kennedy been in office for more extended periods, it is unlikely that our involvement there would have been as deep or as extended as it was under Johnson. The learning time for each president who faced the Vietnam problem was itself costly in human lives and material resources.

The six-year term, nevertheless, does vest additional power in the office of the presidency and, for that reason, should not be instituted without other changes to balance that power. The Twenty-fifth Amendment to the Constitution provides that, when the elected president vacates office, the succeeding vice-president shall nominate a new vice-president subject to a majority vote of each House of the Congress. In place of the Twenty-fifth Amendment, we should adopt a provision that would call for a special election to fill the unexpired term of the vacating elected president, if he leaves office with two or more years of his term to be completed. As Senator Edward Kennedy has pointed out, the appointment and congressional confirmation of either of our two national leaders is not "consistent with our democracy and the principle of government by the people."

The vice-president is elected on the constitutional coattails of the president. The people have little to say about his selection, and cannot cast votes separately for president and vice-president. Under those circumstances, to permit the vice-president to serve more than two years of the unexpired term of the elected president and to nominate his own successor is, indeed, contrary to our democratic system. It could tend to render him and, during his incumbency, the presidential office less responsive to the will of the American people. Moreover, as brutal and exhausting as the presidential campaign has become, much of what a candidate endures sharpens his ability to lead the people, and can summon the best or expose the worst elements of the common personality characteristics described in Chapters IX and X. The attention that the experience with Gerald Ford and Nelson Rockefeller has focused on the Twenty-fifth Amendment should be sustained in a national dialogue directed at its repeal and modification.

The six-year presidential term can not be considered in isolation from congressional reform (or other changes suggested in this final chapter, particularly those related to campaign financing and access to television). The six-year term for senators should continue, with re-election an unlimited option. The legislative check and balance corollary to the longer presidential tenure is to increase from two to four years the term of office for members of the House of Representatives.

The length of the term for House members has been sporadically debated from the time the founding fathers set it at two years in the Constitution. Even in those early days of constitutional wrangling, James Madison favored a three-year term. In the debates, the arguments ranged from terms of one to three years. The *Federalist Papers* suggest that the two-year term for House members was one of the more tentative judgments of the framers:

> As it is essential to liberty that the government in general should have a common interest with the people; so it is particularly essential that the branch of it under consideration should have an immediate dependence on, and an intimate sympathy with the people. Frequent elections are unquestionably the only policy by which this dependency and sympathy can be effectually secured. But what particular degree of frequency may be absolutely necessary for the purpose, does not appear to be susceptible of any precise calculation; and must depend on a variety of circumstances with which it may be connected.

Circumstances have changed since the original thirteen colonies became the first states under the Constitution. Present two-year terms have turned most House members into distracted, trampoline politicians, bouncing up and down on airplanes to and from their home districts. Unless they are blessed with a safe district, they begin to campaign for re-election on the day after they are elected. Many Congressmen spend more than half of their two-year terms running for re-election. Their families are often torn apart by the Tuesday-to-Thursday in Washington, Friday-to-Monday in the congressional district lives they lead most months of the year. So personally brutalizing is the life of a young congressman that many good politicians refuse to run for the office.

A two-year term barely permits a congressman to focus on a single federal budgetary cycle, much less acquire any profound understanding of the federal government. It tends to increase the advantages of those congressmen who are in safe districts, and thus can accumulate seniority. Not only do they usually have more power and higher rank in the committee structure of the House, but they also have significantly more time to devote to substantive legislative issues than their less secure congressional colleagues. This, in turn, tends to give the president fewer, more powerful, and less immediately representative men to deal with in the House.

The statistics of the congressional work load constitute a

convincing brief for extending the term of House members
to four years. In the very first Congress, 142 bills were introduced resulting in 108 public laws. By the 93rd Congress
(1973–1974), almost 22,000 bills were introduced, more than
500 of which were enacted into public law. If the congressmen worked each of the 365 days in a year (and tried to look
at those bills), they would be considering an average of almost 60 bills each day and passing more than 1, in addition
to servicing their constituents. And excluding the thousands
of military officer nominations, the 93rd Congress acted on
6,788 civilian presidential nominations.

The society in which we live has become inordinately complex, and the need for deep federal penetration into a variety
of areas renders many legislative items infinitely more difficult and significant than they were a generation ago. As result, the sessions of Congress have grown increasingly long.
In 1904, the Congress adjourned in April. By 1958, the Congress adjourned in August. Since the mid-sixties, the Congress has usually adjourned in December, often without
completing its work. As the discussion in Chapter III indicates, so many committee meetings are necessary that the
job of scheduling them has become infinitely more difficult
than setting class schedules at a multiversity with tens of
thousands of students.

No political official, be he governor, senator, state legislator, or even president, has more pressure on his time than a
member of the House of Representatives in a contested district sincerely trying to perform his duties. In today's climate,
congressmen do not have enough time to vote their own
conscience intelligently and thoughtfully. They barely have
enough time to vote it even emotionally. The two-year term
renders such members political sitting ducks for any shrewd
president, too often dependent on the smallest of presidential favors and fearful of the least presidential slight.

The usual argument against increasing the two-year term
is that the original framers designed a House of Representatives so deliberately insecure as to be sensitive on a daily basis
to their constituencies. But that was at a time when it took
days, or even weeks, for news and congressmen to travel

from Washington to their home districts. With modern communications and jet planes, this is no longer the case.

There are any number of ways the four-year term for House members could be put into effect. The best might be to have a geographically distributed half of the House elected each two years. To the degree congressional district elections reflect the view of the people on national as well as local issues, this method would provide a biennial barometer of the public mood. It would retain a limited sense of continuity with the original concept of a body of the national legislature acutely sensitive to the wishes of a large segment of a broadly based population. To the extent wide congressional elections around the nation reverberate on the conduct of the White House, the staggered system would provide that impact every two years. But the method chosen is less important than the adoption of the concept.

The Senate deserves credit for providing the most effective political roadblock to the establishment of a four-year term for House members because most senators do not want representatives who are able to run against them without forfeiting their House seats. The parochially self-interested nature of this argument should be enough to dismiss it. Several governors and mayors are in a position to run against incumbent senators without leaving the state houses or city halls and that has not affected the security and continuity essential to the more careful, "longer view" deliberation with which the Senate is supposed to inform the legislative process. The added competition might contribute to increasing the responsiveness of our political system.

As a matter of practical politics, incumbent senators have a veto power over any attempt to extend the term of House members. There may well be no realistic possibility of obtaining the necessary legislative action to establish a four-year term for House members unless incumbent representatives are precluded from running for a Senate seat without resigning as members of the House. If so, and outrageous as is that position, the importance of the four-year term in the restoration of the House and the entire Congress to an equal as well as separate status with the presidency appears to justify reluctant acceptance of such a limitation. The four-year term for House members is an essential element of restoring balance between the legislative and executive branches even with the existing four-year presidential term. It would be foolhardy to extend the presidential term to six years without increasing the term of members in the House of Representatives to four.

The key goals of presidential accountability, responsiveness, and credibility cannot be achieved without a major reorganization of the executive and legislative branches and the way they conduct the public's business.

Recent presidents, particularly Johnson and Nixon, recognized the need for vast executive reorganization. Johnson was distinctly more successful in pursuit of this goal, but both he and Nixon fell far short of the need to reshape the federal executive along functional lines. The expert task forces that studied this subject in the 1960s and early 1970s all came to essentially the same conclusions. Several domestic program departments, agencies, and bureaus should be reorganized into four functionally oriented departments: Natural Resources and Development, Economic Affairs, Human Resources (Social Services), and Housing and Community Development. Ideally, such a reorganization would eliminate several agencies and all cabinet departments except State, Justice, Transportation, Treasury, and Defense. Under the best of these recommendations, however, some of the remaining departments would lose certain of their present functions; for example, the civil functions of the Corps of Engineers would move to the new Department of Natural Resources and Development.

Under the existing executive branch departmental structure, working as the president's domestic affairs assistant is like driving on a superhighway with a horse and buggy. Anyone who has labored in the executive branch senses the desperate need to rearrange old-line agencies and departments and place responsibility more clearly in accord with authority. Coordination is no substitute for getting the organization charts in shape, for giving the president one man with enough authority to be held responsible for transportation or natural resources. In turn, a functional reorganization will more pointedly render the president himself responsible and accountable.

As we have seen, the traditional stumbling blocks to proposed reorganizations have been the special-interest groups and the Congress, aided and abetted by their allies in the existing executive bureaucracy. Business, labor, and farm interests want constituent-oriented departments who see their role as protecting the interests of their constituencies. Intractable resistance has come from the congressional committees that fear loss of jurisdictional power as much as many entrenched executive branch bureaucrats do. Major executive reorganization can go forward only with a change in congressional attitude.

The political key to any such change may be the simultaneous reorganization of congressional committees essential to reinstatement of the legislature to equal partnership with the executive. The committee system of the Congress should be reshaped to reflect the realities of life in the last quarter of the twentieth century. The Senate and House committees should be structured along functional lines to give the Congress the organizational capability to fulfill its oversight responsibilities. Congressman Richard Bollings's ill-fated 1974 *Report on Committee Structure and Procedures of the House of Representatives* proposed some significant steps in the right direction. Based on that report and the numerous executive branch task force reports, the House, the Senate, and the president should form a joint commission to reach agreement on a joint reorganization of the executive and legislative branches. Since the Congress itself needs reorganization as urgently as the executive, the two branches should pursue the problem simultaneously, matching restructured committees with restructured departments. A joint reorganization of the executive and legislative branches is as important to the future of democratic government in our nation as any substantive programs presidents are likely to propose and Congresses are likely to enact.

With the budget legislation enacted in 1974, the Congress

moved to establish its own budget office to support the newly organized House and Senate Budget Committees. In the 1960s and early 1970s, the Congress had precious little independent information and no modern analytical capabilities on which to base its judgments. Legislators are—and should be—sensitive to the desires of their own constituencies. But they do not have any real sense of the data (or much of it) on which so many of the federal programs are based. If they desire to obtain information to develop their own programs, they must go to the executive department concerned to obtain that data. As a result, they often vote on complex programs without any true understanding of the impact on their constituencies or the nation.

To consider and act intelligently on presidential proposals and to produce some of its own, the Congress must develop an institutional capability (a) to analyze public policy alternatives and their implications in the context of any currently pending or imminent legislative proposals, and (b) to assess the problems coming in the future and the future implications of its current actions. The 1974 budget legislation provides the framework for achievement of this institutional capability. The Congressional Budget Office it authorizes should be nonpartisan with a substantial multidisciplinary staff of professional analysts whose energies would be directed solely to substantive problems. To an extent this would be similar to the way in which the Congressional Research Service works. But the work would be more costly and substantive, requiring a major analytical, computer, and information retrieval capability. The millions of dollars such an organization is likely to cost annually will be one of the best investments the Congress could make to regain its status vis-à-vis the presidency. With such a capability, the Congress could intelligently and independently consider executive branch policy and legislative proposals, analyze the National Posture Statement discussed earlier in this chapter, and develop its own independent legislative initiatives.

The Congress also needs its own institutional assistance in anticipating the kinds of problems that this nation is likely to face in the future, particularly to alleviate technological future shock. Recent examples of its failure to do this in the past are the environmental and energy crises. The Office of Technology Assessment, authorized in 1972, provides the institutional framework for this task, if it is properly funded and staffed.

During the late 1960s and early 1970s, there have been a number of suggestions for actions related to the president's staff. Most proposals are variations of three themes. They usually relate to the size of the White House staff (cut it), the sole power of the president to appoint senior staff members (subject them to confirmation and the obligation to testify before congressional committees), and the confidentiality of their communications with the president (eliminate or sharply restrict the extent to which such communications are protected under the doctrine of executive privilege). All three themes are played on the same chord, to render presidential aides accountable.

The size of the White House staff, which hovered between 550 and 600 during the early 1970s, is largely in the president's control. He can temporarily assign members from throughout the federal bureaucracy or use them indirectly. During the early 1970s, the White House staff was too large for the president to control the vicarious power that anyone with a White House telephone on his desk can exercise. The Watergate scandals undoubtedly account for the 10 to 20 percent staff reduction from 1972 to 1974 and it is likely that Ford and future presidents will somewhat reduce the size of the White House staff. But the only way to achieve lasting reductions is to reorganize the executive departments so that the president can look to cabinet officers and agency heads and hold them realistically responsible for functional areas. Any president assuming office with the executive branch organized as it has been in the 1960s and early 1970s will soon experience the gnawing frustration caused by the functional irrationality of the existing executive departments. For the reasons discussed in Chapter II, any president will respond by establishing a strong White House staff along functional lines.

The proposal for Senate confirmation of senior aides is a hollow gesture, as well as an inappropriate one. When a newly elected president, on assuming office, submits to the Senate for confirmation those men whom he has chosen to be his immediate aides, along with his cabinet officers, the Senate will confirm his initial selections, probably within twenty-four and certainly within forty-eight hours. Not only would Senate confirmation of top White House aides be a relatively useless charade, but it might also give the American people a false sense that a greater check on presidential power existed than was actually the case.

Senate confirmation of presidential aides is contrary to the personal staff system that operates in all three branches of the government. No one has suggested the confirmation of the clerks of the Supreme Court justices, aides to the majority leader of the Senate and the Speaker of the House, or, for that matter, to any senator or congressman. Those clerks and aides often have more influence and power than many presidential appointees confirmed by the Senate. The need for personal, confidential aides is recognized as essential to those principals in fulfilling their roles. So the president, the chief executive of the nation, should be entitled to have men of his own choice as his personal aides.

It is just as critical that such aides can be confident—absent the kind of criminal activity that precipitated the 1974 Supreme Court decision on the Nixon tapes—that their communications with the president will be protected. Requiring that certain senior White House aides, notably the top assistants for national security and domestic affairs, testify about their official duties and actions in pursuit of legitimate presidential public policy objectives could seriously impair the free flow of information, ideas, and debate before the president.

Nixon and his aides did to executive privilege in the early 1970s what organized crime did to the Fifth Amendment in the 1950s. Issues were so extremely drawn that the participants polarized their positions. Absolute claims of privilege, like the chauvinistic assertions of Attorney General Richard Kleindienst, rightly infuriated many members of the House and Senate. Presidential attempts to use the doctrine of executive privilege to hide criminal activity grotesquely distorted the rationale on which executive privilege was soundly based.

Over the long run, it is essential that most communications between a president and his immediate staff be privileged and protected from release without the consent of the incumbent president and, in some cases, for an extended period after he leaves office. Presidents need uninhibited advice and it is already difficult enough for them to get it. The most sophisticated business, labor, and congressional leaders pull their punches in the awesome chambers of the Oval Office and the Cabinet Room. During the Johnson administration, I witnessed men as powerful as William Fulbright and Henry Ford temper their remarks about the Vietnam War or economic policy in the presence of the president. There were a few, like Senator Wayne Morse and George Meany, who did not. But for every Morse and Meany there were hundreds of Fulbrights and Fords. Unless they establish close and special relationships with the president, most cabinet officers and White House aides also tend to pull their punches with him, even when they assume their communications will remain confidential until long after they have left the presidential staff.

The interests of full and free discussion of issues within the president's family must be balanced against the interests of disclosure even after the president leaves office. There is a genuine interest in maintaining privileged communications in a variety of situations—doctor and patient, priest and penitent, lawyer and client. That interest also applies in the public arena. Senators and representatives have claimed that their communications with their staff members are privileged. Reporters have claimed that the privilege of maintaining the confidentiality of certain sources is essential to the exercise of First Amendment rights and the gathering of news. No one suggests that these privileges end as soon as the doctor is discharged by the patient, the reporter by the newspaper, the lawyer by the client, the staff aide by the senator, or when the sinner leaves the confessional. Similarly, not only while the president is in office, but for some reasonable period thereafter, executive privilege should protect communications within his officially intimate family. Political scientists and congressional critics cannot in one breath decry the isolation of the president and in another urge that little or no privilege attend communications between him and his closest advisors.

The attempted use of the privilege to protect criminal activity during the Nixon administration should not obscure the real need for confidential communications between a president and his top personal staff. The perpetual tension between the chief executive and the other institutions of our society over this issue will continue; but the give and take should be conducted within a general recognition of the need for executive privilege.

At the same time, the contours of executive privilege must recognize the need of a functioning democracy for information and the distinction between advice and orders. The special committees of the House and Senate conducting the re-examination of the work of the Central Intelligence Agency since its inception must certainly have access to orders that have been issued during past administrations and to current administration policies and procedures. Without such information, those committees cannot conduct the kinds of investigations essential to fulfillment of the congressional legislative and appropriations responsibilities. The Senate Select Committee, for example, carefully limited its initial request to copies of White House orders and national security memoranda authorizing or providing guidelines for CIA activities. The rationale for confidential communications between a president and his close aides does not appear to justify withholding such material from the Congress.

There are new powers which, if given to the president, would likely increase the accountability and responsiveness of the office and the executive branch. One set relates to economic policy; the other to the more cost-effective deployment of public program funds.

By and large, the American people hold the president

personally responsible for the operation of the American economy. If there is inflation, he is condemned for his failure to stop it; if unemployment rises, it is the president's policies which are putting people out of work. Yet the president's ability to control the economy is remarkably limited. Essentially, he has the power to recommend a budget to the Congress, sometimes to reduce government spending below what Congress appropriates (or at least to control the time at which certain funds are spent), and to propose tax measures to the Congress. For a brief period, President Nixon was given power to control wages and prices, but the Congress did not extend that stand-by power when it expired in early 1974.

Limited in his powers, the president's true ability to tune the economy depends largely on his ingenuity, his moral suasion, his use of such blunderbusses as the antitrust laws, his willingness to jawbone business or labor, luck, and his political spine in withstanding congressional and special-interest pressures when federal expenditures are delayed and highways are not built, federal grants are not made, and federal guarantees are not provided. This limited power puts the president in the position of shouldering the political responsibility for the economic welfare of the nation without adequate legal authority to fulfill that responsibility.

Authority and responsibility can be reasonably meshed if, on a continuing basis, the president were given limited additional powers. He should have the stand-by power to impose wage and price controls selectively or across the board when economic indicators and projections suggest their necessity. The inept use of this authority during the early 1970s should not discredit a sound concept. As former chairman of the Council of Economic Advisers Arthur M. Okun has said, "Perhaps the most unfortunate fallout of that experience is the bad name the Nixon administration has given to wage and price controls by its incompetent use of those tools." The mere existence of such authority on a continuing basis can be a potent tool in the hands of a president who skillfully uses his power to establish voluntary wage and price guideposts or to engage in jawboning.

The president should also be vested with authority to alter tax rates to some limited degree, up or down, with residual power in the Congress to approve or disapprove within a specified period of time. Such powers have been discussed since the early 1960s. Presidents Kennedy and Johnson made cautious attempts to obtain them, but retreated in the face of congressional opposition. The concept makes even more sense in view of the persistent double-digit inflation and high unemployment of the early 1970s.

The president's impact on interest rates and monetary policy is indirect. He can limit government capital investments like those in housing and federal construction. He has certain appointment powers, for example, with respect to members of the Federal Home Loan Bank Board and the Federal Reserve Board. But Federal Reserve Board governors regard themselves as the Supreme Court justices of money and banking and do not take presidential directives. As with the Supreme Court, the president must win a majority of votes from the Federal Reserve Board for his viewpoint to prevail.

The relationship between the president and the Federal Reserve Board is a particularly delicate one to change. In many cases, existing staff relationships and the rapport between the chairman and the president assure the necessary coordination. But the occasions on which the Federal Reserve Board acts without any prior consultation with the president and his economic advisors are not as infrequent as most Americans believe and such occasions often involve major economic policy judgments. Thus, two relatively limited steps appear worth taking. The term of the chairman of the Federal Reserve Board should be set to coincide with the term of the president. This would give the incoming president an opportunity to appoint a Board chairman sympathetic to his economic policies and yet preserve the over-all independence on the Board, an independence of value both as a check on the president and as a proven incentive to the maintenance of one of the ablest staffs in Washington. The second step would be to require the Federal Reserve Board to notify the president of any proposed major decisions (increases or decreases in the discount rate, for example) and to give the president and his economic advisers an opportunity to present their views on any such proposed actions to the full Board. That opportunity could be a confidential one until the final action was announced, if economic conditions justified such secrecy. But it would at least give the president and his economic advisers a right to be heard by all the Federal Reserve Board governors and contribute to the more effective coordination of the application of governmental leverage to economic policy objectives.

The other set of additional presidential powers relates to domestic programs. As the analysis in Chapter II indicates, the explosion of domestic programs operated by the executive branch between 1960 and 1969 qualitatively changed the office of the presidency and the executive branch. The federal executive now probes deeply into the smallest neighborhoods and intrudes upon the most intimate family relationships.

Some new programs work; some fail. Some existing programs become obsolete; others need to be strengthened and redirected. The time gap between operational recognition of success or failure and effective corrective action is too long and expensive for the people to whom such programs are intended and for the American taxpayer. The president should have authority (subject to congressional approval or disapproval) to move money from one domestic program which is not going well and into another which is progressing beyond original expectations. Such authority should be limited to programs designed to meet similar problems. For example, if the federal government is operating a dozen manpower training programs and one is significantly more successful than the others, while another is a total failure, the president should be able to move funds and resources from the failing program to the cost-effective one.

Under clearly defined standards, the president should also have the power to eliminate obsolete programs, subject to congressional veto within a limited period of time. Where a new program provides for all the needs that had been filled by an old one, then the decision whether to continue both should be made promptly and the burden of that decision, at least initially, should fall on the executive branch.

The president should also have a fund of several million dollars to operate experimental programs, so that major domestic program ideas can be tested prior to substantial federal investment. Reports on these experiments should be promptly made available to the Congress. In all new legislative program proposals, the president should be required to indicate whether there have been any such experiments and their results. To continue to propose massive new programs without some experience makes little economic or public policy sense.

Finally, the president should be given more authority to organize the federal government, limiting the role of Congress only to proposals which would create or eliminate new departments and agencies. The president should be permitted to move and merge bureaus and divisions within departments and agencies without submitting plans to the Congress for approval. Such power seems a minimum organizational corollary to the president's constitutional duty faithfully to execute the laws and his political responsibility to do so as efficiently as possible.

John Gardner alluded to the issues of the efficacy of state and local government cautiously but pointedly in his elegant paper, "Rebirth of a Nation":

> In today's intricately organized society, allocation of powers among federal, state and local levels of government is an exceedingly complex process, to be continuously readjusted in the light of contemporary realities. But the states can continue to be—as originally intended—a constraint on the power of the central government, *provided* that the states themselves are not in decay. It is foolish to hand power back to the states (through revenue sharing or otherwise) without revitalizing state governments so that they can exercise power responsibly.

Institutional changes that stop at the last page of the *Federal Government Organization Manual* will not be adequate to put presidential power in perspective. The intervention of the president's branch is increasingly multijurisdictional. Federal planners recognize that the execution of human and economic development programs in terms of state boundaries is as arbitrary as the lines the pilgrims drew over three hundred years ago. The rhetoric of a revival of states' rights and powers should not belie the reality that the resources and conditions which affect prosperity and poverty, pollution and transportation, often extend over entire regions—New England, the Great Lakes, Appalachia.

The web of government extends into the county commissioner's office, city hall, and the local neighborhood. It is here that government can become a horrendous maze of competing and conflicting jurisdictions. It is here, at the grass (and concrete) roots, where the need for change may be most urgent, if we are to restore a sensible balance between centralized presidential power and decentralized counterpoints of public power.

The ramifications of the kind of radical surgery needed here are singularly difficult to measure, particularly in the context of power balances between the presidency and state and local government, between the efficient use of limited resources and political sensitivity to individual human needs. What is clear is that the existing structure of states, cities, and counties must be subjected to ruthless scrutiny on an urgent basis.

There are simply too many erratically conceived and irrationally maintained city, county, and public jurisdictions within each of the states and among neighboring states. The states must look at themselves and see the extent to which their present arbitrary jurisdictional lines create and perpetuate economic, social, and democratic deficiencies. These states and cities must be reorganized in some context that makes functional and political sense. The racial, economic, social, industrial, and other problems of such a reorganization are staggering. But it is better to face the problems now than to let them continue to fester.

This nation may well be at the point where a truly unhealthy concentration of centralized presidential (and national) power will be permanently consolidated unless the states and cities are reshaped in some system of effective regional government with metropolitan groups within each region. An intelligent determination of what to centralize or decentralize may well require a recognition of what should be regional and what should be metropolitan concerns. Certainly industrial growth, air and water pollution, and traffic congestion have become *de facto* regional problems. The issue whether to establish *de jure* regional institutions to supersede the state structures should be examined thoughtfully and coldly, with special attention to the possible creation of a permanent regional apparatus that would establish an effective group of counterforces for the presidency.

Mere consideration of such radical institutional surgery involves severe conflicts for our people to face, particularly our politicians. Whatever the ultimate source of effective local power to counterpoint the presidency, the states and cities as presently postured simply cannot do the job in the closing decades of the twentieth century. It is naïve to think that we can develop the right balance between central (national), intermediate (state), local (city), and personal (neighborhood) power in this nation, without focusing on new kinds of regional and metropolitan organizations. Sensible solutions require volumes of study far beyond the scope of this book. But it is clear that changes in the Congress and the presidency alone will not suffice to balance presidential power in the last quarter of the twentieth century. Radical surgery is needed at the state and local level and the search for the nature of that surgery deserves the attention of the best minds in this nation.

In the late 1960s and early 1970s the press provided the most effective counterpoint for the American presidency. Yet, the press has never been held in particularly high repute by American society and there is no guarantee that it can continue to perform its critical functions.

The press needs systematic and institutionalized assistance if it is to continue to perform its critical role as a countervailing force to reckon with the exercise of presidential power. The courts must attend the needs of the press to First

Amendment protection with unyielding vigilance. This involves the protection of confidential sources, the skeptical examination of government actions against the media, the maintenance of relaxed libel law standards where public figures and public issues are involved, the opening up of government institutions to the press. The role of the federal judiciary in the balance of power between the presidency and the press is to tilt solidly for the press.

Access to information controlled by the president and his chief aides and departmental heads must be opened. The Freedom of Information Act has helped, but the critical issue, as President Ford's unsuccessful veto of 1974 amendments to strengthen the act reflected, is who controls the classification and protection of executive branch information. Aside from the need to protect the personal communication apparatus of the president and his immediate staff and chief departmental, agency, and private advisors, the power to provide or withhold information should not be in the sole control of the president and his branch. Here again, the federal judiciary has an important role under the Freedom of Information Act and under the Constitution. The congressional override of Ford's veto in November 1974 is an important step in the right direction. In addition, however, the national security classification system and the right of the executive branch to withhold other information should be subject to rules and regulations and prompt case-by-case adjudication by a commission composed of members appointed by the president, the House, and the Senate.

The press and the people (particularly through effective organizations like the League of Women Voters and Common Cause) can put public pressure on presidents to hold press conferences on a regular basis. For example, during campaigns, the press, and institutions like Common Cause, should push presidential candidates to make public commitments, if elected, to hold press conferences each week or, at worst, every other week. Presidents can then be measured against these commitments. There is, of course, no insurance that a presidential candidate will keep this kind of commitment any more than he is likely to keep other campaign commitments. But their existence will play a part in the number of press conferences a president holds. At such conferences, it is imperative that the press be well prepared and give colleagues an opportunity to follow up on nonresponsive or evasive answers.

The continuing media coverage of the incumbent president must be sharpened. The Watergate revelations have added a healthy measure of skepticism to the White House press corps, but the maintenance of that attitude requires that major news organizations (the wire services, the broadcast networks, and the major newspapers) assign, in addition to their usual White House correspondent, investigative reporters permanently to cover the president. The need of the traditional White House correspondent for continuing background information on foreign and domestic policies requires a close relationship with White House staffers incompatible with tough investigative reporting that leaves little room for friendly exchanges with those subject to such skeptical scrutiny.

The press must significantly increase its expertise in the areas in which the president's branch functions—health, education, agricultural policy, housing, transportation, regulatory policies, and the like. As Supreme Court Justice Potter Stewart has pointed out, in its original conception, "the free press meant organized, expert scrutiny of government. The press was a conspiracy of the intellect, with the courage of numbers. This formidable check on official power was what the British Crown had feared—and what the American Founders decided to risk."

There are too few risks for presidential spokesmen and cabinet officials when they speak to the press about government programs. Too often they stand self-confidently before reporters on an informed pedestal, when they should be hopping like bureaucratic cats on hot tin roofs. Some of the major news organizations have begun to seek experts in specialized areas as reporters and consultants, but far more substantial investments must be made in this direction and too few news organizations have the necessary resources to make those investments. Considering the critical role they fulfill in our society, reporters are among the most underpaid professionals in our nation.

The economic viability of the media deserves special mention in any examination of its ability to help put presidential power in perspective. The electronic media is the rich uncle of American journalism. It is, however, not without inhibition because it is so heavily regulated by the Federal Communications Commission. The FCC is presently composed of seven members, appointed by the president for terms of seven years, with the usual regulatory requirement that no more than a bare majority be from the same political party. With television the uncontested champion of communication, FCC members hold some of the most critical positions in our society. The FCC, with its singularly important role, should be at least as free of presidential influence as the Federal Reserve Board, and the quality of individual membership must be sharply upgraded.

The print media (newspapers, magazines, and books) operate on frighteningly tight margins. Many publishers are chronically in the red. Scores of newspapers and magazines have folded during the 1960s and early 1970s. The Failing Newspaper Act, which permits mergers that otherwise would violate the antitrust laws in limited circumstances of financial distress, provides a legislative precedent for recognition of the special public interest in the economic viability of the press. The Congress should tailor the postal laws to protect the press, if necessary even providing free passage through the mails.

The implementation of antitrust policy should be under constant examination to attend carefully to the preservation of the economic welfare of the press, as should the implementation of all other laws and regulations. Particular attention should be given to any general economic regulation as applied to the press (wage and price controls are a good example) to make certain that only minimal financial hurdles are placed in its way. Justice William Douglas, reflecting on his absolutist view of the First Amendment, once asked counsel during an oral argument in the Supreme Court, "Can the Congress pass a law that helps the press exercise its First Amendment rights in view of the flat prohibition in the Constitution?" My answer would be a resounding "yes," particularly where the economic health of the press is concerned. It may well be that the greatest danger to the free press as a counterforce to presidential power lies less in political and judicial assaults on First Amendment rights than in the financial fragility of major press organizations and local newspapers.

The role of the federal judiciary may well be decisive in the relationship of private institutions and individuals to a necessarily increasingly interventionist presidency. As American society becomes more complicated and its resources more strained, the level of governmental intervention is likely to continue to increase. The individual and the family are the critical units of any society which places a high value on freedom. Modern technology has a tendency to render the individual and the family statistical abstractions, just as the complexity of problems like pollution control and energy allocation have a tendency to require more intimate regulation of their everyday lives. In the face of this presidential branch intrusion, the individual and his family must look to the federal courts for protection of their rights to privacy, life, liberty, and fulfillment of their independent talents. The provision of this protection will be their highest duty in keeping presidential power in perspective in the future, as it has so often been in the past. After all, individual freedom in the context of collective security is what the American dream is about.

It is individual Americans, some in positions of great power, others not, who must understand the risks and benefits of a presidential nation and the need to put presidential power in perspective.

The pragmatic reality of the presidency is that it is part of a system of forces faced off against each other, in a division of power designed to protect individual freedom and enhance individual opportunity. The presidency is today the dominant force of that system. Technology, communications, and economics have combined to offer more power to the man in the Oval Office than at any time in American history. Too little sustained thought has been given to strengthening the nonpresidential institutions of society that harbor the potential to put presidential power in perspective. Each power vested in the presidency in well-intentioned pursuit of legitimate public policy objectives can be used to slice away at individual freedom. In the hands of an amoral incumbent, those powers can be turned against the American people they were designed to protect and the rights they were crafted to preserve.

There are any number of laws and regulations needed to block the illegitimate intrusions of the presidency on individual freedom. No attempt has been made to catalogue the myriad suggestions in this area that have flowed from the Watergate investigations of the early 1970s. The focus of this book has been on institutional and systems reform because, in the long run, these are the changes most difficult to achieve and most important to the preservation of our democratic system.

This book does not pretend to have all or even most of the answers to the increasing concentration of power in the presidency and the steady deterioration of the institutional counterforces in the American nation that once held presidential power securely in check. Hopefully, however, it will provide some interrelated ideas for others concerned with this problem. Most importantly, this analysis should provide a recognition that the presidency cannot be considered in political or historical isolation and an appreciation of the special importance of institutions (how they operate, their processes, and procedures) in preserving individual freedom and the public welfare and making a necessarily strong presidency work for all of us.

A strong presidency will be accountable, responsive, and credible only where independently effective institutions are available to temper its exercise of power. We must not unduly inhibit the use of presidential power—for we need a strong presidency—but we should not be deluded by presidential rhetoric that derides as undesirably divisive the inevitable political, economic, and social clashes that strengthened institutional counterpoints to presidential power auger. As Supreme Court Justice Louis Brandeis wrote a half century ago, "The [Founders'] purpose was, not to avoid friction, but, by means of the inevitable friction incident to the distribution of the governmental powers among three departments, to save the people from autocracy."

The personalities of the men elected to exercise presidential power are likely to reflect more common than disparate characteristics. The men who hold the presidential seal in their hands in the last quarter of the twentieth century will be human beings with fallible, sometimes weak, sometimes strong, human natures. George Washington and Julius Caesar were both imbued with human natures. But the institutional constraints on their exercise of power were quite different. The absence of those constraints on Caesar and their presence on George Washington and most of his successors may tell us more about the way one exercised power over the Roman Empire and the others over the American nation than any analysis of their personalities.

If we fail to take any action, one thing seems certain: The forces now at play in our society will inevitably press toward a dangerous concentration of presidential power. The *status quo* means more power to the president. The institutional pressures and the deterioration of potential counterforces have too much persistent momentum to be deterred for more than historical moments, even by diversions as traumatic as the Vietnam War and Watergate scandals.

Nineteen-seventy-six America is not 1776 America. At its bicentennial, America is infinitely bigger, more complex, and more mobile. It is less sure of itself and more powerful. It has the ability to destroy the world. Its 6 percent of the world population consumes 40 percent of the world's resources. It is more affluent and less self-sufficient. It is more cynical, and its people are more self-centered, hedonistic, and ahistorical. All of these characteristics play on the presidency and the other institutions in the system. Most play to the power of the president.

We must face promptly, but intelligently, the consequences of the power we continue to vest in the presidency and deny to its potential counterpoints of power. Americans are human beings and their human nature is no different than that of the Greeks whose affluence eventually led them to a decadent society; the Romans who ultimately acceded to Caesar; the French who followed Napoleon; and the Germans who followed Hitler. As a nation, we are no more immune from the laws of history than those civilizations were.

INDEX